Wisdom is Calling

Geoffrey Duncan spent many years working as Information Officer of the Council for World Mission, the affiliating body of a number of churches in the reformed tradition around the world.

He is the compiler of two previous anthologies of original material for worship: *Seeing Christ in Others*, published by The Canterbury Press, and *Dare to Dream*, published by HarperCollins.

Wisdom is Calling

*An anthology of hope:
an agenda for change*

Compiled by Geoffrey Duncan

CANTERBURY
PRESS
Norwich

© in this compilation Geoffrey Duncan 1999

First published 1999 by The Canterbury Press Norwich
(a publishing imprint of Hymns Ancient & Modern Limited,
a registered charity)
St Mary's Works, St Mary's Plain,
Norwich, Norfolk, NR3 3BH

British Library Cataloguing in Publication Data

A catalogue record for this book is available
from the British Library

ISBN 1-85311-243-7

*Typeset in Great Britain by Rowland Phototypesetting Limited,
Bury St Edmunds, Suffolk
Printed in Great Britain by Biddles Limited,
Guildford and King's Lynn*

To SAMUHA,*

its staff and the communities with whom it works,

for their vision and commitment.

* SAMUHA is a non-governmental development agency working in the state of Karnataka, South India. You can find out more about its work from its website. url:http://www. samuha. org. The royalties from *Wisdom is Calling* are being given to SAMUHA.

Contents

Preface   xiii

Foreword   xv

Introduction   xvii

A New Heaven and a New Earth   1

Ecology and the Environment
   introduced by Sir Ghillean Prance

Love Is Made Perfect In Us . . .   43

Creating Community
   introduced by Peter Millar

Proclaim Jubilee!   109

Fair Trade
   introduced by Michael Taylor

Whole Person, Whole Community, Whole World   137

Health and Holistic Influences
   introduced by Janet Lees

Become People for Justice and Joy   181

Human Rights
   introduced by Anthea Dove

The Whereabouts of Peace   229

   introduced by Fred Kaan

Light for the World   267

Science and Technology
   introduced by Professor John Polkinghorne

Wisdom is Calling   303

Worship and Spirituality
   introduced by David Adam

Magnificat for a New Millennium   383

Index of Authors   391

Index of Titles/First lines   395

Acknowledgements   407

Commendations for *Wisdom is Calling*

This is a wonderful collection full of life and born from the reality of people's experiences.

Dr Sheila Cassidy

On Human Rights

Human rights must never be allowed to wither into a legalistic concept alone. The Universal Declaration in 1948 was an expression of widely held convictions about what society could and should be; it was informed by the traumatic experiences of the Second World War and what led to it; it was also a strategic expression of qualitative concern. Christians have a very special responsibility to play their full part in regenerating that positive, living context. That is why *Wisdom is Calling* is so important.

Lord Judd

Everyone is in favour of human rights . . . especially in the fiftieth Anniversary Year of the Universal Declaration of Human Rights. But human wrongs take ever new forms. Who had heard of 'ethnic cleansing' ten years ago? God became human – but can we? That is the challenge of these texts from around the world.

Dr Roger Williamson,
Policy and Campaigns Director,
Christian Aid

On Peace

Peace can be too easy a word. 'Peace, peace – where there is no peace.' Justice and true reconciliation are painful and demanding as these texts show.

Dr Roger Williamson,
Policy and Campaigns Director,
Christian Aid

On 'Proclaim Jubilee!'

I found this section challenging and sharing a vision of a fairer world where justice, community and hope are realities. This anthology has helpful material that can be used in different settings.

Dr Daleep Mukarji,
Director,
Christian Aid

The contributions which follow serve to remind us that the complexities of our world should not be allowed to obscure the simple fact that the earth exists only because of God's gracious generosity to us. And because that generosity is written into every fibre of creation, then we as God's creatures all owe a debt and it is a debt to God to seek to be likewise generous in our living one with another and with God's good earth.

Rt Revd Laurie Green,
Bishop of Bradwell

Science and Technology

Five years ago I experienced a heart attack. A defibrilator started my heart again. Drugs dissolved the clot. I saw a young man laughing as he wildly rode a jet-ski. His arms and hands grotesquely short, mere stumps from his shoulders. A drug prescribed to his mother. In France an Australian surgeon transplants a human hand. Thank God we have ceased blowing people's feet off with land mines. Good-doing or bad-doing? Choosing the good gifts of science demands uncommon wisdom.

Revd Graham Brookes,
Uniting Church in Australia

It is wonderful to have worship and reflective material which speaks straight to the perplexity of human response to science and technology as we enter the twenty-first century. The optimism of the early nineteenth century is gone but so also is the rigid division between science and faith.

Here are resources which lead us through penitence for the misuse of resources and intercession for people involved in research and application, to a tentative joy in human zest for exploration. The resources explore the boundary between technology and faith, a boundary which was so long the battle front for futile argument from entrenched positions on either side, now open to hope and song.

Revd Janet Wootton,
Congregational Federation

Pretty well everything around us seductively invites us to live present-tense lives in the Land of Me, to live forgetfully, without origins and without consummation, seeking satiation without satisfaction. Hopelessness and despair are never far away. Wisdom winsomely calls us to live with God, the other, the whole of creation, to touch, smell her and feel again: to be open to God's surprising new-making. Wisdom is Calling: Listen.

Revd Graham Brookes,
Uniting Church in Australia

In the wonderful Wisdom literature of the Hebrew Scriptures, Wisdom emerges as a force of creation, a dancing, playing, intelligent, planning sheer delight in creation and discovery. Like a benign harlot, Wisdom calls from the street corners, where men and women are going about their daily lives of commerce and their nightly lives of pleasure and lures them to divine love. For Wisdom is female, both feminine and womanly.

This section of the book delights us with all the same lures. From a rich diversity of cultures, the beauties of creation are celebrated with all the exuberance of Wisdom writing in scripture. Women and men rejoice in the powerful female image of God, finding in Godself the image of humanity in its fulness.

Revd Janet Wootton,
Congregational Federation

Preface

In recent years Christian discipleship and prayer have been considerably influenced by the struggle of people all over the world against injustice and inhumanity. We have learnt to sing the songs of oppressed peoples as a way of affirming our solidarity with them. They have enriched and challenged our understanding of what it means to be Christian.

Wisdom is Calling is a remarkable anthology of voices from many different countries inviting us to glimpse the glory of God in both the joy and the pain of our lives. We are called to be creators of justice and joy, compassion and peace. This is no book for those who are content with where they are for it invites us to go on a journey of spiritual exploration into the experience of others as a way of deepening our own commitments to a world of greater peace and freedom.

One of the most striking reflections in the anthology is that 'the edge is the centre of spiritual renewal'. Many of the contributors are known to me either personally or by reputation and I know they live that conviction in their own lives. Many of them have experienced the loneliness of suffering and others among them have discovered their present way of life through identification with those who are forced to the edges of society. All of them have found strength and encouragement from their daily encounter with the living Christ whose ministry was to the poor and the outcasts of his society.

I hope the anthology will be widely used not only for private reflection and encouragement but also in public worship. Its purpose is summed up in one of the contributions calling us

to be strong with compassion
to be just with insight
and to be active in the cause of right with patience.

John Reardon, General Secretary,
Council of Churches for Britain and Ireland,
Advent Sunday 1998

Foreword

The linguist Benjamin Lee Whorf once wrote, 'Speech is the best show man puts on.' (He was writing long enough ago to be forgiven his sexist pronoun.) Devotion, in its personal form or its communal form, inherits the drama that is resident in speech, for Christians are a people of the Word.

Geoffrey Duncan has once again served the whole people of God by providing words, speech, language, the Word. His two previous books have met with warm response here in Canada and his personal presence at the launch of *Seeing Christ in Others*, for Canadian readers provided a personal dimension to this series of devotional anthologies.

Persons returning home from international gatherings, ecumenical or denominational are always enthusiastic about the experience of hearing afresh phrasing for familiar thoughts. This volume allows the many women and men who miss the experience of travel the opportunity of sharing in a worldwide treasury of devotional literature.

The material in this volume has freshness without its being contrived. It springs from genuine conviction. Some of the works have us saying, 'Of course, just as I've always thought' – though we've not found the words to express it but are pleased someone else has. Others bring us up short, like the African saying quoted by Peter Millar of Scotland,

> Eat and drink together;
> talk and laugh together;
> enjoy life together;
> but never call it friendship
> until we have wept together.

Wham!

It is this kind of penetrating expression that makes this an anthology for mission as well as for meditation and worship.

Celebration of the millennium with its theme of Jubilee has us all searching for fresh material for devotion. Our gratitude goes to Geoffrey Duncan and his contributors for meeting that need.

The United Church of Canada's Publishing House is delighted to be involved in publishing this fine work in North America.

Revd Robert A Wallace,
Minister, The United Church of Canada

Introduction

Wisdom cries aloud in the streets; in the markets she raises her voice; on the top of the walls she cries out; at the entrance of the city gates she speaks. Proverbs 1:20

Come Sing and live a world Magnificat,
the new Millennium with hope embrace.
Now is the time for trust and taking sides:
Say 'yes' in love to all the human race.

So writes Fred Kaan in his Magnificat for a New Millennium. The prayers, poems, liturgies and litanies in *Wisdom is Calling* reflect the themes relevant at the beginning of the 21st century.

The world around us is in need of hope and an immense amount of loving care. People are searching for ways in which to express their spirituality. This is reflected in our societies through: the growing number of charities working to improve quality of life for people; people offering themselves for service through taking 'time out', a career change or voluntary work, and people finding ways to be in partnership and solidarity with others in need.

Recently, my wife and I visited South India. We experienced life in Chennai (Madras), Bangalore and remote villages in the drought-prone area of northern Karnataka State. We learned of the work of SAMUHA, a non-governmental development agency based in Bangalore. SAMUHA is Sanskrit for 'an organized group or society which reflects the belief that development is best sustained when undertaken through group processes'. There are community initiatives which allow people to work for their own good and to overcome divisions between caste, class, politics and gender. Work is being carried out with: children and women who are marginalized in city and village communities; families living in slum dwellings in the cities in the clutches of slum landlords; people with disabilities; people living with HIV/AIDS and semi-nomadic people and Tibetan refugees.

Ultimately, people are individuals and SAMUHA recognizes this in its philosophy.

We also visited Church of South India projects in Chennai and Bangalore where it was a delight to meet with the Bishop of Bangalore and his wife, the Rev Mrs Vasanthakumar, who is passionate in her work of alleviating the suffering of the rag pickers, the street children and the young prostitutes. She is also concerned with environmental issues and the needs of women. She is determined to encourage the Church to make a commitment to working in these areas. Bishop Vasanthakumar conducts worship each Sunday in villages where the majority of the people are Dalits – Untouchables. He believes it is important to be alongside his people who suffer injustices in society. The Church, through its many different members, has a task ahead of it, to encourage Christians and members of other faiths, to work together to show love and care to vulnerable people. Church and society need each other and SAMUHA and the Church of South India offer excellent examples of what can be done.

In Canada I learned about First Nations people. Dr Jessie Salteaux was an Assiniboine elder from Carry the Kettle First Nation, Saskatchewan. Her vision was to involve Aboriginal people in the spiritual leadership of their own communities. As a result of her dedication, the Dr Jessie Salteaux Resource Centre was founded in 1984 at Beausejour, Manitoba, Canada. The centre trains Aboriginal people for ministry and provides cross-cultural education for the larger community. The United Church of Canada supports this work in recognizing that these women and men need to be trained for ministry as they are an integral part of Canadian society. The Church and minority groups in their wisdom will help people grow and work together.

In west Belfast, where the local Methodist church is situated in the Catholic area of Springfield Road, I walked through a metal gate in the Peace Wall from the Protestant area of Shankhill Road to the Catholic area and met some inspiring women and men at the Forthspring Community. These included two mothers, one Protestant and one Catholic, who have set up a group for their children so that they can play together in safety. These two mothers are peace campaigners who wish their children to grow up in a spirit of peace which will enable them to develop and live together in harmony as adults.

In today's society I believe that we need to see Christ reflected in our neighbours, wherever they are in the world, so that we overcome differences of class, politics, gender, sexuality and religion. We may have diverse social and cultural backgrounds, but we all laugh and cry, sing and dance, talk and eat together. We can benefit from each others' experiences as we grow in love and grace through the sheer joy of being equal partners in God's world.

Wisdom is calling us to learn from the spirituality inherent in all cultures and contexts in which people live. It is encouraging us to respect each other for who we are and to recognize Christ in each other. We need to make time for reflection; recognize Christ in each other. We need to be open to the wisdom of God and to allow new visions and fresh insights to shape faith and action in the lives of women and men across the world.

This is an anthology of hope and an agenda for change. In the words of a song written by a Hindu member of the Indian Student Christian Movement, 'We need to do something to change the world and make it a better place.'

The Spirit of the Lord is upon me,
because he has anointed me to preach good news to the poor.
He has sent me to proclaim release to the captives
and recovering of sight to the blind,

to set at liberty those who are oppressed,
to proclaim the acceptable year of the Lord. Luke 4: 18,19

Geoffrey Duncan,
Hertfordshire,
1998

A New Heaven and a New Earth

Ecology and the Environment

We Are Responsible . . .

We live in a far from perfect world today because of what humankind has done to it. The words of the prophet Isaiah that 'The earth lies polluted under its inhabitants' (Isaiah 24:5 NRSV) rings true today in a far more reaching way than just the moral pollution intended by the prophet. However, the two are intimately connected and the environmental pollution is caused by greedy and selfish motives. Our air is polluted with all sorts of industrial wastes turning rainfall as acid as lemon juice in some places and our oceans are the dumping grounds for all sorts of unwanted products from sewerage to nuclear waste. We are using up fossil fuel at such a rate that the increase in atmospheric carbon dioxide is causing the global climate to change; we have destroyed part of the stratospheric ozone layer that protects us from excessive radiation by ultra-violet B light; we have lost twenty-five per cent of our topsoil in the last fifty years and we have lost many biological species and continue to lose them at a rate of more than twenty a day. Species extinction now exceeds the natural rate by about a thousand times. All this because the twenty per cent of the population in the developed world greedily seeks an ever increasing standard of living and uses over eighty per cent of the natural resources. At the same time, the developing world increases its population at an unsustainable rate. Creation is indeed 'groaning in labour pains' (Romans 8:22 NRSV) because of what we have done to it.

How far we have strayed from the biblical command given to the first people to look after the land. 'The Lord God took the man and put him in the garden of Eden to till it and keep it' (Genesis 2:15 NRSV). The Hebrew words translated 'till' and 'keep' literally mean 'to serve' and 'preserve'. We are certainly doing neither to the earth, at present, and the destruction continues. The world does not even take seriously such things as the Climate Change Convention or the Convention on Biological Diversity that emerged from the Rio de Janeiro Earth Summit of 1992, yet these and other international agreements are a beginning of world-wide concern and a small sign of hope. Another sign of hope is the number of individuals around the world that are becoming environmentally aware. On my travels, I have found an encouraging number of people who are both concerned and involved in environmental action whether it be in Bangladesh or Belgium, Lucknow or London. A successful response will lie with each individual.

God cares for the creatures of the world: 'Look at the birds of the air; they neither sow nor reap nor gather into barns, and yet your heavenly Father feeds them' (Matthew 6:26 NRSV). But where are his followers in the caring for his creation? We are called here to repentance for our treatment of creation and not only to meditate on what is happening in the world around us or even what a more perfect world would be like, but to put our thoughts into action and become earth-keepers because we know and love the creator God. This does not necessarily mean that we are to be involved in international affairs. Good stewardship of the planet begins at home with each individual playing their part locally. This can and will make a difference.

Ghillean T Prance
England

Director of the Royal
Botanic Gardens, Kew

Daybreak

As at dawn of creation,
The lake waits light's coming;
Herons stand, grey wraiths
In the swirling mist;
Wing-stretchings, stirrings in
Undergrowth, greet the day;
Questioning chirps from a
Secret world swell to
Full throat's song in the
Strengthening sun;
A Kingfisher – glimpse of glory
Glancing in sunlight –
No wonder God rejoices:
It is very good.

Ann Lewin
England

Spirit of Creation

Spirit of creation, spilling into rivers and oceans,
	cleanse the life-giving waters.
Spirit of creation, rushing through mighty forests,
	spread the seeds of new life.
Spirit of creation, burning in the hearts of your people,
	give life, reborn and renewed.
Spirit of God, water, wind and fire,
	fill us with your love.

Diane Clutterbuck
England

Spirit of God

Spirit of God, by your mighty breath the worlds
were set to spin in their places.
Spirit of God, by your gentle breath you gave life
to the sparrow and the lion.
The great and the mighty, the small and the helpless,
all were created as you breathed over the chaos with holy
  breath.

Father God, creator of life,
in a garden you made a home for humanity,
a garden of peace and harmony,
a place of shalom.

Mother God, creator of life,
in a garden you gave birth to human kind.
Eve and Adam, made in your image,
filled with the sacred breath of life.

But we have sinned, O God.
By our arrogant choices and our ignorant misuse of creation,
we have spoiled the garden.
We have polluted the air
and fouled the rivers.
We have turned the grassland to deserts and forests to
  wasteland.
We have eliminated forever some of your creatures.
We have hurt and maimed the ones like us, made in your
  image.

Forgive our pride and our self-indulgence.
Forgive our self-importance and our greed.
Help us take our rightful place in the great circle of life.
Help us to heal our selfish use of of your wonderful gifts.

Spirit of God, breathe new life,
Father God, open our eyes,
Mother God, birth in us a new vision.

Betty Radford Turcott
Canada

Creation Song

My spirit sings in blessing
of the sacredness of the earth,
of the rootedness of all things
and humbleness to grow.

My spirit sings in blessing.
Alleluia. Blessed be.

My spirit sings in blessing
of abundance freely shared,
of lavish hospitality
and the extravagance of grace.

My spirit sings in blessing.
Alleluia. Blessed be.

My spirit sings in blessing
of life that's lived with joy,
of trust that flows in welcome
and a universe of love.

My spirit sings in blessing.
Alleluia. Blessed be.

My spirit sings in blessing
of the spirit that creates,
of the call to be creator
and partake in God's delight.

My spirit sings in blessing.
Alleluia. Blessed be.
Alleluia. Blessed be.

Jan Berry
England

All Creation Is Yours

All creation is yours;
the steamy rain forests and the barren, rocky desert;
the lonely bedsit and the crowded city street;
the power of the atom and the majesty of the stars;
the dark depths of the Atlantic and the windy heights of
    Everest;
the house marten, the rhino and the pilot whale;
the newest baby at the maternity hospital and the frail old
    person.

Creator God, we are all yours,
conceived in your mind long ago,
brought to birth through the patience of evolution,
redeemed by the love of Jesus.

Help us to realise the neighbourliness of all creation –
Forgive our desire to exploit and destroy.
Bring us to new horizons of kindness and service.
Restore in us reverence for all your works.

And teach us to follow you through Jesus Christ,
who is your pattern for all humanity.

Nigel Collinson
England

The Land Is Holy

The land is from God and we are his people;
the land sustains us so we should sustain the land.
Why do we desecrate the land?
Why do we pump impurities into the air?
Why do we fill the rivers with filth?
Since the earth is the Lord's, let us respect it.
Since the land is holy let us revere it.
Since the world is God's creation, let us honour him
in our enjoyment of the land and all its produce.
God gave us Eden; we made hell on earth.
Now let us return to the Lord and obey his word;
then we shall inherit Eden once more.

Responsive Prayer

Leader: Loving Creator,
           you care for the land by sending rain;
           you make it fertile and fruitful.
           What a rich harvest you provide.

Response: **All your creation sings for joy.**

Leader: When we take care of the land,
           sowing the seed and reaping the harvest,

Response: **All your creation sings for joy.**

Leader: When we keep streams and rivers clean,
           when we respect the purity of lakes and seas,

Response: **All your creation sings for joy.**

Leader: When we refuse to hunt down animals,
           when we take care of them and value their
              work,

Response: **All your creation sings for joy.**

9

Leader: When we recognize that we are one family,
            brothers and sisters together, connected to the
                land,

Response: All your creation sings for joy
            for you bless us abundantly all our days.

            I cannot be an enemy to the land
                for the land gives me life.
            I cannot buy or sell the land
        for it is the free gift of God to the people.
            People and land are one creation
        and when their essential unity is broken
            the land and the people suffer.
                All creation cries in pain
        until the redeemer buys its peace again.

John Johansen-Berg
England

I Saw a New Heaven and a New Earth

Call to Worship

Leader: Where is the beauty of the earth today?
            Air and water are polluted.
            Nature is exploited.
            Wealth matters more than Mother Earth.

All: In Jesus' day animals were rounded up in Israel
            for sport killing in Rome's arenas.
            Hills were de-forested for palaces
            in distant lands.
            People died of lead poisoning
            from water pipes and cooking pots.

Leader: In the beginning every part of Creation
was deemed 'good' – of value in and of itself;
and humanity, a precious part
of that intricate and beautiful web.

All: **With God's help, let us strive**
to bring joy to all creation
that the beauty of creation
may one day shine again.

Leader: Come then, let us worship God!

*

Call to Worship

Leader: Every bud that opens,

People on the sides: *Every bird that sings,*

People in the centre: *Every grain that ripens*

All: **reflects God's love!**

Leader: Every act of kindness,

People on the sides: *Every step in faith,*

People in the centre: *Every time justice is restored,*

All: **reveals God's love!**

Leader: Let us be thankful!

All: **And worship our loving and giving**
God!

Betty Lynn Schwab
Canada

11

Rays of Hope

There is a place in the
　universe
so very far away,
where time and space dance
　pirouettes
and form a unity.

And in that place our sun's
　gone out
(perhaps yet to ignite);
it waits and hopes that one
　fine day
it too will see the light.

But here on earth we find
　ourselves
unique in time and space;
creative, complex, self-
　aware:
the marvellous human race.

Our microcosmic hearts are
　but
brief moments in God's
　scope;
but here we brim with life
　and love,
invested with such hope.

This time for life is but a
　blink
within the universe;
and so it is a privilege
God's drama to
　rehearse.

For in this brief and precious
　time
beneath our local sun,
we have the chance to
　contemplate
that all of life is one.

We think and write, we talk
　and make,
we sing and work and play,
to show what God makes
　possible
when reason meets with ray.

But what will be our witness
when the light we now
　reflect
arrives in that place so far
　away,
our actions it detects?

It yearns for air and sea and
　sky,
the chance to re-create;
to be like earth with fish and
　flower,
its own new forms to make.

And yet it sees this moment
　spurned
by lust and greed and
　war;
by creativity denied
God's moment just
　ignored.

Or does it? Do we yet have time?
New shadows we might cast?
So that, across the universe,
the image of life may last.

Ed Cox
England

Trinity of Earth, Sky and Sea

God of the owls
you know where we are going
and what we must do
to fulfil our potential.
Fly above us
shelter us under your wings.

   God of the owls fly above us.

Christ of the dolphins
when we play in the shallows
or flounder in deep water
you have already been there.
Swim alongside us
sharing our joys and entering our pain.

   Christ of the dolphins swim alongside us.

Spirit of the moles
sent to empower us
to delve tunnels
linking ourselves to each other
burrow within us
making our lives your home.

   Spirit of the moles burrow within us.

Trinity of all living things
of earth, sky and sea
we feel your presence
and worship your creativity.

Trinity of earth, sky and sea
we worship your creativity.

Heather Johnston
England

Multi-coloured Glory

Gracious God,
in the bright multi-coloured glory of Creation,
and the heartbeat rhythm of the seasons,
in the light of Christ we live,
our days and ways illuminated by your Spirit.
We bring our darknesses and our brightnesses –
all the shades and colours of our lives –
our winter, spring, summer, autumn
before you now in worship:
and we pray that as we seek to draw near to you,
we will know you near us and with us as we go.
In Jesus' name we pray.

Stephen Brown
England

Intricate Wonders

To witness an ebony quilt of sky
stitched by beaming stars;
And awaken to ancient cedar's sway
dancing with the wind,
Is to glimpse God's scattering of grace.

14

To recognize an inner flutter and pulse
as new life's movement in the womb;
Or hear a tone so sweetly sung
that heaven opens within,
Is to stand at the threshold of everything holy.

To wonder at the sweep of a whale
breaching the air from concealed depths;
Or gaze at the ripples and curves formed above
by a cloud of wings on the move,
Is to be breathless with praise for the radiance of life.

Keri K Wehlander
Canada

Marking the Swallow's Fall

a swallow's grey wing
like a pointed gravestone
sticks up from the highway
marks
the broken purple
the interrupted green
of the swallow

a trinity of purple-green
flickering above the wing
dips and rises in turn
spins
a tilting prayer circle
of autumnal purple
and vernal green

Norm S D Esdon
Canada

Stargazing

Look up, look up at the stars
twinkling high above the dark village
in the black velvet of night.
Stars, millions of years old;
Light travelling to us before we were born.
Space infinite and beyond our understanding;
Galaxy beyond galaxy baffling comprehension;
Constellation and black hole defying thought.
Look up, look up at the stars!
Open your mind to the grandeur of God.
Untie the string around the narrow box of your thought.
Let God be free – don't try to tame her
or reduce her to your comprehension.
God is greater than our understanding,
way beyond the narrow limits of our thought.
Look up, look up at the stars
and let heart and mind leap in praise and wonder.

Jean Mayland
England

A Restless Star

Creative God, who from the voids of space
Took dust and fire, and into being hurled
A restless star, this softly shining world,
Swept by the wind from darkness into light.
Till ages gone, the green expectant earth
Knew the first agonies of human birth.

And now grown proud, wise in our own conceit,
We twist your laws to ravage and destroy;
Our clamour drowns your Spirit's song of joy
Our strident arrogance derides your Word.
While statesmen barter peace for bitter lands
With uncontrolled destruction in their hands.

Forgive us still, though we confess with shame,
That in our fear-filled selfishness and greed
We reap the spoils, while others sow the seed,
We garner gold, but do not share our gain,
Lured by the comforts of complacency
And lulled by dreams of false security.

Creative God, revealed in Christ, your Son,
Still challenge us to choose the way he chose;
To make the desert blossom like the rose,
To break the barren stones as living bread.
Till deaf ears hear the language of the dumb,
And sightless eyes perceive your Kingdom come.

Jill Jenkins
England

God Give Me a Dream

O God, where has it gone?
Where has it all gone;
flowers and cottages,
the gentle, unpolluted sunset,
a perfect rest
at the end of a satisfying day's work,
friendship on the streets,
life that was golden and good?
As I stumble up the stairs that smell like a toilet,
dance between the needles
and close my ears to the shouting;
my heart aches for long ago.
Where is This England now?

'It's gone, my child,
because it never was.'

This millennium, God give me
a dream for the future,
a dream that one day
will be as real
as the concrete beneath my feet.

Bob Warwicker
England

What Have We Done?

What have we done? How can we mend it?
Why are we killing birds, animals, plants, trees and rivers?

Look into the future. What do you see?
Look into the past. How many differences can you find?

When you listen to the past, what do you hear?
When you listen in the future, what will you hear?

Will you notice any differences? If yes, how many?
I cannot count. I think there are too many!

Katrina Maclean (aged 11)
Scotland

Back to Earth

when I weep for
    the beluga
    the peregrine
    and the giant panda
when I mourn for
    the amazon
    the queen charlottes
    and canada north

when I chafe under
    acid rain
    nuclear snow
    and torn ozone

then I will remember you
    little girl
that rain spattered morning
I spotted you
fingertip-flipping
rain battered earthworms
    from the gutter
    back to the earth

Norm S D Esdon
Canada

Cathedral

Without its walls the pavementing people
are hurrying to spend the sun's hours
moneying in hives of grey granite
while the racecard yelling city
feverishly pounds through another day.

Still there it stands all stony and golden
midst the city's cacophony,
a part of the complex,
like a heart surely beating in a fretful being –
a silent assurance of purposefulness.

Harry Wiggett
South Africa

An Urban Version of Isaiah 35

When God comes as Creator and Powerful Vindicator to the
    urban wilderness this will be the herald's song:

Let the tenement and the derelict parkland be glad,
let the slums and ghettoes rejoice and burst into comfort and
    beauty.
Let them flower with well-kept gardens,
let music and laughter be heard in the streets –
the glory of dreaming spires is given to them,
the splendour too of cathedral and palace;
these will see the glory of the Lord,
the splendour of our God.

Encourage those who have no work,
steady the ones who fall under work's burden;
say to the despairing and the depressed, 'Be strong, don't be
    afraid!
Your God is here to save you,
to bring justice and freedom.'

Then there will be vision for those who were blinded by
    despair
and the people who longed for a friendly voice will hear
    love-songs.
Those crippled by poverty will jump up and run into plenty
and the powerless will find a voice;
for friendship will break out in the slums
and love will explode in joy in the ghettoes.
People's dreams will begin to come true
and their barren longings suddenly possible;
instead of disillusion, hope will grow
in communities where fear haunts the streets!

And this will be the way forward
along the way of peace where travellers go safely
    – the way of just dealing and honest trade,

where neither mugger nor loan shark will be found.
On that road the people will return to God who rescues them.
Free at last, God's people will possess the city
and shout out in delight at God's triumph
and their joy will last for ever!
Gladness and joy will be theirs at last,
while misery and hopelessness will be banished.

Heather Pencavel
England

Simplistic?

We go in our cars,
We do –
Well, we have to,
We'll be late
Otherwise . . .

It's only a little way,
Lots of stops and starts,
Lots of fumes.

It's hot,
The sun burns
Through the haze –
We can't see far,
Only a little way –
Lots of fumes.

We can't see the sky-hole
The sun burns through –
Because of the haze . . .
We do know it's stopped the rain
Somehow, though –
Not here but in other places –

Stopped the rain
So nothing grows
Over there now . . .
Because we drive our cars here
And the rain stops there –
The crops fail –
So
When we drive here

We steal from their begging bowls.

Margot Arthurton
England

Enchantment in the Suburbs

Have you noticed how magic has been seeping out of the world? It's no longer *enchanting*. The world needs re-enchantment. It needs to find a sense of mystery and magic again. *The body needs a soul.*

When God made the Garden of Eden, he made all sorts of trees with all sorts of fruit. As children, we probably have memories of climbing trees, mysterious trees, private cubby-houses away from adults.

Trees are often used in the Bible as metaphors for growth, strength, shelter, protection. As in Psalm One: 'Blessed is the man who does not walk in the counsel of the wicked, or stand in the way of sinners or sit in the seat of mockers. But his delight is in the law of the Lord and on his law he meditates day and night. He is like a tree planted by streams of water, which yields its fruit in season and whose leaf does not wither. Whatever he does prospers'(RSV).

There is a sense in which some Australian suburbs embody a respect for nature, a reproduction of the Garden of Eden in everyone's front yard.

Trees and gardens have some mystical quality. Entering a garden is like entering another world, where time stands still, flowers grow slowly and you can commune with nature. Gardens need nurturing like humans do. If cared for properly, plants and trees stand tall, provide fruit and flowers, contribute to the cycle of life as bees and birds eat from them, drop seeds and fertilize other plants.

A regular recipe for stress is to spend more time in the garden.

It is interesting how much great music and how many great paintings focus on the garden. They tell us that the soul cannot thrive in the absence of a garden. And, more profoundly, they tell us that our soul is like a garden. It needs watering to prevent dryness, protecting from adversity and fertilizing to produce fruit. If this happens, not only is our garden re-enchanted, so is our soul.

Alan Nichols
Australia

Fulfilment

The leaf was made for dancing
and the cloud for shade at noon;
The breeze was made for freshness
when the sea gleams in the moon.
The waves were made for stirring
and mountains to be still,
the daisies made for sunlight
and great trees to clothe the hill.

And everything that you have made
was good in your sight, Lord.
For all things have a part to play
and nothing is ignored.

You lead the way from seed to fruit,
from womb to birth to youth;
You trust us all to be mature,
to handle love and truth;
Now help us, Lord, to give a place
to every living thing,
to know the good that you have made,
that every voice may sing.

Bernard Thorogood
London/Sydney

For the Man and for the Woman

For the man and for the woman,
for the body and the soul,
for the mind and for the spirit,
for the love that makes them whole;
for the person and the people,
for the many and the few,
for tradition and for custom,
for the fresh and for the new.

For the friendship, for the suffering,
for the pleasure and the grief,
for the learning, for the listening,
for the doubting and belief;
for the sound and for the silence,
for the labour and the prayer,
for the rock and for the flower,
for the earth and for the air.

For the harmony of nations,
for the sounds of many lands,
for the rhythm, for the chanting,
for the language of the hands;
for the richness of the senses,
for the colour and design,
for the weaving of the pattern,
for the circle and the line.

In the dancer and the poet,
in the singer and the song,
in the artist and the actor,
on the flute and on the gong,
we will praise you, great Creator,
light of light and fire of fire;
make us one and make us many –
your delight is our desire.

Colin Gibson
Aotearoa New Zealand

Rivers, Mountains and Trees

Albuquerque dawn, like an icon of praise
To a God who paints pictures to lighten our days
Who dances on the morning and opens our eyes
A God who's an artist and who loves to surprise.

North Carolina in the time of fall
A carpet of leaves covers it all
Beautiful sunlight makes everything gold
Brings shimmers of glory to comfort your soul.

Chorus: The rivers, the mountains and the trees
Wind off the desert, walks by the sea
Gold leaves in the Autumn and warm
   Summer breeze

Like a holy touch of mercy that helps us to
 breathe.
The rivers, the mountains and the trees.

Down at Port Alfred you can sit there all day
Watch the dolphins swim past somewhere around ten
Then in the evening they're back without fail
And, if you're lucky, you may see a whale.

Chorus: The rivers . . .

Passing Loch Lomond, heading up to Loch Ness
Passing Ben Nevis but the part I love best
Is the awe and fear as you go through Glencoe.
Such a strict God as the mountains loom close.

Chorus: The rivers . . .

Early one morning I woke up to see
A moment of destiny on my TV
People clasping hands round the trunk of a tree.
They were trying to save it for posterity.

Chorus: The rivers . . .

There's a tale that is told from the Southern Sudan
About a tree where life began.
And it's strange how our myths and our stories agree
There's something quite special that begins with a tree.

Chorus: The rivers . . .

The Hills of Jerusalem now disappear
Wrapped up in concrete and buried with tears.
Up north birds are singing on a mountain by the sea
It happens to be where a man talked of peace.

Chorus: The rivers . . .

Mystical moment – speak to me still
From the Church of St Enodoc next to Bray Hill
Did I feel God breathing – did the earth really shake?
Centuries of prayer – all for our sake.

Chorus: The rivers . . .

Snapshots of beauty returning to me
Make me so grateful for all that I've seen.
Images so wild in the surf and the rain
O the power and there's beauty from a strength that's not
    tame.

Chorus: The rivers . . .

Garth Hewitt
England

Trees

Father God of golden leaves
reflecting your majesty
the swaying branches
bow down in humility.

Mother God of brown leaves
uniting the earth
recreating new life
in your kingdom.

Christ of crimson leaves
life-throbbing blood
flowing with fire
through our veins.

Spirit of evergreen leaves
surging with sap

filling with power
replenishing life.

Trinity of trees
changing
falling
recreating
renewing.

Heather Johnston
England

Tree of Life

Ezekiel 31: 3–7; Proverbs 30: 24–28

Leader: Patient, mysterious forests
Dancing, playful skies
Glimmering, ancient waters –

All: **You blessed and called, 'Good'.**

Leader: Sleek, ecstatic dolphins
Elegant, watchful herons
Persistent, creative spiders –

All: **You blessed and called, 'Good'.**

Leader: Luminous, fragile shells
Intricate, nurturing soil
Drifting, brilliant clouds –

All: **You blessed and called, 'Good'.**

Leader: This beloved expanse of life,
This delicate flow of breath
Must be cherished to endure
Must be honoured that all may thrive.

All: **May we cherish and bless;**
                May we honour and uphold,
                May God declare: 'It is good!'

*

Leader: Ancient strength, this tree of life:
                water, breath and bone.
                Each leaf linked to soil and star –
                no part stands alone.

                Flight of an owl to form a branch,
                scent of a rose to shape the trunk,
                laughter of people to pattern the bark,
                grace of a leopard to fashion a stem,
                song of a whale to weave a root –
                no part stands alone.

All: **May we revere this tree of life,**
                and see it as God's own.
                Walking our days, mindful of all –
                for no part stands alone.

Keri K Wehlander
Canada

Next Year There Will Be No Nest

Based on Deuteronomy 22: 6–7

Next year there will no nest,
the hen is dead. The cock bird
flies his repeated spiral of confusion.
His shrieking lament breaks unheard
against the deafened sky.

29

Can you hear the birdsong
over the traffic roar,
scent the wildflower
on the fume filled wind,
harsh gale of a thousand
passing juggernauts?

The trees, breeze-dancers
of the centuries,
are burned grey ash,
the breathing grass
smothered beneath
grey asphalt.
Where now will the bird rest from flight
the mind from the tyranny of concentration
or the wheel from turning?

O God,
who knows each sparrow's fall,
let there still be time
for our returning,
for the building of nests
and the fragile beauty of the heartsease.

Peter Trow
Wales/England

Climate Change

The earth is the Lord's and the fullness thereof. Psalm 24:1a

The effects of climate change are predicted to include:
more intense storms,
more floods,
more droughts
and more disease.

To keep climate changes within bearable limits, the emission of greenhouse gases,
especially carbon dioxide, methane and chlorofluorocarbon must be significantly reduced.
Industrial countries are the main source of these emissions while the first victims
will be small island states such as in the Pacific
and low-lying coastal countries like Bangladesh.

Despite the risks people and governments are slow to act.

Here we stand Creator God,
Forgive us when we treat this beloved planet
as if we own it and can use it as we wish.
Forgive us when we recklessly exploit its resources and
pollute its complex ecosystems.
Our lifestyle of wasteful over-consumption
in the rich industrial countries is insensitive
to the effects of global warming on
peoples and ecosystems around the world.
We want to express our love and care for all creation.
We know that we must learn more about the problem and
take effective action.
Here we stand wondering and confused
because of the bounty that you have given us.
And here we stand Creator God,
and we ask you to help us to care for the earth
as our responsibility.
Help us to do what we know we must
even at the cost of reducing our lifestyle
so that others may live.
Please help us O God.

National Commission for Mission
Uniting Church in Australia

The Myth of Farming

John was taught that farmers had an affinity with the land. Farming, he was told, was a way of life. People were not farming for money but for the lifestyle. When John moved to a prosperous rural area he was quickly disabused of this notion.

The province had rich soil because originally it was bush covered. The climate never went to extremes. It was a very pleasant place to be. However, in the time John was there two major climatic changes took place. There were often severe floods in the winter and droughts in the summer.

The reason was simple. Farmers cleared most of the bush so that when the winter rains came there was nothing to absorb them. The rain swept off the hills and the result was widespread flooding. Because there was no bush to absorb the water everything dried up. The result was severe droughts.

If we abuse nature there are always consequences. Even people who have an affinity with the land can make mistakes over its use.

Prayer for the Environment

I guess it's a matter of different strokes for different folks,
    Lord.
The idea of a new heaven and a new earth
where streets are paved with gold has never appealed.
Why on earth, Lord, would you want gold streets?
Even as a symbol, I don't see the point.

Now a river of water, pure and clear,
that has more appeal.
An unpolluted river.
There used to be lots of them
but now it is difficult to find pure water.
Our water supply has so many things added,
chloride, fluoride and goodness knows what else.
So it will be nice to have pure water to drink, Lord.

Somewhere else, is it Isaiah,
you speak of the lion and the lamb lying down together
that has some appeal but it seems a little unnatural.
Did you not make nature red in tooth and claw?
If there are no more carnivores what will clean up the dead
    carcasses?
What effect will all these extra herbivores have on the
    environment?

The need for a new heaven and a new earth assumes this one
    is flawed.
We have taken this heaven and earth for granted.
So what will change if we get a new one?

Les A Howard
Aotearoa/New Zealand

Mining and the Environment

We all benefit from the good life. Nearly everything we use
and own has been made from raw materials produced by mining and oil exploration. If we have insurance and superannu-
ation policies then it is possible that some of our funds are
invested in shares in resource development companies. None
of us can escape from being involved in the decisions being
made by mining companies.

For many people, particularly in developing countries, on
whose land minerals are mined, their experience has been one
of devastation and change. Land has been taken away. Special
places have been spoilt. Rivers have been polluted. Land
rights and human rights have been denied.

Creator God,
we love the miracles of modern technology
that produce the variety of material goods on which we
    depend.

33

We enjoy cars, our computers and our labour saving devices.
Our livelihood depends on the continuing availability of
   minerals and oil.

When we consider where these resources come from,
we know that sometimes all is not well,
that our good life is built on the pain of others.
Give us the grace to recognize this inter-relatedness.
Help us to make the connections and bear some of the
   sacrifice,
by recycling, reusing, rethinking and caring
about the cost that people may have paid
with their lives, their community and their land.
Help us to make the changes needed
to protect the environment
and ensure justice for all people.

National Commission for Mission
Uniting Church in Australia

Theoland

How come God and Land,
In theology they speak?
Land was God,
God's land it was.
People spoke to God,
God spoke to people.
The land they possessed
Sacred, Precious and Tender,
Mother-like they cared, shared until Tanha (Greed)
Engulfed them to conquest, occupy.
Roughly used,
Desecrated the land god,
Mother they treasured and revered,
'Give back our mother God'
A cry of people

Raped and polluted
To build a Theoland,
Sacred to the Dispossessed.
God's Land – Land God
Both owned by Landless people
Of the God of the Land.

Shanthi Hettiarachchi
Sri Lanka

Ecology-Theology

God Creator
We the creature
With all nature
Share we this

God is Lover
We beloved
With all other
We are His

God the Son is
Ever Saviour
In our oneness
Thus He gave

Every creature
To our keeping
Made us free to
Spoil or save

Let us hallow
God the Father
Thus to follow
God the Son

With the Holy
Spirit in us
Loving fully
Every one.

Audrey Bryant
England

Pilgrim Bread

Touch tenderly: earth, water, air,
salt, time and broken grain –
this one life
in all. Touch
with loving hands;

hands to make
to shape and mould,
warm, moisty dough,
feeling fleshy,
smelling earthy;

hands to bake,
well crusted bread
set by the sun
transformed by fire,
warm with wonder

hands to break
and break again
pilgrim bread
for pilgrim people.

In the kitchens,
from the tables,
priests of the moment
we dare to serve

this quiet mystery
this risen life
gift of the earth
gift of our hands
for all to share.

Joy Mead
England

Striding Out

Let the earth be fractured with cracks of joy
    infectiously spreading across the nations.
Let new hope echo through city, town and country
    knocking down the fortresses of hate and despair.

In the new millennium, let us find
    the courage to love
    and the strength to cross
the boundaries of our separateness.
Give us the ability to cultivate and share
    the strengths of our diversity;
so that by exploring the countless possibilities
we sustain and enrich our world.

Miriam Bennett
England

Tread Gently

Blessed are you who tread gently on the earth
    for you will be part of the new creation.
Blessed are you who share its resources now
    for you will also share in the feast prepared for all
      people.
Blessed are you who weep at the destruction of the land
    for you will laugh and dance in green fields.

37

Blessed are you when you are hated and insulted because
you show up
the folly of others who do not share your concern for the
earth and its people.
Rejoice in that day and leap for joy because you shall dwell
with God.

But woe to you who exploit the earth,
for you have already received your comfort.
Woe to you who are greedy and ensure your own wants are
met without
a thought for the toil of others,
for you will go hungry.
Woe to you who laugh as factories pump waste into rivers,
as exhaust fumes fill the skies,
as unprotected workers inhale pesticides,
for you will mourn and weep.
Woe to you when bankers and shareholders speak well of
your profits
and ignore your ethics,
for the Lord knows the secrets of the heart.

Jenny Spouge
England

We Recycle

This is a land the Lord your God cares for. Deuteronomy 11:12

Only God can create
the atoms of the earth,
can arrange their planetary song;
We rearrange –
we recycle.

We bring down on our heads
what we pump into the skies;
We breathe, drink and eat

38

what we throw out –
    we recycle.

We and our children will be
what we dump;
Garbage out
is garbage in –
    we recycle.

What we recycle –
poisoned or purified
curse or blessing –
    is our choice.

We can do for the earth
as we would have the earth
do for us;
only God can create –
    we recycle.

Norm S D Esdon
Canada

Your World

We pray for the world –
a world of hunger and deprivation,
a world of pain and self-seeking,
a world of hatred and warfare –
and yet, also,
a world of beauty and music,
a world of nobility and literature,
a world of caring and of learning.

Gracious God,
we believe that this world,
with its mixture of good and evil,

is ultimately your world,
created by you through long ages
and redeemed by you in Christ.

Therefore, we pray that your Holy Spirit
will live and work through
all those men and women
who are receptive to you,
bringing hope and vision
and peace into people's lives.
And as we pray for others,
so we pray for ourselves.
Strengthen our faith,
we humbly pray,
to withstand adversity and temptation
and so to live the Christian life,
through Jesus Christ our Saviour.

Nigel Collinson
England

They Heal Their Bodies . . . They Heal the Earth

She bleeds,
With every slash on her body
She weeps!
The electric saw cuts deep . . . cuts quickly
Into the gentle flesh of the trees.
The trees weep!
And slowly the forests die . . .
The soil dies . . .
The earth dies
And God knows that the earth weeps
And weeps with her.

She bleeds,
With every battering of her body

She weeps!
His hand has power . . . it cuts deeply
Into the gentle flesh of her soul.
We all weep!
Slowly the women die . . .
The community dies . . .
The earth dies
And God knows that the women weep
And weeps with them.

The women resist the saw
The audacious power of the profit seeking contractor.
The women use their wounded bodies
To save their trees.
The only form of resistance open to them
They cling to the trees defying death.
They stop the saw.
They stop the flow of blood.
They heal the forests,
They heal the earth.

The women resist the violence
The arrogant power of the 'brave and strong' one.
The women transcend their suffering and pain
To save their lives.
The only form of strength they have.
They come together into a circle of energy,
They cling to each other's tears.
They overcome the hurt, the pain.
They heal the community.
They heal the earth.

Women of the Chipko movement,
Women of the earth,
Women of life . . .
Women of survivors of violence,
Women of hope . . .
They weep no more,

They heal their bodies,
They heal the earth . . .
And God laughs with uninhibited joy!

Aruna Gnanadason
India

Love Is Made Perfect In Us . . .
Creating Community

A Work of Love

'"Community" is a warm word. Nobody is supposed to be against it. Yet there is a bewildering range of uses of the word. In recent years, we have heard of community development, community studies, community policing, youth and community work, community care, community health and even community theologians! In 1955 George Hillery listed ninety-four uses of the term, the only feature they had in common being a concern about people. A feature which was not included was that of decline, although that seems to be a central theme in the current discussion.'

Kenneth Leech, *The Sky is Red*, (DLT, 1997)

This quotation highlights the increasing use of the word 'community' – a term I hear often in my pastoral work and as a member of the ecumenical Iona Community. During my years as Warden of Iona Abbey, I met literally thousands of people, from around the world, who were involved, one way or another, with the restoration of local communities. Bridge-builders, who were often working in areas where there had been a total break-down of the common life, or where different cultural and religious traditions encountered one another only in conflict and misunderstanding.

Yet in this search for 'community' in our post-modern world which is marked by its plurality, it is not possible to retreat to some notion of the common life rooted in an idealized model of rural living. If the churches of the West are to be prophetically engaged, in the coming century, with the rebuilding of the common life, then this task must be grounded in the vibrancy, fragmentation and extraordinarily rich diversity of urban areas. And on any counts, that is the work which will demand profound spiritual awareness, a compassionate engagement with contemporary cultures and a constant willingness to take risks and be in solidarity with the vulnerable and powerless.

It is essentially a work of love: of reaching out, of accepting the fact that Christ's peace is never going to be 'comfortable' although it may be comforting. In the first Letter of John we read: 'God is love and whoever lives in love lives in union with God and God lives with them. Love is made perfect in us.' Within these powerful and beautiful words is held the primary energy and underlying wisdom of any authentic restoration of community. Or to put it another way: can we reach out to 'the other' without a recognition that Christ is continually reaching out to us in love and acceptance?

In recent years there has been a renewed interest in Celtic spirituality. This growing awareness of our Celtic inheritance has many dimensions and while it is not possible to make an easy transition from the world of the Celtic peoples into our own times, this legacy offers illumination as we wrestle with the reality of community, both locally and globally. The Celtic Christian recognized that Christ is present in the stranger's guise – a truth expressed in the rune of hospitality:

> We saw a stranger yesterday,
> We put food in the eating place,
> Drink in the drinking place,
> Music in the listening place,
> And, with the sacred name of the triune God,
> He blessed us and our house,
> Our cattle and our dear ones.
> As the lark says in her song:
> Often, often, often,
> Goes Christ in the stranger's guise.

We can be greatly strengthened in our search for a more genuine and life-giving understanding of our neighbour, whether next door or far away, when we recognize in her or him the face of Christ. Such a perception of 'the other' propels us out of our often self-absorbed, rather privatized life-styles. It underlines the fact, as the gospel reminds us, that we are not really in a position to understand even a fragment of the mystery of God's love if we have not walked in companionship with our sisters and brothers. And it is this kind of deep-rooted solidarity which will be present within re-energized communities.

Perhaps that is why I have always been touched by an old African saying which has contemporary relevance:

> Eat and drink together;
> talk and laugh together;
> enjoy life together;
> but never call it friendship
> until we have wept together.

As we look at the many social and economic divisions in our own communities we may well wonder if 'community' in any meaningful way can ever return. My own view is that we are living through a time of great searching and uncertainty in which many familiar markers are disappearing. For some people, this present fragmentation is enormously threatening but it is also a moment of possibility for the churches which, when they are seeking to be faithful to the gospel and not only interested in their survival, are signs of real community.

It is not fashionable to speak of mutual accountability but the gospel is always calling us back to this truth. We are bound together in Christ: enfolded as a pilgrim people with many questions and many uncertainties, in the light and forgiving love of the One who walks with us. And it is in this amazing hope that we can begin to find community, not as an abstract philosophy or a warm word, but rather as a vibrant reality revealing many surprises. The last word has not been left with those who believe that individual self-enhancement regardless of others, is the ultimate goal of the human journey. Our times are revealing more clearly than ever, just how interconnected we all are on this small, yet amazingly diverse, planet.

Peter W Millar
Scotland
Warden of Iona Abbey 1995–1998

Seeing Christ

Two
arms of an empty cross;
one pointing up to heaven,
the other out into the world.

'Why
look among the dead
for someone
who is alive?
Jesus is not here;
he has risen.' *

Now,
wherever I turn,
I see
the face of Christ
gazing steadfastly
back at me.

Susan Hardwick
England

* *Luke 24:5b, 6a*

Praise Be to God!

Praise be to God,
who calls the people to new hope in every generation,
who lifts our eyes to see a new heaven and a new earth
which one day will break through the old, tired efforts
and reach into justice beyond our imagining.

Praise be to God,
who leads us on past crucifixions of failure,
rejection and faithlessness,
drawing a picture of a world ready to blossom from the bud,
delicate and fragile,
vulnerable as a baby in Bethlehem.

Praise be to God,
who brings to life the dead bodies of despair
which lie entombed in our souls
and in our churches,
dancing ahead of us undefeated
in the Spirit of truth and healing and love.
Praise be to God!

Dorothy McRae-McMahon
Australia

Love Is Made Perfect In Us

Call to Worship

Leader: The world always asks
who will we include?
who matters?
who's the best?

All: **Even in the church**
we often disagree.
People feel left out and hurt.

49

Leader: Our families and schools, churches and malls
challenge us: does our love show?
does God's love show in us?

All: **God is love.**
And God's love is made perfect
in us.
So let us come before God
in hope and trust,
so that God's Love might shine
through us all.

Leader: Yes! Let us worship God!

Call to Worship

Leader: Christ calls to us, 'Get up!'

People on the sides: *Up out of our indifference!*

People in the centre: *Up out of our self-centred living!*

People on the sides: *Up out of our fears, paralysis and death*
in all its forms.

Leader: Christ calls to us, 'Get up and live!'

People in the centre: *Live justice and peace!*

People on the sides: *Live generosity and harmony!*

All: **Live Christ's Way!**

Leader: So, come, let us worship Him!

All: **Jesus Christ, our Risen Lord.**

Betty Lynn Schwab
Canada

Transform Us

Holy, loving, inviting God
In Jesus you call us to yourself
    and make us into a holy, loving and inviting people.
May we proclaim the good news of your reign
    in all we say
    in all we do
    in all we are
    (in this parish/congregation/community).
God the Sending One, may your love transform us in worship
God the Sent One, may your grace liberate us in ministry
God our Strengthener as we go, may your power lead us
   gently in mission.

Michael McCoy
South Africa/Australia

Move Us On

Move us on, God,
move us on
from these wounded streets

For it seems
in our frozen twilight
we have rediscovered tenderness
and are noticing each other

We have become inexperienced pilgrims,
bringing bouquets, small poems,
sleeping bags, our cluttered stories,
our children and our candles of intention

Move us on, God, together
deep in the present
whilst holding to the past and future lands

With our hearts now all outside us
we should be ready
to enfold the desperate
and prod the powerful

Move us on, God,
move us on
we your faint, unfinished psalms
now crave for your translucent palms

Stewart Henderson
England

On the Edge

Look for us, Lord.
We are on the edge,
vulnerable and afraid.

Search for us, Lord.
We are beyond the pale,
lonely and fearful.

Find us, Lord.
We have wandered far from home,
isolated and rejected.

> I, your God,
> like a good shepherd,
> have known you
> from the beginning of your time.

> I hear your cry,
> I run to meet you,
> as you re-turn to me.

The tree of defeat
has become the tree of glory.
Where life was lost
life has been restored.

Christ is risen.
He is risen indeed!

Kate McIlhagga
England

We Are All Alone

Gordon had only just left Disraeli Road when, carrying a little
   square package, prettily wrapped, Nicki knocked at the
   same house.

Sue's mother opened the door to her.

'I called to see how Sue was.'

'Not too badly, dear, but she's upstairs resting in bed. She's
   rather upset at the moment.'

'Can I go up for a minute?'

'Well, come inside, dear . . . now, what's your name?'

Nicki told her and Mrs Girton went upstairs. There was a mur-
   mur of voices overhead, then almost at once, she was back.

'I'm sorry, dear. She doesn't want to see anybody just at the
   moment. She's had a nasty shock.'

It was a mistake to have come. She was conscious of the faint
   smell of freesia from the bathcubes in her hand. They were
   a frivolity and probably more expensive than was necessary
   but she had felt instinctively that they were the right thing.

'I would like to see her. Can you tell her I'm sorry and I'd like
   to be friends?'

Sue's mother turned again and began to mount the stairs for
   the second time.

'Tell her to go away,' called Sue's voice from above. 'She's
   mucked it all up and I don't want to see her . . . ever.'

'I think you'd better go,' said Sue's Mum.

'Look,' Nicki spoke urgently. 'Will you tell her I do understand. Tell her Steve had a go at me, too.'

She stepped to the foot of the stairs.

'Sue, I am sorry,' she called up. 'Sue, Steve had a go at me, too.'

There was a moment's silence.

'What do you mean?'

'Steve . . . he tried to attack me.'

'I don't believe you. Go away. Just go away!'

'Can't I come up and talk?'

'No. Go away. I don't want to see anybody.'

Mrs Girton opened the front door.

'I think . . .,' she began.

It all seemed so difficult, suddenly.

'We are all alone, aren't we,' Nicki wanted to say. 'We are all
so terribly alone . . . alone most of the time.'

She thought of people spending whole chapters of their lives
unable to communicate.

She pushed the scented package at Sue's Mum and went.

Brian Louis Pearce
England

Sunday Night, after 'Phone Calls

A woman, dear to me, has been held under siege
in the home she was trying to share with her rampaging
daughter.
Living nailed to a cross?

A woman, dear to me, is returning to her home,
knowing it holds all the loneliness from which she had fled.
Living in an empty tomb?

Sisters, will you find any resurrection time tonight?

A woman, dear to me, is learning to live alone
in a quiet house, cat and radio her best company.

Living in a pre-dawn garden?

Sister, will you recognize the new day when it comes?

And very early on the first day of the week, when the sun had risen,
they went to the tomb. They had been saying to one another, 'Who
will roll away the stone for us from the entrance to the tomb?' When
they looked up, they saw that the stone, which was very large, had
been rolled back.

Mark 16:2

Living God, roll away the very large stones before us.
Give us a sunrise picture of our lives
bursting forth with new joy.

Gillian Hunt
Australia

Prayer Walk

My garden gate opens out on to the world.
The world of my neighbours.
As I walk past their homes,
their lives come to mind.
There's the elderly man who cares,
day in, day out,
for his wife with Alzheimer's disease.
Two doors on,
a woman, widowed a year ago
but her wounds of grief are still very raw.
Across the road,
the teenage son has dropped out of college.
He stays in his room
all day and out of the house
most of the night
and will hardly speak to his worried parents.

Lord, how should I love my neighbour?

Into the main road –
solemn faces gaze from a passing bus –
anxiety?
Anticipation?
Boredom?

You know, Lord, what they are thinking.

At the post office –
signed books proffered under the glass partition,
double stamped
returned with pensions or allowance.
Money carefully counted, pursed and pocketed.
The means of survival ensured for another week?

Dear God,
a name on a booklet
may signify a benevolent government's acknowledgement
that a person exists
but You know the real needs
and entitlements of that human being.

Help us work for a caring and just society.

Returning I pass the doctor's surgery and
recall that today a friend goes for blood test results.
Anxiety, hope, despair, joy.
Just a few words will make all the difference.

Back at my gate,
half an hour
and half a mile later.
It was more than just a walk to post a letter.

Rowena Webster
England

A Malagasy Story

Jao and Vony moved to town with their three children aged two and four years because life in the country was no longer viable: crops were stolen when they were still in the fields, their hens were killed by disease or stolen. They decided to move with a hope for better living conditions, knowing nothing about life in the big cities. They wandered about trying to find jobs, sleeping under the arcades or the bridges, fighting against the police and the other homeless people, doing all kinds of odd jobs – just trying to survive.

While he was washing cars, Jao met a middle-aged couple. He told his story which aroused their sympathy. They engaged him as their guard and gardener. Also, Vony could help with the housekeeping. The couple said that if Jao and Vony did well in their work they would reward them accordingly. And they did: they paid for Jao's driving lessons and provided Vony with materials needed at the church women's group for knitting and sewing. They paid school fees for the children.

Everything is going well for the family. Jao and Vony are saving for the young villagers they have left behind and whom they intend to help. They are thinking of setting up a youth centre in their village where young people can learn skills that will help them in life. Their motto is, 'You are freely given so you must freely give.'

Naliranto Ranaivoson
Madagascar

Proclaim Jubilee

Generous God, you created this world for all to share,
Unclench our hands to let go of the greed which robs the
    poor,
Unclog our ears to hear the agony of all who cry for justice,
Unbind our hearts to recognize those who are oppressed by
    debt,

Open our lips to proclaim Jubilee in our own time and place,
May our care be thorough and our solidarity active,
May this community be a sign of hope,
For now is the favourable time.

St Michael's Parish
Liverpool
England

Love Thy Neighbour?

I was hungry
And you formed a humanities group
to discuss my hunger;

I was imprisoned
And you crept off quietly to your chapel
and prayed for my release;

I was naked
And in your mind you debated the morality
of my appearance;

I was sick
And you preached to me the spiritual shelter
of the love of God!

I was lonely
And you left me alone
to pray for me.

You seem so holy,
so close to God!

But I am still very hungry
                    – and lonely
                              – and cold.

Crosspoints
Sri Lanka

Community of Love

She rediscovered her religion in St Joseph of the Mountains
In the little Episcopal church in the Honduran town
At San Pedro Sula where she joined the congregation
And drew strength from the Eucharist in a community of
   love.

Chorus: She found strength in a community of love
              She found love in a community of faith
              She found faith in a community of God
              She found God in a community of love.

She turned on her TV and heard the bishop speaking
After the 10 o'clock news and before the evening film.
He told her how God loved her just the way she was
And she could come and join the family in a community of
   love.

Chorus: She found strength . . .

She was welcomed to the family of the carpenter of Nazareth
Where those who are forgotten find strength to start again.
They find mercy and forgiveness and in linking arms
   together
They are lifted up to a dignity in a community of love.

Chorus: She found strength . . .

Garth Hewitt
England

On Entering a Manila Slum

My first visit to the Philippines was a baptism of fire. I have vivid memories of almost every detail especially when I stayed with a family in a Manila slum. Tiny shacks made of waste cardboard, wood and plastic were crowded on either side of a narrow alleyway. The home of my host family had a tiny entrance through which you had to crawl. Once inside you could not stand up. When I first arrived I found the husband and wife on their hands and knees mopping the plywood floor. They were doing what families do the world over when they get word of an unexpected visitor: a quick tidy up. In a space about seven feet square and in the most appalling conditions they were living and bringing up five sons with great dignity.

I walked into their home with my shoes on and very soon discovered my mistake. They taught me to remove my footwear at the entrance to leave the filth outside. The plywood floor was also their table and their bed. Some time later I realized that I should have taken off my shoes anyway, for I was on holy ground. This family, the poorest of the poor, shared with me their rice but they gave me much more than food. In the evening, with their neighbours, they prayed and discussed the happenings of the day and the problems they had experienced. They read from the gospel and talked about it together, discussing its implications for their lives.

Vin McMullen
England

A New Village?

People once lived in a village with an extended family. We have seen in the recent past, with people needing to move to get work, the breakdown of the extended family and the advent of the nuclear family.

I see the economic and other pressures on a husband and wife. It is a very heavy responsibility for a young couple to care for little children on their own. People are expected to work harder and longer hours. A father may not be able to give his wife and children much time. A mother may feel she needs to get back into paid employment to maintain the family's standard of living. For many couples, it becomes too much. I wonder if we are now seeing the breakdown of the nuclear family.

Around us there are a number of groups of home units being built, four or five in a row or in a cluster. Usually these are occupied by older people, some alone, others with their spouse. When one person in the group is hospitable, it can become a little community. They watch to see one another's blinds go up in the mornings, someone fetches in all the newspapers, occasionally they meet for a cup of coffee.

We need a new way of living together. Perhaps the cluster of units can provide us with both the support and the independence we need. A young solo mother moved into a unit in one group. The older people delight in her young child. Someone is always happy to baby-sit or to help with homework. When the child appeared in the school play everyone went along to watch.

Maybe we have here a vision for caring and community in the new millennium.

> O God, let our hearts and minds be open
> to the needs of our neighbours and our own needs.
> O God, let our hearts and minds be open
> to new ways of caring and living together.
> O God, let us know your Spirit
> touching and empowering us for loving.

John Hunt
Aotearoa New Zealand

God of Town and Village

Matthew 9: 35–38

God of city and street,
town and village,
we thank you for our communities
and for our homes.
We pray for all who live and work in cities.
We pray for those who find the city an unfriendly,
uncaring place and
for those who live on its streets.

We pray for all who work to improve cities and
the life within them
for planners, architects and builders,
for street cleaners and gardeners,
for those who work in the social services,
voluntary organizations and churches.

Lord, in your mercy

People: Hear our prayer.

Jenny Spouge
England

Illumined By Love

One day, village, you will sing,
Voices rising in hope,
Sinking never in despair,
But finding truth and honour and strength
In your song.

And when the fiddlers take up their bows
And guitars resound to heaven,
When the organ adds spiced dissonance

To the throbbing harmony,
Then shall you rise up, people, to dance for joy,
Young and old within the house of God,
Holding hands, turning and circling
With arms held heavenward
In love and communion
With your maker.

Then, falling silent, form a mighty circle
Bowed in prayer, united in stillness,
Drawing to yourselves
The poor, the hungry, the dispossessed
And at the centre,
Illumined by love,
The living Christ.

Marlene Phillips
England

A Creed of Commitment

We believe in a community
that opens its doors to people who flee war,
hunger and poverty in search of a better life.

We believe in the power of love,
not the power of violence.

We believe that we are called to share our lives,
so as to free each other from poverty,
racism and oppression of all kinds.

We believe that the resources of the earth
are to be shared among all people
– not just the few.

We believe in a community that has as a priority
a response to those who are denied
basic human rights and dignity.

We reject a world where people are denied access
to warmth, food, shelter
and the right to live in peace.

We want to believe in justice,
in goodness
and in people.

We believe we are called
to a life of freedom,
of service, of witness, of hope.

We reject the idea that
nothing can be done.

We believe that a time will come
when all people will share in the richness of our world
and that all people will be truly loved and respected.

We commit ourselves in the name of God
who created the world for all to share,
of Christ who leads us to freedom
and of the Spirit who calls us to action.

Today we commit ourselves to work together
to make this belief a reality.

Catholic Fund for Overseas Development
England

Street Cred.

Walking through a town in the Midlands, UK, I am greeted by an elderly road-sweeper, pushing his cart. He told me he was made redundant from a good, steady job nine years ago but was not to be put down. Now he brings dignity, pride and I suspect a real pastoral ministry to this 'other' career.

Dropped, as litter is
Without a thought upon
A windswept street
Aged fifty-four, this finely
Printed fragile package
Of a man is past his
Economic sell-by date
And well might blow away
Upon the city breeze
And be forgotten.

But caught within this packaging
A person lurks who
Will not be defeated
Nor easily renounce his
Hard-won self-respect
Nor draw his dole
Nor watch the seconds
Of his life
Blow by and sink
Into a premature oblivion.

This other then strips off
His pride and battered dignity
To sweep the streets amidst
The scattered dog-ends of the world
And smiling greets a passer-by
Or hears the lonely stories
Of a wasting worn-out world
And in so listening

Sanctifies
The streets for God.

Edgar Ruddock
England

Monday Afternoon at the Job Centre

The queue snakes between grey ribbons from the door
shuffling murmuring waiting hoping
hot in winter coats. Nothing this week
no vacancies part time only three pounds twenty-five an hour
claims at that counter it is signposted if you missed it
wait again . . .
I was here first, two hours standing bored
child in pushchair what else to do with her
yes I can find a minder
if I get a job – you have to pay them – now she's crying
I'm crying too inside do they know what it's like
having to ask for money beg for work
at least they've all got jobs
how would they like to stand here
with nutters and no-hopers and this yelling kid
waiting all afternoon
afraid angry helpless tired.

The queue is nearly out the door that's thirty-eight
since lunchtime
wanting money wanting work wanting hope wanting wanting
this claim has been disallowed appeal how long
do you want work or don't you
this looks like fraud well dodgy anyway
this one comes every week we still can't help
and he is sad polite understands even smiles
papers numbers people . . .
desperate short-staffed sickness spending cuts
not enough of us and more and more of them

with baffled rage and yelling kids
they curse me blaming shouting
wanting money I can't give them
sympathy I can't afford
how would they like to work here
facing the endless stream of hopeful hopeless ones
waiting all afternoon
afraid angry helpless tired.

Heather Pencavel
England

Neighbours

The disciple questioned his Master saying: 'I have two neighbours, each as dear to me as I to them. But both worship falsely. At eventide I hear them pray. The one on the right of my tent chants this:

> Even as my Beloved unlatches the door, so do you visit me Great Goddess veiled in dark attire. Watch over us and all creatures with your myriad eyes. And to my children grant protection during this hallowed night.

The one on the left of my tent sings this:

> Infinite God, lodge in the deep caverns of my heart as my Closest Friend. Shadow the eyes of the snake: entrap the robber in his own pit. Bestow that knowledge which sees Thee in the moonlight as it refreshes the weary, guards the sleeping and bathes the hearts of lovers with light.

Neither invokes the Most Blessed Trinity: neither prays to Christ, the Holy Son of God. Thus the truth is not in them. Are they damned?

The Master sat in silence for a long while. Then he replied:

Know these two things, my son. First, that the Lord Christ, Who is the Universal Word, speaks with a multitude of accents. Walking through time, He draws around Himself the cloak of many histories. Second, that truth is unbounded and in the spot of time called a life we understand but its smallest part.

Go now. Learn from your friends how you may unite your prayer to theirs.

Derek H Webster
England

Mr Vasapa

Medak District, Andra Pradesh, South India is dry and barren. Dirt tracks and the occasional tarmac road dissect dusty fields of crops or grasses but mostly there are great expanses of thirsty, rocky soils dotted with the occasional coarse bush tree and large patches of red, open soil through which gullies have been carved by seasonal rains, like bleeding wounds on the rugged landscape. Centuries ago these lands would have been forested but now very few trees remain and the area resembles a moonscape. Recent agricultural practices have not helped. The government has subsidized pesticides and irrigation schemes in order to promote sugar cane farming to supply its local sugar mill. More land for cotton growing is likely to be made available. Both cash crops require intensive agricultural techniques which use a great deal of water hence lowering the water table and leaving the soil exposed for certain periods which leads to severe erosion.

The Deccan Development Society (DDS) has assisted schemes to develop large areas of wasteland around villages by removing rocks and planting hardy trees. Hundreds of villagers have been involved in growing certain medicinal crops and herbs in an attempt to reclaim some of the lost traditional remedies. Women have been involved in environmental campaigning and marching in protest against cotton growing and its impact.

With the help of DDS, Mr Vasapa dug an open well, fifteen feet deep, to supply water for irrigation for a small farm he was establishing. Since then he has had to remove thousands of small red rocks which now form chest-high walls around his plots in order to leave a little workable soil. He grows all kinds of produce from mulberries to sorghum. He supplies papaya to the local balwadis (nursery schools) in the district and acts as a local garden centre where mango saplings and other hardy plants are grown for distribution to farmers who are committed to re-forestation. The water from his well irrigates twenty-two acres of land that is farmed by a sangham of forty-four women. Mr Vasapa has rarely left his farm. In fact, when his daughter was married in Hyderabad he told her he would not be making the journey: 'If I come,' he said, 'all my trees will get lonely.'

Ed Cox
England

One Family

People come and go in the market place;
they see others in different hues;
here there are black and white, indigenous and immigrant,
a rainbow people but truly together,
a people of one family.
We seek to bear each other's burdens;
we seek to share each other's joys;
we share our happiness and our sorrows;
why then do some seek to make us enemies?
We are one family, God's people,
a rainbow people whose song is love.

Responsive Prayer

Leader: Give strength to hands that are tired.
Tell everyone who is discouraged,

Response: **Be strong and do not be afraid.**
God is coming to rescue you.

Leader: For the people who leave a land of poverty
seeking assured food for their children.

Response: **Do not be discouraged: God is with you.**

Leader: For people who flee from oppression
seeking freedom in a far land.

Response: **Do not be discouraged: God is with you.**

Leader: For those who have come to a strange country
and find themselves subject to insult and
discrimination.

Response: **Do not be discouraged: God is with you.**

Leader: For those who offer their gifts in the community
and find that they are rejected.

Response: **Do not be discouraged: God is with you.**

Leader: Tell everyone who is hurt and fearful,
Be strong and do not be afraid,

Response: **God is with you; you will see his love and**
power.

What gives us our unity and strength?
It is the law which gives to each
rights upheld by courts.
What gives us our unity and trust?

It is the social contract which gives to each
rights and responsibilities.
What gives us our unity and peace?
It is the covenant-offering to all from each
a compassionate relationship of love.

John Johansen-Berg
England

For Personal Meditation

The dogma that 'there is no such thing as society, only individuals' is profoundly untheological.

*

The Christian community was intended to be a reflection of
the community of heaven itself.

*

When we pray about the home, we pray for those who are
lonely and for those who ensure we are not lonely.

*

Today we watch 'Neighbours' rather than talk to those living
next door and we watch 'Play Your Cards Right' rather than
engage with our family!

Martin Wallace
England

Living in Society

Living in society, we should share the sufferings of our fellow citizens and practise compassion and tolerance not only towards our loved ones but also towards our enemies. This is the test of our moral strength.

Tenzin Gyatso
The Fourteenth Dalai Lama
exiled in Dharamsala, India

Waves of Change

Many people are living their lives in the face of immense waves of change which affect relationships, work, homes, values, sympathies and self-understanding. Merely to maintain their balance and keep a sense of direction is a huge achievement and demands great nerve as they face the future.

However, there is no shortage of people who want to apply themselves to questions about the future:
who care about the community of human beings,
who will insist on more than a meagre safety net of
social welfare,
who believe in the morality of taxes,
who value social and cultural diversity,
who refuse to accept that human life will ever be reducible simply to economics,
who resist the notion that the earth is a dustbin but
who wish to use technology for its best purposes.

I want to keep faith with them, their visions and their ability to find solutions for the world's problems and I believe the Christian Church should keep faith with them too. Sometimes it will seem like skimming through successive waves of change with not too many of the resources that were available to previous generations. There will be repeated calls to take up old certainties that worked in another world but are inadequate for the future which will be either an exhilarating place or an extremely frightening one. We constantly need to teach each other how to keep faith and learn to do more than survive in what some of our forebears would regard as a rather thin atmosphere.

Nigel Collinson
England
adapted

You Ask Us to Wait

Patient God,
For you, one day is like a thousand years,
and a thousand years is like one day.
Be with us in our impatience.

For the red-faced baby
    crying out with pain as her first tooth emerges;
For the fidgety child
    longing for the sound of the home-time bell;
For the angst-ridden teenager
    yearning for the moment to declare his passion.

With these waiting people you ask us to wait:
Be with us in the waiting time.

For the woman at the bus stop,
her cold hands scored by heavy shopping bags,
    as empty cars pass her by;
For the man in the dole queue,
consoling his bitterness and shame with a nod and a wink
    to his Job Centre companions;
For the prisoner in her jail cell,
counting down the years
    until the Home Secretary gives her more years to count.

With these waiting people you ask us to wait
Be with us in the waiting time.

For the single person in the church,
avoiding the matchmakers and waiting, not for a partner,
    but for equal treatment in her own right;
For the tired church leader
driven on by the vision of what might be
    but held back by the reality of what already is;
For the elderly resident of the nursing home,
longing for the last time
    he will be wheeled back to his bed.

With these waiting people you ask us to wait:
Be with us in the waiting time.

For the lonely Nigerian asylum-seeker,
terrified at the prospect
    of being returned to her death;
For the African child growing up with HIV,
wondering whether his last sneeze
    is the beginning of the end;
For the Palestinian activist,
as he steps into the busy Jewish market,
    heart racing, one final time.

With these waiting people you ask us to wait:
Be with us in the waiting time.

But we cannot wait any longer Lord;
we are crying out for justice;
we are calling for the one who makes all things new.

But you ask us to wait.

Patient God,
For you, one day is like a thousand years,
            and a thousand years is like one day.
            Be with us in our impatience.

Ed Cox
England

Multi-cultural Living

To you, Almighty God, we all owe praise and thanks. Yet
in Jesus you came among us as a slave, as one not to be
served but to serve. He laid aside his rightful glory to
give himself as a ransom for many.
Shake us out of that smug complacency which assumes
that our ways are your ways and that others should
conform to them.

Help us
>   not to be ruled by our preconceptions but to be open to
>   the
>   insights of those whose cultures are not our own;
>
>   not to be dominated or terrified by fear of the different
>   but to
>   welcome other ways of describing and understanding
>   reality;
>
>   not to try to impose our accepted ways on others merely
>   for the
>   sake of our own convenience,
>   that we may live as those who know that in Christ
>   there is no distinction of race, gender, class or culture,
>   for Christ is all and in all.

Ian Gillman
Australia

Living with People of Other Faiths

You shall also love the stranger . . . Deuteronomy 10:19

*People of other cultures and faiths are now our next door neighbours. They
are our work colleagues. They experience homesickness as they seek a new
home in a strange land. God's people are commanded to have a special care
for them.*

Father God:
You commanded your people of old
'You shall also love the stranger . . . .'

Help us to remember
they are your beloved children;
people for whom Jesus died
and apart from whom, we will not be saved.

Grant us confidence
to witness peacefully to the heart of our faith,
and the path
you have called us to follow.

Help us to be hospitable,
and to listen to our neighbour's story:
their aspirations, hopes and fears.

Save us
from asserting our own righteousness
and from judging others
by our own narrow grasp of truth.

In a society where so many spirits are broken,
help us to be people of peace, justice and love.

*National Commission for Mission
Uniting Church in Australia*

Inside Out

Black, white and gold
Are the colours of life –

For sorrow is black;
And the small seed of kindness
Unseen;
And the velvet of night
That hides love . . .

And the colour of skin.

For whiteness is pure,
And the breathless potential
Of dawn
Is revealed in the light
That hides nothing . . .

And the colour of skin.

For gold is of joy;
And the shining of sunlight
Unspent;
And the heat of the fire
That heals all . . .

And the colour of skin.

If the colours of life
Are the colours of skin –
Which clothes and encloses
The essence within –

Then the blood and the tears
Are the same.

Margot Arthurton
England

77

Racism

Why this strong temptation
to shy at creation
and boil down every person
to inferior parts?
We're all different
    special
    valued
far from perfect, but with impact
for we're fashioned in the image
of a bright imagination!
Resist the chance to hurl abuse
and praise instead the God who gives
us huge variety
to broadcast thanks!

Peter Comaish
England

One Village

Human migration ever since humanity
Made world diverse and pluriform
migration continues
No law, rule, legislation ever stop
Mixture like rivers
Into mighty ocean?
Different to rivers
Assertive, seeking uniqueness
Multi faith multi culture multi ethnic multi linguistic
Pluralism granted
But No to Global village
Too much, too many to be just One
Oneness endangers, pretentious
Of the stark diversity
Undermines it

Solidarity, Trust and Mutuality
The way to be
Be for future.

Shanthi Hettiarachchi
Sri Lanka

What Have They Done?

Some are called untouchables or outcastes,
Yet all are created in God's image.
Some are called street kids,
Yet there is none whose birth place is Kamuzu Procession
    Road.*
Some are identified as refugees or asylum seekers,
Yet the whole world is God's parish.
What have they done to be called by such dehumanizing
    terms?

Some are not given jobs because of colour and tongue,
Yet our God is no respecter of persons.
Some are denied ordination because they are female,
Yet both sexes are found in God.
Some countries are called the first world, others the third,
Yet God alone created the heavens and the earth.
What have they done to endure such discrimination?

Some domestic workers go unpaid for months,
Yet our God advises not to withhold the wages of someone
    until morning.
Some are in detention without trial.
Yet God is full of justice and righteousness.
Some are busy dumping nuclear waste in others' oceans,
    lakes and rivers,
Yet endangering animals' and peoples' lives.
What have they done to deserve such punishments?

Millions exist on empty stomachs every day,
Yet others have plenty of food and even dump some in
    rubbish bins.
Aren't we told to do to others what we want them to do for
    us?
Some are killed in the name of religion,
Aren't we brothers' brothers and sisters' sisters?
Yet God commands love for one another without condition.
Sometimes I wonder what have others done to deserve all
    these things.

* Kamuzu Procession Road is the name of a famous road in Malawi

Goodwin Zainga
Malawi

Bread and Wine

Your bread-body broken
Your wine-blood shed
Have I ever really come to your table?
Feeling enough
    to break?
Caring enough
    to bleed?
Have I ever really
come to your table?
Sustained
    by your life-giving bread?
Or consumed
    by my bread-seeking life?
Breaking and bleeding
    for my Judases?
Or breaking and making
    my Judases bleed?

But still you invite me
to come to your table . . .

80

Break my stubborn indifference
Shed my venomous pride
Make me one with the ones
whose life in the Son
I share
in the Bread
and the Wine

Norm S D Esdon
Canada

Birthing a New Creation

When it seems beyond my ability
When all I want to do is give up
When there seems no way forward
Your presence calms my dread and trepidation.

I look into your face
Your hand squeezes mine.

*It will be alright you know.
You will survive!
Don't give up.*

You speak words that lift up my broken spirit,
give energy to my tired body.
You encourage me to breathe in rhythm with yours.

*Breathe with me
In, out, in, out.*

*You are doing well.
Keep going!*

You wait as a midwife at my side,
A midwife to your people.
You have been through it all,
the pain of birthing a new creation.
You wipe my brow
and your touch quells my fears.
Your words of comfort and assurance
are enough to get me through.

Rest a moment now and then get ready to push.
It's on its way!
It's almost here!

Then tender and inexperienced hands
reach out to receive this new wet, screaming embodiment of
hope.

And I know, by the look on your face, that your joy equals
mine.

Helen Richmond
Australia

An Ordinary Day

The Journey

An ordinary day became surreal, hallucinatory.
Horizon out of focus in the surge of people towards
Bethlehem.

No better than any other place to trace back family roots.

We travelled through Joseph's childhood,
paid homage to the past and carried the future
uncomfortably.

Do I remember being afraid of anything more than this?

It takes some kind of fool to believe that God can have a hand in this mess.
I've seen it all before, the dawn will come and everything will fall into place.

This child will be mine.

Arrival

Stillness takes hold of my fear, suspended in the air
it gives light to the make-do bed of hay.

Sounds become irrelevant, advice echoes around, never lands.
The powerful waves of pain are the only words I understand.

All my breath is used up. Deflated.
I have no body. It shrank into the darkness.

All I am is a space for God.

God help her, she cannot do this on her own.
Even the shepherds are paralysed, hands too dirty to touch her.

We are outsiders. Curious yet superfluous.
Spectatorship on a scale yet uncharted.

Will this child be mine?

Adoration

He is more than I expected. His flesh is real.
I imagined the birth of something quite different.
Speculation denying my experience.
Undermining the memory of a promise I made.

My bones entwined with his in the miracle of life.

I touch his skin, brush his cheek and find the softness
   belongs to me.

*Light-headed from holding my breath I sit at the side of the
   bed.
He is exactly as I remembered from the dream.*

*This rudimentary home is appropriate for the birth of someone
who turns things upside down and inside out.*

I am his father and I am his son.

Valerie Shedden
England

Keziah, My Goddaughter

A baptismal sermon based on Revelation 12: 1−6

I have been getting into all sorts of bother trying to write a
sermon for your baptismal service. It scares me, Keziah, to
realize that by the time you are the age I am now, I shall be due
to retire. The year of my birth will seem to you a distant
historical era. By then, God knows what other gulfs than age
might separate us: gulfs of political opinion, musical taste, of
aesthetic sensibilities. More significantly, if it survives, what
will our wonderful planet then be like? What will we have
bequeathed you, how angry will you be with us for the state
of things? Above all Keziah, in spite of the promises made
today by your parents and Godparents and on behalf of God's
Church by the members of this congregation who can say if
well into the twenty-first century you will be a disciple of
Christ? Will humanity have made any progress, laid any
foundations on which you can build? Will the Church have
learned the cost of discipleship? Posing the questions as
sharply as that, makes me wonder if we will even be on speaking terms.

   You see, Keziah, at this service celebrating your birth and

God's love, I feel compelled to intrude a note of sobriety. Much as a Jewish Bride and Groom smash the glass from which they have drunk their bridal wine as a symbol that suffering must not be forgotten even where there is great joy, I want to remember that the world is a hard place in which to live. Your namesake, Keziah, was the second daughter of Job, and she would only have had to ask her father about the nature of suffering and what a story she would have heard. Your parents too, soft as they are, have noses hard enough to tell you the truth. The world is not all the cuddly toys, warm blankets, loving and familiar voices that are your world today. I have heard and seen small children in Shepherd's Bush, Somalian refugees, drawing pictures of their fathers being murdered. I have had my senses violently assaulted by pictures, sounds and stories of genocide in Rwanda. I have visited Bosnia and seen the effects of 'ethnic cleansing'. There is evil in the world, sometimes so strong that you can taste it, sometimes so subtle that it hangs almost unnoticed on the breeze. I hope, Keziah, that the innocence of your childhood is never cut short and I pray that you are never so isolated from the world that you become an adult without knowing that there is real evil in the world and that we are all responsible for it.

The Bible reading I chose for your baptismal service is as lurid, as dangerous, as vigorous as the world I have just been writing about. Its author was acquainted with suffering. He had seen many friends die because they were Christians. He himself was an exile because it was too dangerous for him in his home city. Out of suffering he dreams a dream. A picture written on the sky conceived with the passion of a prophet and with the imagination of a poet. As a child you will have less difficulty than I with this strange world of moon and stars, and symbolic women, and evil seven headed dragons. Some may think it a peculiar choice for a baptismal sermon text. And yet, Keziah, it is about the birth of a child, the birth of a child into a world where evil waits hungrily for it, ready to devour it as it is delivered from its mother's womb. It is a passage that frightens me. It is a passage that gives me hope. My scholarly books tell me what the symbols stand for: the woman for Israel or the Church, the dragon for evil, the child for the Messiah Jesus; and the wilderness into which the woman flees, represents a time of preparations and reflection. But I read this passage, Keziah, more with my feelings than my mind. As a poem it loses something of its mystery when it is explained, unpacked, dissected, applied, so too do dreams! They are given to be breathed in, lived with, stored and treasured. In this vision, the evil is fierce and powerful, but, Keziah, it does not win, for the goodness of God is far stronger than the wickedness of the dragon. Dream on that.

Baptism in the strong name of the Trinity, the dreams of an old poet in exile on a Mediterranean island, these are after all threads in the same fabric, intersecting weaves in the same pattern: suffering and hope, cross and resurrection.

I hope that one day you too, my Goddaughter, will wear the dream.

Stephen Plant
England

Jesus Falls the First Time

Today

Nirmala, aged seven years, collapsed in the classroom of a village school in Uttar Pradesh hardly had school begun for the day. The teacher asked Shanti, Nirmala's sister, who was in the same class, what was wrong with Nirmala.

In a weak and timid voice Shanti spoke, 'Today was not Nirmala's turn to have breakfast.'

Nirmala and Shanti belonged to a family of seven children. Their father, a farmer, could not afford to feed his children. So they took turns. Some ate while others starved.

Reflection

In the first fall of Jesus on the road to Calvary we think of all those in the world today who at this moment are starving, their bodies denuded of flesh and drained of blood, reduced to frightful skeletons for want of food.

Overcome by weakness they stumble and fall, or sit listless waiting for an end to their misery.

Perhaps, many of us are too familiar with hunger, not as it painfully affects us but as it affects others.

Our social landscape is too crowded with vivid sights and scenes of hungry men, women and children eating out of bins, wasting away by the road-side, that we have grown immune.

But hunger is a cruel thing when you are forced to experience it.

'Hunger,' wrote Pablo Neruda, ' feels like pincers, like the bite of crabs. It burns, burns and has no fire. Hunger is cold fire.'

As we look at Jesus crushed under the cross of hunger in the person of our famished brothers and sisters, let us examine ourselves:

Do we take for granted that because we have money, we can spend it as we please?

How often have we indulged in an over-kill in the matters of food and drink through our wild celebrations on the occasion of a birthday, christening, first communion or marriage?

How often are we guilty of wasting food?

If a person is starving the living image of God is wasted ... the empty stomach means an insult to the image of God.

Kosuke Koyama

Cedric Rebello
India

Children in the New Millennium

Compassionate God,

We pray for the children around the world.
Bless them,
       heal them,
              protect them.

Teach us to love our children, well.
Forgive us when we have abused them
in many and different ways.

Help us to see
Your face in their faces;
experience the child-like awe
and wonder.

May we learn from their ability
to trust,
eagerness
to learn
and spontaneous joy!

Bless the children
and may the children
bless us.

In the name of Jesus,
lover of children.
Amen.

Elizabeth S Tapia
Philippines

Lamentation and Dreams of a Streetchild

Because I am a girl . . .
Because I am a child . . .
Because I am homeless . . .
Because I want to live . . .
I was denied my human rights.
Why? Why? Tell me why.

    While other children
        are enjoying their homes and gardens;
    The garbage heap is my garden, the dirty street my
        home;
            Why? Why? Don't tell me why.

    When they sing 'Jesus loves the little children . . .'
        am I included or not?
    When they say I am special,
        do they really mean that?

But I must keep going . . .
I want to survive.
I want to dance.
I want to dream.

I dream of chasing butterflies and dancing with bamboo
    trees.
I dream of a safe and loving home, good-smelling clothes
and colourful story books.
I dream of going to school.
I dream of becoming a medical doctor
        to heal broken bodies, cure children of diarrhoea,
    TB and AIDS.
I dream of becoming a teacher,
        to teach grown-ups how to treat children well.
I dream of becoming a farmer,
        to produce enough rice, beans, carrots for all.

I dream of becoming a mature woman;
    strong and gentle; loving, peaceful and wise.
    And why not?

Elizabeth S Tapia
Philippines

Litany for Children

We Pray For Children

who leave chocolate fingerprints all round the house
who like to be tickled
who jump in puddles, oblivious of the consequences
who have no sense of time or routine
whose shoes are often missing at school time
who handle the 'phone like experts

And We Pray For Those

who have never tickled their palate with chocolate,
who have never had a pair of new shoes
who have never made daisy chains or taunted the dog
who are born in places we would rather not think about
who have been forced to grow old too young
who only know a world of abuse

We Pray For Children

who give us sticky kisses and fistfuls of dandelions
who hug us in a hurry and forget their dinner money
who sing their hearts out to their own tune
who exhaust us with their energy
who ask naïve questions and don't listen to the answers
who have imaginary friends and conversations

And We Pray For Those

> who don't have any personal space
> who can't find any bread to steal
> who watch their parents watch them die
> whose minds are filled with violent memories
> who don't feel important to anyone else

We Pray For Children
> who spend their pocket-money before it's actually in
> their pocket
> who throw tantrums in the supermarket and pick at
> their food
> who hide their possessions under their bed and leave a
> ring round the bath
> who get visits from the tooth fairy
> who set video and tap computer like second nature
> whose tears can make us laugh and whose smiles can
> make us cry

And We Pray For Those

> who will eat everything they have chance of
> who have never had an ability test or visited a dentist
> who live in grinding poverty
> who see the hours through the night and wait for the
> dawn of another day
> who do not know the meaning of security and comfort

We Pray For Children

> who long to be loved and hugged and called by name
> and for those who fill our lives and make us feel special.

Rosemary Wass
England

And What Is Love?

In many parts of the world parents are abandoning their children. Education is poor or non-existent for millions of people and their chances of well paid employment remain near the zero mark. Living in makeshift single room houses on land no one else is prepared to build on leads to an aggressive society of crime and drug dependency as a way of escaping the nightmare we call life and living.

Jesus of Nazareth came from a background of poverty and deprivation. He knew about being poor and his experience taught him to seek for a more just and equal society. People who have been kicked to the sidelines of rich and powerful communities need the love of Christ. They are the outcasts of our modern society and their children are the casualties. The circumstances contained in the meditation are based on a real situation.

I am a child and my father is dead, killed in a feud over cocaine brought from Colombia. It was to be taken through Venezuela to the USA. My father took some of it for himself and my mother. We live in a house with one room twelve feet square built from hollow clay bricks. Electric light is taken from a line to a neighbour's house. We have a tap and water which is not always clean. My mother cannot get work because of my baby sister and there is no government money. My brother has gone to live under the motorway bridge with other boys who scavenge for food at night. My mother went out the day before yesterday and I am left here with my sister. I do not know if she will return. I feel sick and hungry. Dear Lord of love and compassion did you die for me? Did you take the sin of the world and let it be nailed to a cross so that I would not suffer or did you let them kill you so that I might know how to deal with my suffering? One day I will grow into the beautiful woman you have created me to be but I do not want you to see the slimness of my limbs or desire me for the pools of honey from which you created my eyes. I need your love, the gift of yourself for me.

All the people I have ever known want to trade their love for mine. My father cared little for me. He needed me only to go on errands to men who stared at me. Their eyes pierced my thin T-shirt and saw my nakedness. He gave me money that was not enough to buy anything. My mother needed me to look after my sister because when my father gave her the white powder she sat in a chair not moving for hours and my sister cried and needed attention. Later, she would hug me and want me to hug her but only because my father would not.

My brother is the only one who sees my real needs. He comes back now and again to bring me food he has found or stolen. He asks for nothing in return.

Are you telling me that real love is the gift of myself to others? Are you saying to me that today I must begin to collect all the good in myself in order to give it to another because they need it like I need you and your true love, for me? Is that why you knelt down and washed the feet of your followers? If we have a gift that we selfishly keep for ourselves or cannot find the courage to give, then the love we have for ourselves is perhaps too great and we are like the rich man who came to Jesus looking for eternal life but wanting to give up nothing that mattered to him.

When I pass the houses of the rich people they tie a dog to the gate to guard it but it is they who are tied to their palaces. The woman who lives across the way has a job as a secretary and she will do nothing for her neighbours if it interferes with her work. I expect she wishes she could feel free to do her job and be part of her community without fear of losing either.

I begin to see that all our life, our problems and difficulties make it impossible to forget ourselves. Was it only you, Jesus, who was able to die to your own self and serve only the needs of others? Is that why it led you to the cross, because the real love of God demands that we submit to ourselves being crucified for others? Are you asking me Lord to be crucified so that the rich can continue to live without changing their ways?

Jesus chose of his own free will, the authentic true love of God and gave it expression in his life and in the manner of his death. He did not stop loving because he never stopped giving and it was in his giving that he received the power of God.

They are coming to take my sister and me away to an

93

orphanage* because we have not eaten for six days and we have become ill. Can someone show me a mother's love and a father's love so that I can find the way of love that leads to God?

* *There are more than thirty abandoned children being looked after at the San Sebastian Orphanage, Caracas, Venezuela.*

Roger Dawson
England/Venezuela

You've Got to Be Joking Me

Who, me?
Believe in God?
Come on, man,
You've got to be joking me.

What do you say?
Have I thought about it?
Oh yes, I've thought about it,
Not a lot, I'll credit you – but I've thought about it.

But this is me you're talking to,
Me with the designer jeans and the baseball cap . . .
Think of my street cred.

What's that you say?
The crucifix?
Oh yes, I wear a crucifix around my neck.
It's cool, see – a symbol of my street cred –
No more than that.

But God, Jesus, and all that stuff,
That's something else.

What's that you say?
Jesus had street cred?
Come on, man, you've got to be joking me.

Mind you, I grant you, everyone followed him.
Cheered him, fell at his feet
Wherever he went.
Wow.
That's street cred.
What a thought.

What's that you say?
The crucifix?
Oh yes,
My mates think
I wear it to be like them.
But I wear it for Jesus –
Symbol of real street cred –
Jesus, the coolest dude I know.

Pat Marsh
England

Taking the Roof Off

Based on Mark 2: 1–12

Boarded up – in or out?
It's hard to tell
but here we need
to do more than
take the roof off!
Carpenter Christ,
teach us your trade,

that we too might practise life-giving forgiveness.
Share the tools of community building with us,
so that here, together,
we might create a place of healing.

Janet Lees
England

Confession

We pray 'Ancient of Days'
and misuse this name to
allow the past the upper hand with our
'tried that before – always done it like this' responses.

We pray 'Word made Flesh'
and misuse this gift
to exclude people and build barriers
with our pages of dusty legalism.

Silence or Sing The Kyrie

If dry bones can live
then so can we!
Breathe on us, renewing Spirit.
Turn the pages of legalism
that your word may fulfil
your life-giving promises.
May we know you as the Living One,
in whom yesterday, today and forever
are related in endless and uninhibited movement,
in which chaos and glory are crafted
by the same Creator.
May we live to grow together into this inheritance.

Janet Lees
England

Into Egypt

The bucketing, banging wind is stilled
and the moon is cold and clear.
Castles like candles guard the coast
and the moon is ringed with fire.

> The coble's ashore and the logs are cut
> the moon rides alone in the sky
> until the shivering sliver of light appears;
> the star in the east, the sign of hope;
> rising to claim its place
> in the hearts and the hearths of all the earth,
> proclaiming the dawn of peace.

Open your hearts and your homes tonight.
Welcome the dawn of hope;
throw wide the arms of your love today,
embrace the dawn of love.

> Then the freezing wind returns
> the sky is streaked with black.
> The glory is gone
> the hills remain,
> distant and coldly white.
> The sea retreats
> the castles stand
> and the moon is hidden from sight.
> The child is restless,
> the refugee cold,
> the mother afraid once more.

Then is the time to know it's true.
Then is the time to cling to hope.
Then is the time to pray for love:
when it's dark and cold
and hope is scarce;
when it's windy and wet and sad.

Then is the time to hope for faith
in a world the Creator made.

So open your hearts and your homes tonight,
throw wide the arms of your pain
against all the odds
despite all the hurt
risk the piercings of the wind,
risk the demands of love.

Kate McIlhagga
England

The Good Samaritan

Hug me,
Pray for me,
Sit with me in the stillness please.

I have a grief as deep as oceans
And a need as high as mountains.
So hold my hand,
Hug me,
Sit quietly by my side,
But I beg of you
Do not,
Do not weep for me.

For you see only
Grief
Echoing from my heart,
Oceans of pain reflected in my eyes.

And you are right.
Your eyes do not deceive you.
But come
And stand in my shoes.

If you could look through my eyes
Then what privilege it would be
To know
The joy of being
The stranger who is loved,
Unconditionally loved,
To feel the warmth of your compassion,
Drink in the fragrance of your tender prayers.

If you could see
Through my eyes
You would see beyond the pain,
Beyond the mist of tears,
To glorious glimpses of amazing love,
The healing and eternal love of God,
And know
That you were meeting face to face
The Good Samaritan
On the dusty road.

So hug me,
Pray for me,
Sit with me in the stillness please
But do not
Do not weep for me.

Pat Marsh
England

Sing Me Your Bethlehem

tell me more –
tell me
     what all these words mean
     to you
speak the Word in your own words
     how you wrestle with

how you celebrate
the Holy in your everyday
the Word made flesh
in you
dance me
your bondage to pharaoh
your fear of the desert
sing me
your bethlehem
your epiphany
your easter
dance me
the Song made flesh
in you
that I might dance
free of my pharaoh
through my desert
to my own bethlehem
my own epiphany
my own easter.

Norm S D Esdon
Canada

My Name Is Goodness

They would have me believe that since my birth, light and warmth have fled the home where I was born. No *shareen* leaves adorned the doorway spreading the joyful news that I had come, a princess sent by God to bestow comfort on this woman and man who together called me into birth.

Mother, do not weep for me. They cannot rip God's kiss from my beating heart for I know who I am and I was marked in goodness. And you, Father, dare to be brave, defying all those customs meant to deny me a rightful place equal to my brothers.

Surely you have love enough to embrace us all! I know who I am, your daughter but God's first and all that God has made is good. My Mother has endured and I will too, God will not be mocked by those who try to steal the Truth.

O Father, how often you think that I am comforted when you pat my head and give such tender *pyyar* calling me *beta*, the greatest of your compliments. This title is not mine for though spoken in love it reinforces my inferiority claiming that only Son is good.

O Father have you never seen that Daughters, too, are beautiful? How is it that you never give *pyyar* upon my brother's head and call him *beti* tenderly, making him my equal? Would you deny my birthright, be blind to what is good? The daughters of God must be free!

O hear me well, my Mother, no longer shed a tear for me. All you have wept is swept away, an ocean overflowing, love enough to bathe the old ways in forgiveness, depositing a top-soil, so rich beyond the imagination, dreams come true bring life and God has called it good. This new *shareen* will sing for all!

Patricia Boyle
Pakistan

shareen – the leaves of this tree are hung above the doorway at the birth of a son
pyyar – a loving gesture or blessing on the head of a young person
beta – a son
beti – a daughter

Love Is Like Yeast

Matthew 13:33

Love is like yeast,
growing organically,
multiplying unseen
from the microscopic.

Love is a living thing,
so hard to kill
but fragile and dependent
on the right conditions for growth.

Love brings transformation;
enlarging our perspective,
swelling our compassion,
forcing out the rigid boundaries
of our assumptions about truth.

Love is like yeast,
generating warmth from within,
lightening the heavy heart
as life fizzes over
with rising bubbles of joy.

Peter Trow
Wales/England

I Saw You, Jesus

I saw You, Jesus
    in the victims
        of violence, hatred and exploitation,
        of race and colour-based discrimination!

I saw You
   downtrodden and outcast,
   counted as the scum of our society!

I saw You
   rot in dungeons, prisons and camps,
   living-dead in slums, ghettos and favelas!

I saw You
   in the agonizing cries that reach no human heart,
   in the uplifted arms that touch no human hand,
   in the burning gaze that penetrates no human eyes!

I saw You
   in the young,
      whose eyes brighten in no twinkle,
      whose lips part in no happy smile,
      whose tender-dried up frame that no clothes warm,
      whose hands,
         stranger to books and pens and toys,
         have hardened with chisel and hammer!

I saw You
   in the young of heart,
      who with gaze levelled and back straightened,
         dare to speak against unscrupulous money,
         and arrogant might!

I saw You
   in those who, with earnest zeal
   and love-filled heart, strive to double
   'the Urchins' Priest of Turin' *
   and 'the little brown saint of Hindustan',†
   and thus to heed Your call to Beatitudes!

And I turned away my gaze!

Yes, Lord – no sooner than I saw You,
I turned away my gaze;
For to meet You I have great fear;
If I did, I feared,
You might ask me to follow You closer!

I know, I thus made You once again sad,
Like that rich young man of long ago,
Whom You looked at with tender-deep love,
But who left You plunged in ever deeper sorrow.

I lacked courage and a sense of venture,
I was not generous to change the texture of my life,
And I did not have great zeal for You
And for your Kingdom,
And I felt little love for my brothers!

Lord, today I want to meet You;
For, despite all, You did love me so,
And, I know you'll ever do!
Bid me come and stay with You, Lord,
Give me love to be another 'urchins' priest'!

Joseph Pulikal
India

* *Don Bosco (1815–1888) spent his whole life for the welfare of the street boys of Turin. Here the author would like to call him 'the Urchins' Priest of Turin'.*

† *Mahatma Gandhi was styled by many as 'the little brown saint of Hindustan'.*

The Promised Community

Through the waters of baptism
we entered the life of Christ
and joined the Christian Community.

Male and female, Jew and Greek
we are all one in Christ.
Such is the promise
but what is the reality?
For centuries Christians have enslaved others.
For generations men have oppressed women.
For years Church leaders have controlled the people of God
and the promise of new community has remained sterile.
But now 2,000 years since Christ dwelt on earth
we have a chance to begin again;
to make real the gift of our baptism,
to value each baptised person for themselves,
to enter into the promised community
of equality, love and truth.
Do we dare to be different in the new millennium?
Do we dare to make real the community
enshrined from the beginning in God
the Holy Trinity, a Unity of love?

Jean Mayland
England

Marginal God

Gracious God,
persistently loving,
consistently faithful,
unfailingly compassionate,
we praise you
as we wrestle and reflect
on your purpose for us.

We pray for the heart of the church,
and rejoice that our heart is disparate –
found wherever people hunger and thirst
after their right relationship with you.
We pray our heart is strong;

we pray our heart beats the life blood
of Christlike discipleship
through the arteries of our churches.

We pray for the heart of the church.
And we pray for the margins of our church,
for people sitting on the fringes of our fellowship,
lives shy of commitment, lives wary of piety,
lives battered and broken and aching for love,
and sense, and sustenance.

We pray for courage, for imagination, for good sense,
for passion, for clarity of vision:
that people on the margin
will know the love, the mercy, the grace and the peace
you alone can give – even through us
in the name of Jesus Christ our Lord, we pray.

Stephen Brown
England

Christian People Sing Together

Tune: Hyfrydol or Bethany
Any 8.7.8.7.D

Christian people sing together,
All united in one voice.
Though we come from many backgrounds,
Yet in Christ we all rejoice.
In our daily lives we're scattered,
Serving God in various ways.
Then in worship we're united
Giving him our thanks and praise.

God created countless faces,
Yet in Christ we all are one.

Though we look from many angles,
All our views reflect the Son.
So we bring each gift and talent,
Offering what we have to share

And God blends us all together
In one body of his care.

Teach us Lord, to trust each other,
Though our ways are not the same.
As you call us to your purpose,
Bless our working in your name.
In the world of daily living
Each uniquely serves your will,
Show how every person matters,
As our calling we fulfil.

Marjorie Dobson
England

* Voice-over God, Our Lover and Creator

Tune: Finlandia

Voice-over God, our Lover and Creator,
whose Word transformed disorder into peace,
who gave to all that is a name, a calling,
by whom all human wisdom was released,
God! Give us confidence in living, loving,
the mind, the mood to make this life a feast.

Com-panion Christ, in human terms among us,
let your redeeming, freeing presence teach
and help us not to measure those around us
by culture, race, by gender, creed or speech,
to look for that which is of God within them,
reach out, give thanks for what is good in each.

Ennobling Spirit, source of strength and passion,
inspire our hearts to hear the voiceless cry,
our will to break the shackles of injustice,
　take down all barriers that demean, divide,
　to give the hungry bread, the homeless shelter:
life in all fulness, that will *never* die.

Fred Kaan
England

* *The use of the word 'voice-over' owes its origin to the world of film, radio and television where an unseen voice is sometimes used to hold a play together while the actors each have their own role to play. The first and final words are often spoken in 'voice-over' mode.*

Proclaim Jubilee!

Fair Trade

A Growing Opportunity

The conventional wisdom that now calls us is that opportunity, not charity, spells good news for the poor. It is growing opportunity that brings them hope and joy and makes them want to celebrate.

This is wisdom we can readily embrace except for saying it is not just true now; it has always been true. The poor have never been particularly enthusiastic about charity, and the difference between them and the rich is not that one is lazy or dependent or lacks initiative whilst the other is hard working and self-reliant. Both rich and poor can be lazy. There is no moral difference between them. But if they want to help themselves and stand on their own feet, as most of us do, some get the opportunity to do so and others don't.

If then we want to act and pray for a more celebratory world we shall ask not so much how we can help the not-so-well-off and the poverty stricken, but how we can open up opportunities for them to seize.

The rapidly growing campaign to cancel the unpayable debts of the world's poorest countries under the banner of Jubilee 2000 is a good example of removing the obstacles that rob the poor of opportunities. If your country is already poor and has to spend a large percentage of what it does manage to earn on debt repayments (many of which cannot be justified in the first place) then it has no money to spend on keeping its own people healthy, or educating its children for the future, or investing in new industries and creating more jobs. The road of opportunity is blocked.

It is not enough of course to take the blocks away. There has to be life after debt in a better-organized world where the same old problems of exploitation don't occur all over again. That is why it is important to act and pray, amongst other things, for fair trade as well as debt cancellation.

Many of the products we have ample opportunity to buy and enjoy are grown and made for us by poor people in far away places. Some are made by poor people in towns and cities remarkably close to home. There is a nasty sweatshop industry on our doorstep as well as child labour, bad working conditions, pitifully low wages and insecure workers who can be hired and fired at will in other countries.

They don't have the opportunity to question what is going on – they would lose their jobs if they did. We do, and the supermarkets for example are very sensitive to what their customers have to say. They want our business but they should only get it on our terms or, if you like, fair terms. We can and should demand that they adopt codes of conduct which ensure that their suppliers give their workers a fair deal: the opportunity to have a decent job and a decent wage so that they can support their families like the rest of us.

A fairer world where more and more members of the human family enjoy the opportunity to earn a living will not come about by drawing up a wish list – which is what our praying can often amount to. We shall have to understand quite difficult issues, put pen to paper, question MPs and supermarket managers, make a noise, create a disturbance, accept the compromises that move things on, find ways of mutually supporting each other, test what we are about against our visions and values, reinvigorate ourselves in the dynamics of worship and meditation and celebrate our own joy and hope.

But one last cautionary note. The world of opportunity for everyone will not come easily – God made that clear in the crucified Christ, if we didn't already know – and it will not come tomorrow. Meanwhile huge numbers of those who watch and wait for it will live and die in poverty. We had better share what we have with them without pretending that is the answer to their poverty or ours, otherwise all our campaigning will sound hollow – like breaking bread but keeping both halves of the loaf.

Michael Taylor
England

Former Director of Christian Aid
and President and Chief Executive
of Selly Oak Colleges

A Vision of Shalom

The Spirit of the Lord is upon me, because he has sent me to bring good news to the poor . . . to set free the oppressed. Luke 4:18

Call to Worship

Leader: In Jesus' day
           beggars called out in every town;
           taxes were due for the Temple and for Rome;
           selling your child into slavery
           was one way to make ends meet.

**All: Today families are wounded by
               unemployment.
           Cash crops from distant places
           mean people there starve in those lands.
           Debt overwhelms many of us –
           and whole nations.**

Leader: Yet God raises up within us
           a vision of Shalom –
           a vision of places and people
           living in justice and abundance.

All: Jesus Christ is the Way into that Vision.
Come! Let us worship Him!

Betty Lynn Schwab
Canada

Grace

Give us, we pray, a loftier view of life
That we may watch the Earth
Upon its axis turn –
That we may not forget
How rains may flow to flood
And sun relentless burn . . .
And harvests fail . . .

Thus may we now give thanks
For all Earth's goodness set
Before us here –

And in this moment's quiet space
Together met,
We beg that You who generous gives,
Accept our simple, humble grace.

Margot Arthurton
England

God of Rice and Chapatti

1 Timothy 6: 17–19; Isaiah 55: 1–3a

God of corn and bread, of rice and chapatti,
we thank you for our food
and for the immense variety available to us.
We thank you for research that enables food
to be grown

114

without destruction of the earth,
for developments that improve storage
so we waste less.
We pray for all who live and work
in rural communities,
for all who work the land
in this country and all over the world.
We pray for a more equal sharing
of the resources of the earth.

Lord, in your mercy

People: **Hear our prayer.**

Jenny Spouge
England

The Ploughman

A patchwork of layered fields
Stretch across the valley.
A farmer works
Steering the heavy plough
Through soft oozing mud;
Guiding the pair of sturdy oxen
Carefully, skilfully,
Around the curves,
So that each small field is tilled.

As I stand and watch
It seems I have stepped back in time.
This living history is painted before me,
Framed within the mountains and hung
      in the crisp still air.
It's the twentieth century
      the age of technology
      computers, space travel;

Yet here
the rush of the modern world
seems to have passed by and
Time has paused.

Alison Stedman
England/Bhutan

Paddy Fields

Hooved feet
tramp the dust
in an endless march;
Shoulders drag
a heavy wooden plough
turning over clods of rich soil.

Then the fields are flooded;
Hard steps
become shining miniature lakes,
layered mud-beds.

Finally
with skirts held up
tucked in tight belts,
backs bent
feet bare
legs wading through wet slime;
Busy hands
tenderly root
green rice-plants
deep into the murky soil;

Colouring in the valley
with the lush green promise of harvest.

Alison Stedman
England/Bhutan

A Loan to Die

'I reflect on the injustices of our lending to other nations and hope there will be a radical change in our attitudes and practices. . . .'

You took the shoes
    from my feet
    because I couldn't pay the debt
    then let me borrow
    to buy some more.
Then you came again;
    took the shoes from my feet
    and the shirt off my back
    because I couldn't pay the debt
    but you said I could borrow
    to buy some more.
You came again
    took the shoes off my feet,
    the shirt from my back
    and stripped me naked
    in front of the world
    because I couldn't pay back
    the debt that I owed.
Then, with a smile,
    you offer to help
    with a loan for a while
    so I can start again.
But shoes and a shirt
    are no use without food
    so I will borrow once more
    to pay for my death.

Richard Becher
England

The Homeworker

She makes green gowns of paper,
green gowns for hospitals
to aid the healing of the sick.
Piled high in her tiny front room,
green dust settles on every surface.

She is a quiet woman, small framed
and nimble fingered – she has to be.
At £5.00 per thousand you have to be quick
or you don't earn enough to pay
for the running of the machine.

And then there's the packing –
each gown folded and packed in bags of ten.
That's included in the price.
She packs in the evening when the rattle
of the machine
would disturb the neighbours.

She is black with little English.
She is white. She is disabled.
She is a single mother working to buy shoes for
    the kids
(whose home is full of green paper and dust).
She lives in your town.

She sews, she packs, she assembles, she finishes.
Her work lines the shelves of every shop.
Her poverty lies behind that 'hand made' item,
    that bargain.
(Now you know how they make them so cheap)
but her sweated labour is behind that designer
    label too.
Her toil lines the pockets of another with gold.

Sewing green gowns for the healing of the sick,
her labour is the fruit of our own economic sickness.
She pays the price with numbed fingers at thirty
and her children with asthma from the green dust.
So pray for the healing of the sick.

Anne Morris
England

Forgive Us Our Debts

'Forgive us our trespasses
as we forgive those who trespass against us.'

Too many 's's in that for my liking.
In Scotland, we say, 'Forgive us our debts, as we forgive our debtors'.

The story Jesus told of the king forgiving the servant who owed him a lot of money and that servant not forgiving another servant who owed the first servant just a little, is a very good reminder of what this petition in the Lord's prayer means. 'Forgive us our debts, as we forgive our debtors'. If we are not prepared to forgive others who have done us wrong how can we possibly expect God to forgive us? If we want to be *forgiven* people, we need to be *forgiving* people.

Debts enslave. They imprison people till the money is paid off. When debts are so great as to be unpayable the prison sentence is lifelong and is more akin to sheer enslavement.

No one would suggest that the world today does not have nations that are very rich and nations that are desperately poor. We are a divided world. The point of preaching the good news of Jesus to the world is to make much wider the community of faith that is the church. The point of our praying

'Forgive us our debts as we forgive our debtors' is precisely to build that community not on slavery but on love.

Stephen Brown
England

Grant a Release

Open your hand and grant a release.
The biblical injunction is for priests and people;
the scriptural imperative is for business and government.
For too long the poorest in the world
have bent beneath a load of debt, not of their own making.
It is time to give release.

The farmers work the land
but their produce brings them little profit;
the women work with thread and cloth
but their labours bring them little return;
the children work on farms, in factories,
but to little benefit.
They work to pay the debts of oppressors;
middle men reap the profits, often in far lands.
It is time to open our hands and grant a release.

Responsive Prayer

Leader: Comfort my people, says our God, comfort
                them.

              For those who live in poverty in shanty towns,

Response: Comfort them, says our God.

Leader: For those who are refugees, fleeing from
                violence,

Response: **Comfort them, says our God.**

Leader: For those who are burdened by high interest on unpayable debts,

Response: **Comfort them, says our God.**

Leader: For those whose relatives have been victims of landmines,

Response: **Comfort them, says our God.**

Leader: For those who are the victims of discrimination,

Response: **Comfort them, says our God.**

Leader: For those caught up in inter-tribal violence,

Response: **Comfort them, says our God.**

Leader: Comfort my people. Tell them that our God is coming.
He will take care of his flock like a shepherd;

Response: **He will gently lead them to new pastures.**

I bend my back to farm the land;
I grow coffee beans for your delight
but you pay me little in money.
You turn on your machines;
you produce a fine finished product
but you charge me much for this small radio.
So you grow richer and I become poorer
yet still you call it fair trading.

John Johansen-Berg
England

Baa-baa . . . Barmy World

Tune: Baa-baa black sheep

Cash-crop producer have you any bread?
No sir, no sir,
I grow coffee beans instead.
I'm ripped off by the middleman,
I haven't any choice.
Whilst you fill up your cafetières
I dream of eating rice.

Supermarket owner have you any qualms?
No sir, no sir,
he decides what he farms.
I have to make a profit,
I haven't any choice.
Shareholders wouldn't listen
if I tried to raise my voice.

God of justice is there nothing you can do?
Yes sir, yes sir,
for I make all things new.
Give up your endless wanting,
your cries of 'more, more, more.'
And try instead to satisfy
the priorities of the poor.

Ed Cox
England

Coin Considerations

Exodus 22: 25–27; Luke 16:13

Leader: Structures of budgets
Cycles of bills,
Seasons of spending,
Fascinate and frighten us.

All: **How can we sing God's song in this land?**

Leader: Climates of wealth,
Chasms of poverty
Committees of reckoning
Concern and confront us.

All: **How can we sing God's song in this land?**

Leader: Recessions and reductions,
Banking and balancing,
Credits and calculations
Subjugate and startle us.

All: **How can we sing God's song in this land?**

Leader: Divide and conquer our fear,
Multiply our wisdom,
Subtract our apprehension,
Add justice and compassion:

All: **So that we can sing God's song in this land.**

Keri K Wehlander
Canada

The Use of Money

We feel guilty, Lord, because we have been given so much while others have so little.

Help us to recognize our responsibilities, Lord

– to give our money in ways which will help the most, sometimes in regular giving to a known cause; sometimes spontaneously as the need arises;

– to spend our money fairly, remembering that what we pay is meant to help others to a reasonable standard of living;

– to invest our money ethically, so that in sensible provision for our own future we are also supporting those industries and commercial enterprises that treat their workers justly, or those mutual groups which offer beneficial financial support to each other;

– to use our money wisely for the well-being of family, friends and community and in support of those initiatives which will help to shape your world more effectively into your pattern.

Forgive our occasional extravagances Lord, for you are a loving and understanding God, but teach us how your extragavance works in your total and outrageous generosity to your children. Help us to learn from you Lord, that sacrificial giving is also demanded of us and our guilty feelings about the poverty of others are one of the ways in which you urge us to take action.

Lead us Lord, into an understanding of your will in the right use of our money – for your world's sake.

Marjorie Dobson
England

The Golden Idol

It flings itself along the river bank, this idol, belching
flames like a modern Moloch,
consuming people like an ancient one.
It is, of course, to save the people. Taxes will be lower,
there will be jobs.

The road signs say, This way to the Casino. No anxiety
about taking a wrong turn. You can't miss it.

It offers opportunity, promises, promises and promises. It is
   red and gold, its floral
arrangements plush and disciplined. There is food and music
   and happiness.
There goes a famous person, and there is a rich one!

The people carry this idol. They carry it on their
indebted, gambled backs. It is carried through breaches
of family trust, through pay days emptied of cash . . .
it takes sacrifices for the good of the community, the State, the
   economy.

Let us place all false offers of redemption in a
cucumber field.

Give thanks to God for fields and for cucumbers and
other things that grow and for redemption that is free.

National Commission for Mission
Uniting Church in Australia

A Penny for Your Thoughts

A basket is passed around and each person is invited to place a penny in the basket and name how money can be a curse in life. Once everyone has had a chance to do this, the basket is passed around again, and this time, each person is invited to take a penny from the basket and name how money can be a blessing in life.

A Prayer

Leader: God of all hope:

All: Hear our prayer.

Leader: When money becomes a prison:

All: Free us to choose life.

Leader: Where wealth turns into addiction:

All: Free us to choose life.

Leader: When income determines worth:

All: Free us to choose life.

Leader: Where poverty equals invisibility:

All: Free us to choose life.

Leader: When economies deepen injustice:

All: Free us to choose life.

Leader: Where greed invents new oppressions:

All: Free us to choose life.

Leader:	When finance rules every decision:

All: **Free us to choose life.**

Leader:	Where consumption replaces compassion:

All: **Free us to choose life.**

Keri K Wehlander
Canada

Prayer of Confession

Leader:	O Christ, you open up the closed-minded you soften the hard-hearted you lift up the downtrodden.

A moment for sitting with Christ

Leader:	We confess
People on the sides:	*We have been closed-minded and hard-hearted.*
People in the centre:	*It freezes us.* *Soon we are too numb to care –* *about ourselves or for others.*

A moment for private confession

Leader:	We confess
People on the sides:	*We have experienced the pain of being shut out,* *downtrodden, excluded, unwanted.*

127

People in the centre: *It freezes us.*
Soon we are too numb to care –
about ourselves or for others.

A moment for private confession

Leader: O Christ,

All: **forgive us.**
Warm our spirit
until with your grace
we, too, open up the closed-minded
soften the hard-hearted
and lift up those who are downtrodden.

Betty Lynn Schwab
Canada

Bringing His Justice

Injustice weighs us down
A rock
Unliftable, unchangeable
Guilt ridden, spreading
Covering the earth with deeper cloud.

Justice drips drops slowly
One by one
Little by little
Almost unseen, unheard
Wearing away the wrongs of the world.

God's time goes slowly by
Minute by imperceptible minute
Moving hands forward
Working on hearts
Bringing His justice into His world.

Lesley K Steel
Scotland

Living with the New Economic Order

Governments all over the world are selling the new economic order as humankind's saviour. But, based on privatization and profit, it means hardship for many, probably the vast majority. India is a good example: while some 250 million people will benefit, the other 750 million will be poorer than ever.

God, who calls us to community:
We pray as people committed to a new community in Christ.

For the sake of the poor, your people of old
did not reap to the edge of the field,
or pick up the loose ears,
or the fallen grapes.

But now forests are privatized
and the poor can't pick up fallen branches,
or hunt,
or gather.

The new idol, Profit,
has made thieves of us all.

We proclaim your love and justice.
But we need your help lest we become deceivers,
full of words,
unable to do anything
to strengthen the weak
and share the burden
of those for whom you have a special care.

Have mercy on us.

National Commission for Mission
Uniting Church in Australia

A Prayer for Economic Justice

When daily toil leaves empty hands
    and an unfilled belly,
When others prosper while the poor
    slump into the hole of debt.
Fill the hearts of all who strive
      for economic justice with hope in their struggle
      and despair against indifference.

Philip Freier
Australia

In the Beginning Was Globalization . . .

God
you have always seen planet earth as a globe.
You made it that way,
spherical, on purpose, to dance and spin
to the rhythm of the universe.

It is we who have been flat-earthers
afraid of falling off the edge,
afraid to venture far outside
the walls we build
of colour, race and culture
creed and custom,
always persuaded that our ways are best
evangelical in promoting western ideas –
Big Macs and big Bibles – everywhere.

And now
convinced by our own discoveries,
first of foreign markets eager for our wares,
and then of unfair competition

from exploited children in Chinese carpet factories
or making electronic goods
putting our local factories out of work,
we find ourselves beginning to believe
that – incredibly – the earth is round
for a reason!

Help us, God of wisdom and mercy,
to trust your wisdom and believe your Word,
who made the heavens and the earth to be
one universe
beautiful beyond imagination
founded on covenant love and justice.

Show us how to build a global community
redeemed and restored by that same love
expressed in justice
in fair working practice and just trade
in peaceful government and mutual care.

Through Jesus Christ, whose arms spread wide at Calvary
express the global nature of unending love. Amen.

Heather Pencavel
England

The Millennium Dream

Petitions,
and pressure
brought to bear,
to cancel the debts
which shackle
and cripple
our third-world
family.

'The Jubilee Principle?
A <u>nice</u> idea,
my dear.
But,
tell me this,
do –
<u>who</u>
would buy
our arms
if we did
such a thing?'

And so,
God –
will your
millennium dream
turn in the end
into
your nightmare?

Susan Hardwick
England

To Blossom Like the Rose

On a pilgrimage of reconciliation in Israel Palestine, we had
planned to meet the people, the living stones, as well as to visit
the holy places. One memorable visit was to an area of the
West Bank where local arabs were working to make terraces
on the stony and barren land. Their task was made possible by
gifts from the United Reformed Church in the United
Kingdom. These enabled the hire of machinery which
removed large stones for the terracing. Looking over the parts
where the scheme had been in operation for some time the
contrast with the untreated landscape was remarkable. The
beauty of the newly terraced land and its potential for fruit-
fulness made us realize that here truly 'the desert shall rejoice

and blossom as the rose'. We appreciated that the Jewish people who had come into the Land had made a tremendous difference, enabling the wilderness to bear fruit, but here was evidence that the Palestinians too could do the same, given similar resources. If they combine their gifts and resources together, what a transformation there will be throughout the Holy Land.

John Johansen-Berg
England

The Time for Jubilee

Chorus: This is the time for Jubilee
This is the time for setting free
From chains of debt and poverty
Bring wholeness in community.

There are tables to be turned
So all can join in living
Rules that must be changed
Debts to be forgiven
There are dreams that must be dreamed
A loving God to follow
A new world to be born
That brings a new tomorrow.

God's heart is beating close
A heart of love and giving
Our world can't hear the sound
For it moves to a different rhythm
Our eyes have been made blind
By the God of greed we follow
Let the God of love increase
And bring a new tomorrow.

Chorus: This is the time for Jubilee . . .

So we can be the light
We must endure the burning
The pathway to what's right
Beginning with the learning
Of what must change in me
To heal a world of sorrow
So we live the Jubilee
That brings a new tomorrow.

Garth Hewitt
England

Jubilee and Celebrations

Jubilee has a biblical basis in several scripture passages such as in Leviticus 25, Isaiah 61 and Luke 4. From these passages Jubilee seems to emphasize the following: fallow land, forgiveness, freedom, justice and jubilation.

Leader: Let us begin our observance of the Jubilee by turning to God and His word in order to grasp its true meaning.

Response: God, may your spirit be upon us to proclaim the year of the Lord's favour.

Leader: Let us remember the instruction to let the land lie fallow, as we grant rest both to our environment and to our bodies.

Response: Lord, help us to remember the Sabbath principle in every walk of life.

Leader: Let us remember not only to forgive others' sins but even their financial debts to us.

Response: Lord, help us to truly grasp this principle of forgiveness as we endeavour to relieve third world countries of some of their unbearable financial burden.

Leader: Let us endeavour to work for justice, so that good
           news may be brought to the poor and freedom to
           the oppressed.

Response: **Rejoice in the Lord, always. Again, we say
           rejoice for we now live in the year of the Lord's
           favour.**

National Commission for Mission
Uniting Church in Australia

Shake the Foundations

For group activity

Read Jeremiah 6: 13–15 or Acts 17:6

Leader: When greed shapes the walls of our structures,
           When callousness hinges the doors of decision:

All: **Let the foundations be shaken and God's
           realm begun!**

Leader: When ruthlessness reigns in the stairwells of
           power,
           When deception is basic because control is the
           key:

All: **Let the foundations be shaken and God's
           realm begun!**

Leader: When prejudice is stored in our hallways of
           habit,
           When denial shelters the hearth of our fears:

All: **Let the foundations be shaken and God's
           realm begun!**

Sing an appropriate song

Cornerstone Reflection

Each person is given a good sized stone with smooth surfaces and a felt marker. They are invited to write a word/phrase on the stone that reflects an element they would like to see valued at the foundations of their church/society. When everyone has finished, each person is invited to share their 'cornerstone' with the rest of the group and place it in the centre of the group.

Prayer

Unsettling God,
Dizzy with your vision,
May we craft our living
With realized mercies
And unfashionable hope.

Transformed by your message,
May we disrupt idolatrous norms
With the vigour of justice
And the plain language of faith.

Resolute in your embrace,
May we form new foundations
With the endurance of love
And a passion for grace.

Keri K Wehlander
Canada

Whole Person, Whole Community, Whole World

Whole World

Health and Holistic Influences

Sharing in the Work of Healing

In my daily work as a speech therapist and theologian I find that I am continually required to make connections. This is a somewhat counter-cultural activity in a western European context, where splitting things up and ordering them in their respective boxes is a well-supported socio-political system of operating. It is one that can be useful but which needs, I believe, to be balanced with a connective way of working.

I am approaching forty years old, married and the parent of one child, now nearly five years old. I have worked in the British National Health Service for seventeen years. It would be easy, according to a commonplace way of thinking in some mainstream Christian churches, to get on with life concerned only for my personal salvation and that of my nearest and dearest, with a thought or two once or twice a year in the direction of 'those less fortunate'. According to this model of Christian health, all I need to do is concentrate on having the right relationship with God through Jesus and I'll be 'healthy, wealthy and wise' in this world and the next.

But this model began to fall apart for me about twenty years ago, when as a young person meeting Christian partners in India, I had my first encounter with eastern culture. The weaving of a new pattern of understanding is still in progress but has incorporated strands of understanding from many parts of the world, most especially western feminism, South African liberation theology and the experiences of children with speech and language difficulties and their families.

It would be easy to define healing and wholeness simply in terms of physical well-being, where God would reward us by physical healing if we were disabled, just as the Jesus of the Gospels healed people. However, this view ignores and insults the experiences of millions of people with disabilities world-wide, both inside and outside the Church. We need to develop a theology of healing and wholeness which takes the experiences of people with disabilities as its starting point.

There are ways in which we can co-operate in the struggle for wholeness on all levels; ways in which science has a place as much as mysticism, words as much as silence. We need to make connections, embrace a multiplicity of perspectives and weave them together to promote wholeness for individuals, communities and the whole world. There are six ways in which local congregations and individuals might become involved in this world-wide work of healing and wholeness. These are:

> **by being a place of healing,** where there are opportunities for worship and prayer in respect of health and healing, including prayer with the sick and for forgiveness and reconciliation, the sacraments, anointing and laying on of hands, creating healing liturgies, the training of healers and the promotion of healing gifts;

> **by being a caring community,** which promotes opportunities both in and outside the congregation to share in the ministry of healing and reconciliation, to support the poor, marginalized and oppressed, in serving members of the community of faith and the wider society, encouraging them to choose life, health and wholeness;

> **by being a teaching place,** which promotes learning and teaching on health through Bible study, Christian education for all ages and other methods of health education so that participants might learn to take personal responsibility for health;

> **by being a promoter of justice, peace and the integrity of creation,** where people can explore the interconnec-

tion of life on this planet, including developing partner-
ships with other organizations through the world-wide
church

by being a contributor to primary health care, as a promoter of the availability of good basic health care in a convenient place, including discussion about how health care
might be funded, staffed, accommodated and organized;

by being a supporter of healing work, as a promoter of
co-operation with community health care programmes
and health professionals both within the community of
faith and in wider society, including both traditional
medicine and alternative therapies.

This agenda for health is an example of the ministry of connections to which we are called. It is an agenda in which health
is about the physical, mental and spiritual aspects of people's
lives and it concerns both the theologian and the scientist, just
as it happens inside and outside the church, for of such is the
commonwealth of God.

Janet Lees
England

A Litany of Thanks

Psalm 9: 1–2

Leader: To wake from sleep into this day –

All: Is gift enough for thanks.

Leader: To hear a child's delights in laughter –

All: Is gift enough for thanks.

Leader:	To sip a glass of clean, cold water –
All:	**Is gift enough for thanks.**
Leader:	To watch the sunset paint the sky –
All:	**Is gift enough for thanks.**
Leader:	To share a moment with a friend –
All:	**Is gift enough for thanks.**
Leader:	To smell the fragrance of moist soil –
All:	**Is gift enough for thanks.**
Leader:	To feel the comfort of clean clothing –
All:	**Is gift enough for thanks.**
Leader:	To form the words that make a prayer –
All:	**Is gift enough for thanks.**

Keri K Wehlander
Canada

A Prayer for Abundant Life

O God,
Where hearts are fearful and confined:
    Grant freedom and daring.
Where anxiety is infectious and widening:
    Grant peace and reassurance.
Where impossibilities close every door and window:
    Grant imagination and resistance.

Where distrust shapes every understanding:
    Grant healing and transformation.

Where spirits are daunted and dimmed:
    Grant soaring wings and strengthened dreams.

Marion Best
Canada

Sensitive God

Sensitive God,
conductor of musical bird-song,
painter of cloud shapes and sunsets,
planter of pine-scented forests,
grower of mouth-watering melons,
unfurler of soft, silky rose petals,
awaken all our senses to the variety and extravagance of your
    world.

As we rejoice in the many ways we can see, hear, smell,
taste and touch your creation, make us also aware of
those who lack one or more of these senses. Lead us, caring God, to the discovery of sensitive ways in which we
can help all your children to enjoy the beauty and variety
which you have provided for us.

Marjorie Dobson
England

Monday's Angel

*A thought and a prayer after dealing with a visitor to the rectory on
a winter morning.*

Hearing the hands
The old hands

Cold hands
Of the hungry man
Feeling the cracks
The harsh cracks
Silent cracks
Of his fading voice
In the cold.

Cold wind

Touches my eyes
Cataract eyes
Ego eyes
Tearful and blinded
By ease and
Opens my heart
And my door to the closeness
Of God.

Edgar Ruddock
England

Disability: Gift and Struggle

A Different Perspective

For thirty years people have encouraged me to overcome my disability. Yet, it is part of me and it gives me insights and a perspective that I would not have if I didn't have Cerebral Palsy. I have always apologized for the inconvenience caused to other people through my disability but it is part of me. As I grow in self confidence I learn that my disability does not have to be a source of shame, rather it can be a gift that can be offered to others.

Disability is part of life that God gives us.
It does not diminish wholeness
Being human, fashioned in the image of God.
Wholeness is living life to the full
Being at peace with oneself and with God.

Disability is part of life that God gives us.
It is a challenge to live with it.
Attitudes of others and inaccessible buildings
Do handicap and make life difficult
However we share this world with others.

Disability is part of life that God gives us.
We discover the gift in different ways.
Come let's share this gift together
Partners in the struggle of being human
Rejoicing in the diverse experience of life!

Vicki Terrell
Aotearoa New Zealand

Being There

In the deepest depths of pain
Of tiredness
Of vulnerability and fear,

I need you.

I do not need your words
Or wise advice.

I just need you.

You and me together
In the stillness.
Holding my hand as I weep,
Cradling me in the warmth of your love.

In the silence,
Together.

Easing the loneliness,
Sharing the pain.

Just being beside me
In your unknowingness.
Knowing that you cannot know the detail
Of my tortured mind,
Can never plumb these depths of pain.

The comfort of your presence
Brings healing.

Your hand on mine.
Your thoughts
So closely intertwined with mine
In a deep embrace
Of love,
A deep acknowledgement of my needs . . .

That I need you

Just

To be there.

Pat Marsh
England

The Dream of Wholeness

A song based on the San saying:
'There is always someone dreaming us'

Come and dream, the dream of wholeness
The wholeness of the world
For there's always someone dreaming,
Someone dreaming us.

Come and dream, the dream of wholeness
The wholeness of the world
I see Moses and Elijah

Meet Christ the servant Lord
Who will give himself for us
His cross to hold the world.

Peter, James and John are dreaming
The wholeness of the world
On the mountain God is sharing
A dream that shapes the world
Through his suffering and his dying
Our prayers will dream the world.

Douse the candles, mist is rising
Wake the sleepers for the dawn
We are not alone for God cries
I'm hurting for my world
We will give ourselves with him
His cross to heal the world.

Wake now Mary stop your dreaming
In the garden all alone,
You have dreamed the dream of wholeness
Run and spread the news
Come my friends and join our dreaming
Dream the wholeness of the world.

Bob Commin
South Africa

The Kiss of Life

It was a particular treachery that had Judas betray
his Lord with a kiss. Perhaps he was cowardly –
perhaps, even then, he was trying not to implicate
himself: kissing rather than pointing.

But, be that as it may, it was still a 'kiss of death'.

We have a 'kiss of life'. Paul tells us that we are entrusted with the ministry of reconciliation: sharing in the life-giving that brings . . . a 'kiss of life'.

In evocative words from the Iona Community, we are asked, 'Will you kiss the leper clean?' The community might just as easily have written, 'Will you kiss the Aids patient clean?' Or, more generally, 'Will you kiss the outcast clean?'

We have a kiss of life.

Our calling is to embrace the world and not fear being embraced by the world: finding Christ in the face of the poor and the prince; moved to work for justice: to live the love of Christ for the world.

A kiss of life, a breath of renewal, a shared rising.

Don't point! Kiss! Don't betray! Embrace!

Stephen Brown
England

Rainbow

One flame in a thousand panes
one flame at a thousand angles
a list of names, that is all,
that is enough.

In the church we queued to light
many candles, we pinned up
many names on the notice board,
pinned up memories.

One flame, and darkness is incomplete,
one name and oblivion is breached,
one tear at the world's fabric;
redemption yet awaits.

One flame in many flames,
one heavy moon in each one's eyes,
a many-coloured quilt of flesh and spirit,
our rainbow.

Harvey Gillman
England

The Evolving Mystery

I believe that contemporary spirituality cannot and must not ignore the growing issues of sexuality. I would suggest that the issues of the sexualities and the spiritualities are bonded together for the whole of our lives.

Also, I believe that next to the gift of life itself is that of our sexuality, our sexual orientation and our gender. It is this which links our sexualities and our spiritualities. Therefore, any unnatural interference with one inevitably interferes with the other, bonded as they are, as partners for life, nurturing one another.

Spirituality today must not continue to ignore the importance of the emerging issues around psycho-sexual and spiritual growth. I would suggest that a healthy sexual or spiritual experience is like being caught up in the beauty of a sunrise or sunset; in the exhilarating score at the football match; of an all-absorbing concert; or being involved in dervish-type disco dancing. These experiences, I believe, touch on our basic needs. In so doing they highlight very complex issues that an evolving spirituality must find ways of accommodating and challenging.

My experiences suggest to me that all our sensual feelings are linked into the sexual and spiritual aspects of our lives. They are like the bridge linking body and soul; inner and outer; soul with soul; person with person; masculine with feminine; hardness with softness; justice with truth; co-creation with procreation; living with dying and dying with living. They are the Yin and Yang of life.

It is in these areas of our lives that 'wisdom' is calling us to be attentive to the evolving mystery of our sexualities and our spiritualities. These issues demand from us a kind of listening, that is unafraid and open to hearing how, with others, we may encourage a healthy and holistic growth into the fullness of our own life potential.

Bill Kirkpatrick
Canada/England

All One in Christ Jesus

There is neither Jew nor Greek, there is neither slave nor free, there is neither male nor female; for you are all one in Christ Jesus. Galatians 3:28

Our sexuality is an important part of our identity as persons. Ministers in their pastoral visiting have often had to sit with and talk and pray with gay and lesbian people who are desperate to be affirmed in their place in the Christian community. Within a short space of time they had to sit and talk and pray with members for whom any acceptance by the church of homosexual relationships constitutes an assault on their understanding of God's will expressed in the Scriptures for human sexuality.

Prayer

Gracious God, stand among us as we talk about our sexuality. Be with us in the ongoing study, prayer and dialogue so that we can create an environment of grace and openness in which:

* deep issues will not be glossed over,

* respectful listening to those whose opinions and experiences differ from our own will take place,

*   we will seek to regard each other first and foremost as
      sisters and brothers in Christ, broken in our humanity
      yet recipients and agents of the grace of Christ.

National Commission for Mission
Uniting Church in Australia

Sexuality

O God, who made us male and female in your image,
enable us to see in our sexuality a witness to our
constant need of you, as well as of each other.
Help us, in all matters sexual, to treat each other with love-
    tempered responsibility,
together with avoidance of the exploitations and
over-ready condemnation of others.

Ian Gillman
Australia

Words With Mother

Dear Mother,

Thanks for making me a
heterosexual, so that I will
not be identified as 'pagan'
and suffer discrimination as
well as humiliation from the
majority of people.

Thanks for giving me a
church where I can obtain
sisters' and brothers'
support. Unlike homosexuals
who are expelled from the
Church, I can enjoy the
Church's fellowship. They
must wander outside.

My dear daughter,

How can you have forgotten
love makes no difference
between rich and poor,
between different sexual
orientations?

How can you have forgotten
when I was in the world, I
struggled with the sinners,
prostitutes, those who were
oppressed and discriminated
against?

Thanks for giving me faithful pastors. My spiritual life grows under their pastoral care. Unlike those homosexual Christians who are being neglected as lost sheep, I do not have to search for a way of life on my own.

Thanks for making me holy, for accepting me as righteous and for allowing me to worship you and praise you in the Church of high prestige, unlike those homosexual Christians who worship you secretly and walk near you suffering others' blame.

Thanks for bestowing me with wisdom to differentiate between the sinful and the innocent. Unlike those stupid Christians who are willing to walk with homosexuals, worship you with them, feast in their house, infringe upon your name.

How can you have forgotten I left the other ninety-nine sheep and went looking for the one that got lost until I found it?

How can you have forgotten I asked you to go to the disregarded Samaritan?

My daughter, now you view the Church as your own property and reject the ones I love. Now you view your sisters and brothers as sinners. You see the speck in their eyes but pay no attention to the log in your own eye.

My daughter, the one who hurts me is not them but you.

Winnie Ma
translated by Ling Ho
Hong Kong

Dreaming Denied?

I am lying down in my cramped two-bedroom apartment,
My sister is sitting on the chair.
As I look around this congested apartment
I enter my dream-house.

> I see a home I shall build for myself, a house,
> A house perched on a pleasant mountain, with birds
>   singing in the trees.
> I tell my sister of my dream-house.
> Its rooms, I say to her shall be spacious, airy and sunny.
> My sister looks at me long and silently and thoughtfully,
> Then she says to me, 'Ga re itse mma, these are the days
>   of AIDS.'

I am on my way to work; I pass by homes, beautiful homes
With evergreen and climbers, twirling and twisting down the
    edge.
I see a fusion of white, red, pink and yellow roses.
I breathe deep and I am infused with sweet smell of spring.
I stoop down to pick a flower and as I smell it, I enter my
    dream-house.

> I dream of a day I shall plant trees in my own yard,
> I dream of jacarandas, bougainvillaeas.
> Each tree planted with love and tended with love.
> I dream of the many days I shall watch my plants grow.
> I dream of a day I shall come back from work and be
>   welcomed
> A fusion of flowers climbing down my hedge,
>   proclaiming life.
> But then I hear my sister's voice saying, 'Ga re itse mma,
> These are the days of AIDS.'

I am in my apartment, I hear the happy sounds of children
    playing outside.
I go to my window and peer outside; I see them playing ball.

They bounce the ball, they call, they shout, they chase each
other and they laugh
And I enter my dream-house.

I dream of the many children I shall bear through the
years,
I dream of how they shall run to me,
Crying 'Mama, Mama, Mama,' and all hug me
When I return home from work.
I dream of the years to come when I shall be a grey-
haired old woman.
I dream of how I shall be an adored old woman
With a horde of grandchildren , and great-grandchildren
and
Children of my children.
I dream of how I shall sit around the warm blazing fire,
Telling them stories of my own grandmother. 'Gatwe e
kile'
I dream of how they shall sit, spellbound, by my magical
stories.
I dream but then I hear my sister's voice, once again
saying,
'Ga re itse mma, these are the days of AIDS.'

I try to dream of the cows I shall raise
And hear my sister saying, 'Ga re itse mma,
These are the days of . . .'
I try to dream of the fields I shall plant
And hear my sister's voice saying, 'Ga re itse mma . . .'
I try to dream of business I shall start
And my sister's voice says, 'Ga re itse mma'
I try to dream and I am stopped.

Is dreaming denied?

I turned to my little boy sitting on the chair, sweaty and
dusty

From the business of playing.
I put a question to him:

'Tell me what's your dream, boy: Tell me what's your
     dream, boy,
Tell me what's your dream, boy.'
He stands up quickly and looks me in the eye saying,
'You always were the black queen, Mama
You always were the black queen, Mama
I am going to buy you a limousine, Mama
I am going to build you a mansion, Mama
I am going to build you a mansion, Mama
I am going to build a church, Mama, with all playing
     grounds, Mama
Soccer fields, basket ball courts, swimming pools, Mama
I am going to build a very big church, Mama
And all the children shall enter freely in the
     playgrounds.'

I realize then that dreaming can never be denied.

Musa W Dube Shomanah
Botswana

Just Being Human

These short prayers are intended for use in worship around the theme of sexuality. There can be different readers with the prayers separated by silence or music.

Creator God,
we praise you with the bodies you have made,
we glorify you by being fully human, fully alive.

Jesus, you know what it feels like to be hurt,
I know that you share my vulnerability.

God, who calls each of us by name,
forgive us when we put labels on other people.

God of Compassion,
pick me up when I have fallen down.

Encourager, Heart of my own heart,
help me to overcome fear.

God of Justice, inspire us to anger
when we see our sisters and brothers
misjudged and mistreated.

Jesus, our friend,
help us to be there for each other
in good and bad times.

Healing Hands – strong and gentle – holding us
up,
restore our trust.

God of Love, you know me intimately,
sometimes taking me by surprise;
I yearn for your presence:
in it I am filled with delight.

Loving Parent, help me
to take responsibility for myself
and to care for those close to me.

Companion, walk with us on the way,
be with us when we break bread.

God of Laughter,
help me to see the funny side.

Creative Spirit, set us free to live creatively.

God of Truth, help us to be true to ourselves.

Jan Sutch Pickard
England

Wrestling the Unnamed to a Blessing

night crouches behind
the stones by the river
devours the last of
twilight's bones then
pounces
pins and drags me
to the brink
tosses and turns me
face to face with God
knows what –
a mask staring from
fathomless depths with
night-filled night-filling
eyes –
     the I that decks itself
in others' standards
to procure their blessing
     the I that grabs
what-is by the heel
to haul it to what-I-prefer
     the I that would rather
run than wrestle
whose every action
     is a reaction

I want to run but
something holds me back
some nocturnal thing

that dares not speak its name
that knows – if I could name it
I might tame it
recloset it behind the stones
    so I could run again
but something
has me pegged
knows my given name and
the one I should have had
perseveres only to bless
    me with it now

I cannot run –
some nocturnal
unnamed thing
lames me
blesses and
renames me
tells me
    I won.

Norm S D Esdon
Canada

Happy Are Those Who Are Merciful to Others

Matthew 5:7

A Call to Worship

Leader: Scripture says:
        You shall love the Lord your God
        with all your heart, all your soul
        and with all your strength.

All: **Faith then is not a head-trip.**
        Our body matters.
        Our body counts.

Leader:	When God created human beings
	God was very pleased.

All : **May we hallow our bodies**
their strengths and limits
their joys and pain.

Leader: With body, mind and spirit, come.
Let us worship God!

Betty Lynn Schwab
Canada

Wholeness

What makes for my wholeness?
I am one person but a subtle combination
of body, mind and spirit.
When my body is exhausted
my mind finds it hard to function;
when balance of mind is lacking
the spirit loses something of its vitality.
When the spirit lacks its creative spark
then body and mind are exhausted.

What makes for my wholeness?
I am one person but in a complexity
of relationships with others.
I cannot live for myself alone
but must think of the need of neighbours.
I cannot find fulfilment in selfish pleasure
but must seek it in service gladly given.
When I lack relationship with those around me
then I am not fully myself, not truly healthy.

What makes for my wholeness?
I am one person but in communion

with the Creator who made me.
I cannot live as though the world were mine
since all things exist by God's grace.
I cannot be fully a human being
if I am not in harmony with the divine.
When I lack a relationship with my Maker
I am not in a state of true health.
How then shall I seek to live a healthy life?
When I am bound to my neighbours
in compassionate concern,
when I am in communion with God
and at peace within myself,
then I am truly whole, a healthy person.

Responsive Prayer

Leader: God is coming to help us.
             The blind will be able to see,
             and the deaf will hear.

**Response: The lame will leap and dance,
             and those who cannot speak will shout for joy.**

Leader: Loving God, for those in our society who are
                 anxious or depressed,
             for all who suffer mental anguish and
                 experience hidden fears,

**Response: Give them healing and may they thank you
                 with joy.**

Leader: For those in our community who suffer from
                 sickness or disease,
             for all who have been injured or experience
                 pain,

**Response: Give them healing and may they thank you
                 with joy.**

Leader: For those around us who have never known
faith in Christ,
for those whose faith has lapsed or who
experience doubts,

**Response: Grant them a vision of your glory and may
they thank you with joy.**

The Saviour stretched out his hand
to touch the leper and to heal the sick.
So we too release the flow of health by touch;
the hand on the shoulder of someone in deep depression;
hand clasping hand, black and white, in mutual care;
kneeling beside the man in destitution, offering a
helping hand;
taking the arm of the blind woman that we might
walk together;
fingers placed on the face of the outcast, tracing love's
forgiveness;
hands of priest and people pray by touch for the
healing grace of God.

John Johansen-Berg
England

Beyond: A Love Poem

Beyond the boundaries
Love exists
and welcomes us with a
heart so full of tenderness:
ooh, I could sing and dance
in the freedom of life
beyond the boundaries.

But perhaps we never reach
that beyond. Perhaps the
ooh comes from the
intimate knowledge that we
must push ourselves constantly
over the border, onto the edge,
into the no-go area, the risky
ground that beckons.

My love for you lies in the
border area – in the
subtle, shifting, supple
ground where clarity has
nothing to do with clear lines
but rather with a sense,
a perception, that *this*
is the shifting ground
on which I choose to stand.

And the ground shifts
within the confines of a
border, a boundary much
more subtle, but secure –
it is the solid rock that I
know lies beneath the ground.

Ruth Harvey
England

Light

Within the innermost of souls
There strains a light concealed
By jealous guarding –
Reflecting only self
Upon itself,
And in the outer edges
Only blackness,
And potential lost.

But the light released
Is as a vital source,
And boundless in its reach –
To merge and join,
And burgeon into one.

So guard not jealously the light within,
But let it be revealed –
That it may grow,
The earth to show
In perfect unity –
The safety of Eternity . . .
And in the joining of the light
May the work of life be done –

For the wholeness of light is forever . . .
And the Light has no edges.

Margot Arthurton
England

The Gatherer

It is the God in me who gathers,
collects up every thought of you,
loosens the roots of every hurt,
shakes off soil that clogs
paled fibrous memories.
She tugs, plucks out every anger,
pulls away the broken stems.

Searching out every bloom,
of what was right and good,
she breaks them off admiringly.
Stripping stems of every leaf
she breathes in the pungent crush
of lives once broken open
each to the other.

God is this woman in a field
gathering plants in her apron front
for the healing brew.

Viv Stacey
South Africa

Stewardship of Self

O Holy One – we lose ourselves
  in worlds of our own making
Help us to find ourselves
  in your creation – in a cleft of the rock
  where stone and wave and heaven meet
  where body, mind and spirit knit
  where your Word made flesh again in us
  restores in us your bread and wine
  of the Christ's self-giving love

    Open a cleft in our self-made worlds
      where your healing presence
      can give us pause – give us rest
      where our rendering unto Caesar
      becomes an offering unto God

Blessed are you, O Holy One –
  in each body, mind and spirit
  you raise again your temple of
  the Christ's self-giving love.

Norm S D Esdon
Canada

Words

When I was young
I could barely talk.
Words were frightening things.
Once released, they could never be recaptured.
They had the power to defame and to destroy.
'Sticks and stones will hurt your bones,
Words will never hurt you,' I was told.
This was and is not true.
Telephones should come with licences
Like shotguns.

One day, bleeding deep inside from wounds caused by
    horrible words,
I discovered print.
First books, then newspapers.
I stared and stared
At these ancient, powerful enemies of mine,
Captured
Held
Controlled.
Manipulated and moved around
To mean exactly what they were intended to mean
And not what the air had distorted them into
In mine or someone else's mind.
Oh how I admired the people who wrote those books
And those newspapers.
How I would escape into them.
How I longed to be able to write.
And how more rarely I opened my mouth to speak.

I discovered it was possible to learn to write,
Here was a craft, like carpentry, that could be studied.
I became indentured,
An apprentice, to a newspaper.
But they were hard, those years.
What battles I had
With those early words

Those monstrous, slippery, twisty things,
Those fearsome missiles
Capable of such random, horrible destruction
When spoken out loud or even,
I found, despairing,
When wrongly used in print.

'She is aloof,' they would say of me.
They were wrong. I was simply scared.
How I recall
The sweat, the years, the agony
Of learning to take those frightening creatures
And break them, calm them,
Make them things of beauty, mystery and spirit,
Lead them in a dance across a page
To a tune of my own invention
Or better still,
The harmonies of truth.
But then came the guilt.
It remains with me and always will.
The stories I have written
That have hurt people as I myself was hurt.
How ashamed I am.
And still, I could barely speak.

And now has come the miracle of the modern age
Communication by the written word
With people across the continents.
The marriage of modern science
With the Word.
What heaven.
To 'speak' with someone a thousand miles away
Without having to pick up that hated weapon of destruction,
The telephone.
What freedom, liberation, bliss.
And suddenly, comes a glimpse of my own Apocalypse.
A revelation, an explosion in the distance

Prefiguring the dawn of the new Millennium
A time when,
By the Grace of God,
I might no longer be afraid to speak.

Ruth Gledhill
England

Forever Creating

Birthing is painful for both baby and mother,
A process through which partners support one another.
The pain and the suffering a mother endures
Because in the end a new life it secures.
Pain notwithstanding
Birth is demanding.

Most fathers seem awkward, not quite able to cope
With the pain of their partner way beyond scope.
They fuss and they flutter and make matters worse,
Instead of tender and loving they come across terse.
Fathers, remember
To be tender.

But what of the baby who goes through this process?
Leaving comfort and warmth for a kind of osmosis.
It faces the trauma of bashing and bruising
To enter a world where life is confusing.
In baby's birthing
Distress lurking.

Now the picture of God is quite down to earth,
It's of one who continually brings things to birth.
Like mothers the process is one of much pain
But it is one God endures for it produces great gain.
God's pain
Our gain.

People dwell too much on what was the past.
The past it is over, the present won't last.
What endures is persistent creative rebirthing,
It's a continuous process that's forever occurring.
Forever creating
Never abating.

If more like God we aspire daily to be
The process that leads there is not hard to see.
If we're made in the image of the God of creation
We too will create for that's our main station.
God of creation
Creative relation.

Les A Howard
Aotearoa New Zealand

Prayer of the Barren Woman

Take Lord, receive my emptiness,
for those who are empty from circumstances, from rejection
and not from choice.

Take Lord, receive my emptiness,
that the space inside
may be a shelter and peace for the poor and dispossessed.

Take Lord, receive my emptiness,
that it may hold the children in spirit
that I will never know in the flesh.

Take Lord, receive my emptiness.
May I embrace the pain with courage,
not filling the void with counterfeit, deadening the anguish.

Take Lord, receive my emptiness,
for those who abuse their bodies
and know thereby barrenness and bitterness of spirit.

Take Lord, receive my emptiness,
that it may hold the seed of life for others,
even though I experience no flowers or fruit for myself.

Take Lord, receive.

Elizabeth Ruth Obbard
England

Spiders and Eternity

When I was thirteen and had erupted in acne, there was an experience in school which memory has never rinsed out. The physics laboratory was always gloomy, always cramped and its overseer, Mr Tyson, impenetrable. One autumn morning, attempting to unriddle the coefficient of expansion of a metal rod, things were especially depressing. Trapped between tedium and fear, I glanced outside. Clouds hurried endlessly across a cold sun.

Then it happened. Unshuttered, sunlight flared across the school field. Damp earth and grass were lit as a thousand spiders' webs rippled for the wind. Each, hanging with dew, reflected a rainbow light. The angle was crucial. Sitting awkwardly but still, I managed to hold it and watched the miracle disappear and return again and again.

Mr Tyson's finger accused the emptiness of my note book. After school that afternoon, detained to complete the experiment, haltingly I tried to share my vision. Unresponding, his blank stare taught me that education was not about those things which brought joy and were ineffable, but about things that were public and measurable. From that time I began to understand that education had to do with the objective and the general and not with the subjective, the sensuous or the imaginative. With bitterness I realized that education was abstract not personal, that it held no place for poetry. Cycling home alone in dark beating rain, I wept that the spiritual had fled from schooling. It was, I was told, an emotional fantasy which would disappear with the acne.

Of course Mr Tyson was wrong – though I did not understand why until I had finished school years. He had fallen into a subtle trap. His own picture of education held him captive. It was a picture which required us to achieve mediocre competence by reproducing received truth. Sadly it had no time for unlocking our own creativity and fostering independent thinking.

Derek H Webster
England

On Baby Milk

Voice One	Voice Two
Here I sit:	Here I sit:
discussing development,	flies gather round dirty
conversing on the course of	water,
childhood	I get sick and waste away.
Low birth weight,	Low birth weight,
failure to thrive,	failure to thrive,
the vulnerability of infancy;	the vulnerability of infancy;
I have statistics on them all.	I live with them all.
Our meeting is sponsored	My life is cut short
by the misery of those we	when you fail to see who
seek to serve.	you really serve.

Both voices

It's coffee time – drink up!

Nurtured Christ,
with your intimate knowledge

of the vulnerability of infancy,
help us to see
our God is no wheeler-dealer,
faceless financier or greedy multinational.
Sponsor us to challenge
the markets of misery,
where the world is divided between
those who have chocolate breaks
and
those who are broken by them.
May we never be satisfied
with the warm coffee-time feeling
but struggle on together
to share the fruits of your commonwealth
with unending hope.

Janet Lees
England

Head-injured Survivors and Their Carers

Voice One – A Carer: *'It's been a long and tough struggle to get to where we are today.'*

Leader: Showing our care, we pray for those struggling for justice and dignity after head injury.

Response: **Through our lives and by our prayers Your kingdom come.**

Voice Two – A Carer: *'I think a lot of families cannot understand the frustration that people with acquired brain injury have.'*

Leader: Showing we care, we pray for tolerance and openness in our

	communities, that they may be healthy places for people of all abilities.
Voice Three – A Carer:	*'I get a break once a month when I go to a carers' meeting.'*
Leader:	Showing we care, we pray for supporters and volunteers; for the practical expression of love and care they offer. *(Headway and other voluntary organizations which, if known to local congregations, can be named).* *
Voice Four – A Survivor:	*'I want to talk faster, but it takes hours to come out. People think you're stupid, so I change the subject. It doesn't always work. I just feel as if I missed a big gap in my life.'*
Leader:	Showing we care, we listen with open hearts, ready to learn, to support each other and work in partnership through our lives and by our prayers.
All respond:	**Amen.**

Janet Lees
England

* *see Acknowledgements*

Hope Not Frustration . . .

'Hope not frustration is the key to improvement!' says Ramakrishna.

Ramakrishna is a determined sixteen year old whose philosophy has brought him this far and will undoubtedly carry him through his promising future. He was affected by polio at

172

the age of two years and left with paralysis in both legs. At that time, in his home village in South India, there were no services for people with disabilities in the area where he lives. So, unchecked his condition worsened and he developed severe contractures which twisted and stiffened his legs.

Ramakrishna was ten years of age when he came to SAMARTHYA. *

Following a combination of physiotherapy, surgery, sheer grit and determination, his legs were straightened and he received his first pair of callipers. Now he walks the two kilometres to school where he is just completing his school leaving examinations. The next step is college and then. . . ? 'Unlike earlier, I have a standing now and can manage my life on my own. I intend to study further. I will not let anything deter me.'

*

A Few Hesitant Steps

Budappa's face was creased in concentration as he rose and took a few hesitant steps. As he fell down, he clapped his hands and turned to his delighted mother.

Budappa is three years of age and he has delayed development. Luckily for him SAMARTHYA* works in his home town. This has given him an advantage over most children in the district where he lives in South India – the chance for early intervention. His mother has worked hard with him, taking advice from Ayyalappa, the disability worker. Now she is reaping the rewards as he is beginning to walk and speak a few words . . . and he loves laughing!

Ruth Duncan
England/India

* SAMARTHYA – a Sanskrit word meaning 'potential' – is a community based rehabilitation programme working with people with disabilities. It is based in north-east Karnataka, South India and began work in 1989. There are eighteen staff who work across eighty-five villages in Raichur and

Koppal Districts. The programme also provides an assessment and advice service to people from neighbouring districts. At the time of writing SAMARTHYA is working with over 500 children and adults with disabilities and provides the only disability services in the area.

Beatitudes for a Place of Healing

for Great Ormond Street Children's Hospital, London
Based on Matthew 5: 1–10

Blessed are the poor in resources
They will always find ways of being imaginative

Blessed are those who despair for the future
They have a place in paradise

Blessed are the team builders
They will know co-operation

Blessed are those who struggle
They will encourage others

Blessed are those who embrace hard choices
They are the children of God

Blessed are those who remember
They will have much to celebrate

Blessed are all those who answer the 'phones,
clean the toilets, serve the meals,
run the tests, listen most carefully
and do all manner of similar things in the service of others.
The Kingdom of God is like this.

Janet Lees
England

Turn to Me and I Will Heal You

Lord, we come before You,
Sick in body or mind.
We try to heal ourselves
To work out our own problems.
We have intelligent minds
We have all the benefits of modern medicine,
We don't need You.

Turn to me and I will heal you, says the Lord.

Lord, we come before You
With the problems of our land.
We see the abuse of drugs and drink
The break-up of families, the homeless,
The feelings of worthlessness.
But we can fix that, Lord.
We have democracy and social services
We don't need You.

Turn to me and I will heal you, says the Lord.

Lord, we come before You
With the broken of the world,
Those injured or destitute through war,
Those starving through the greed of others,
Those exploited because they are poor.
We give some money
Then we turn away, our duty done.

Turn to me and I will heal you, says the Lord.

Heal us Lord as we turn now to You
So we may go out in Your name.
Bring us wholeness,

Fill our hearts with love.
Only in You can we find
True healing peace and renewal.

Lesley K Steel
Scotland

What Peter Knew . . .

What energy did he tap
that day at the Gate
called Beautiful?
Something deep within himself
reflected in a beggar's eyes;
something treasured in his heart
since that first healing day
when Jesus said 'Tell no-one.'

Sick, lame and demon-possessed;
broken bodies, hot, sweaty and dusty,
smelling of suffering:
they had all come,
searching out the one
whose looking was love,
whose touch could liberate
body and mind.

All day Peter followed
into the place of unknowing
where imagination
ran riot – his own confusion
a first step
to healing.

Sometimes he knew
the holiness
of ordinary moments
fully lived.

Other times
the knowing
and the unknowing
were like a fever

in his own home:
a chance setting
for a miracle
and a living, wordless way
of learning.

There,
Jesus took a nameless
woman's hand
and attended with his being
to her need, and her longing.

So she could take
her own next step
and rise again
to welcome all the marvel
and messiness of human life
waiting, always waiting
at her door.

All are in need
of healing – Peter knew
as he looked with love
into the eyes of one man
that day at the Gate
called Beautiful

and saw himself: a man walking
    not on water
which he quickly understood
is not an element
for walking . . .
but step
by creative step
gently on the earth.
That was freedom,
that was the miracle –
walking his way
with love and wonder
every day
on the good earth –
knowing the element
for which he was designed.

Joy Mead
England

Let Nothing Be Lost

'Gather up the fragments. Let nothing be lost', *
Jesus instructed his disciples
on that far-away hill
on that long-ago day.

After two thousand years
his words echo still.
Between each fragment
of our broken world
is a space,
a dark place,
into which we are called
to follow Christ;
who,
after his death,

descended even into
the darkness of hell
to reclaim lost souls.

It is he who calls us now
to descend with him
into the living hells
of injustice,
pain and fear,
to gather up the fragments
which we find there . . .

'. . . in
order
that
nothing
may
be
lost.'

* *John 6:12*

Susan Hardwick
England

Become People for Justice and Joy

Human Rights

Let Justice Flow . . .

On 10 December 1948, the General Assembly of the United Nations adopted and proclaimed the Universal Declaration of Human Rights 'as a common standard of achievement for all peoples and nations, to the end that every individual and every organ of society, keeping this Declaration constantly in mind, shall strive by teaching and education to promote respect for these rights and freedoms'. Such rights include the right to life, liberty and personal security. No-one shall be held in slavery; no-one shall be subjected to torture. Such freedoms include freedom of thought, conscience and religion and freedom of opinion and expression.

This declaration is consistent with the teaching of Jesus Christ who taught his followers to love and serve one another, to treat all men and women as brothers and sisters. In St Paul's letter to the Colossians we read, 'there is no longer Greek and Jew, circumcised and uncircumcised, barbarian, Scythian, slave and free: but Christ is all and in all' (Colossians 3:11).

The teaching of Jesus and the declaration of the United Nations are often disregarded. Countries like Turkey and Indonesia are notorious for their failure to recognize human rights. But those of us who live in developed and so-called civilized countries have no reason to be complacent.

In Britain, only recently, a woman prisoner was manacled during labour and a young man on remand kept in handcuffs as he lay dying of cancer. Also, up to five times more black youths than white youths are subject to stop and search in Britain; black defendants are more likely to be remanded in custody and more likely to be charged with the most serious offence possible. More black defendants are sent to prison and for up to nine months longer for the same offence. What is often overlooked is that black people are three times more likely to be victims of street crime, twice as likely to be burgled, twice as likely to be assaulted and more likely to be victims of theft than white people. The majority of asylum seekers are denied welfare entitlement. In the words of Cardinal Basil Hume: 'It seems to me that the reception given to those applying for asylum is an illuminating indicator of the state of a society's moral health.'

Our brothers and sisters who come to us seeking asylum, our fellow Christians whose skin happens to be black, our neighbours who live in poverty, are some of the people who all too often are treated not only without the respect due to them as human beings, but with indifference, contempt and cruelty.

We need to reflect on our attitude to others as well as our treatment of them. Loving our neighbour, truly respecting the rights of humankind, is far from easy. Whenever we make judgements on people or gossip about them we are coming dangerously near to violating their human rights. The United Nations would have us treat people of different races, different faiths or different abilities with respect. But Jesus goes further. He would have us treat them with reverence and love.

We need to take action. Where we see injustice we should not keep silent. We can write to newspapers and politicians. We can join with people who work for justice. We can support people like the Ploughshares women who risked their freedom to take a stand against powerful business interests. We can join Amnesty International and write letters on behalf of prisoners of conscience. We can give financial support to organizations such as the Medical Foundation for Victims of Torture which works unceasingly to help and heal those who have suffered from a violation of human rights.

We can pray, in silent solidarity, with people whom we are unlikely ever to meet: the powerless, the weak and the courageous; the people whose rights and freedoms are denied.

Anthea Dove
England

A Place at the Table

For everyone born, a place at the table,
for everyone born, clean water and bread,
a shelter, a space, a safe place for growing,
for everyone born, a star overhead,

> And God will delight when we are creators
> of justice and joy, compassion and peace:
> yes, God will delight when we are creators
> of justice, justice and joy!

For woman and man, a place at the table,
revising the roles, deciding the share,
with wisdom and grace, dividing the power,
for woman and man, a system that's fair.

> And God will delight . . .

For young and for old, a place at the table,
a voice to be heard, a part in the song,
the hands of a child in hands that are wrinkled,
for young and for old, the right to belong,

> And God will delight . . .

For just and unjust, a place at the table,
abuser, abused, with need to forgive,
in anger, in hurt, a mindset of mercy,
for just and unjust, a new way of life,

And God will delight . . .

For everyone born, a place at the table,
to live without fear, and simply to be,
to work, to speak out, to witness and worship,
for everyone born, the right to be free,

And God will delight when we are creators
of justice and joy, compassion and peace:
yes, God will delight when we are creators
of justice, justice and joy!

Shirley Erena Murray
Aotearoa New Zealand

A Dalit's * Cry

I am called a Dalit and not a Human Being –
A forced identity for me.
An identity to distinguish me from others
An identity symbolizing my less-than-humanness
An identity for the survival of the others.

My identity is being misused
Both by my oppressors and so-called sympathizers.
Hundreds of conferences are being organized about me
Pages of literature are available about me
Debates and rhetorics are innumerable
Hosts of leaders are mushrooming every minute.

Yet, my Dalitness remains as it was.
Do these rallies and conferences fill my empty stomach?
Do these books cover my naked body?
Do these solidarity talks give me shelter?

I don't want any titles
I wish to live as human as you are

I am hungry and shelterless and illiterate
And have no job to earn my livelihood.

For the sake of others I am kept where I was.
Save me if you can from the Dalitness.
I am being exploited and humiliated
I am tired of being hired out for rallies.

I do not want to be internationalized.
But I wish to be humanized.

Jeevan Babu
India

* These are the outcasts of Indian society.

Voices of the Indigenous People

All: **Creator God of all grace and compassion,**
             hear the voices of the Indigenous People:

Leader: We mourn for our Aboriginal People,
             who in days gone by were:
             hunted and killed as the spoils of colonization;
             physically, sexually and spiritually violated;
             bought and sold into slavery –
             whose children were stolen,
             deemed unfit to be classified as human . . .

All: **God, hear our cries.**

Leader: . . . the sons and daughters
             of the stolen generations,
            who were imprisoned as inmates
             in missions and reserves;
            who were segregated from their People,
             families, mothers and fathers,
             by those who came to 'save them';

who suffered brutality, violence and hatred
  at the hands of their white 'Protectors';
who were nothing more than the pawns
  of the immoralities of the white society;
who endured racist labels
  like 'boong', 'coon', 'nigger' and 'gin'.

All: **God, hear our cries.**

Leader: We cry for our Aboriginal People,
who today have
  no access to clean, running water and
  no homes to keep them warm
  from the cold desert winters;
whose mothers, daughters and sisters,
and whose fathers, sons and brothers still die
  in the hands of the white prisons;
whose poor health and atrocious living
    conditions
  come as a direct result
  of over two centuries of neglect
  by those who supposedly
  came to be their friends.

All: **God, hear our cries.**

Leader: We pray for our Aboriginal daughters and sons,
  who tomorrow will be our leaders.
Let them not be born into a world of hate,
  rather a world of love.
Let their human rights and dignity
  be recognized and acclaimed.
Let the world rejoice
  when our future generations
  take their rightful place
  as those born of the earth,
  as stewards to creation,
  and as the heart that beats

with the land,
as rightful owners of the land.

All: **God, hear our cries.**
We are reminded of our past
and of our failings in the present
and lament for those who have suffered
the brutalities that our society
has inflicted upon our sisters and brothers.

Anne Pattel-Gray
Indigenous Australia

Aboriginal Land Rights

For two hundred years the people who settled in Australia, who farmed the land and built the cities and mined the gold, treated the land as theirs. They claimed the land and disregarded the rights of the indigenous people who had dwelt there for forty thousand years. Now the nation seeks a remedy for old injustice. Interests clash here: claims escalate; justice for one party becomes hardship for another.

Putting right old wrongs is never easy,
for injustice twines like a creeper
around the walls of human society,
attached to every crevice,
crumbling the hardest stone.

Give us singleness of heart
and clarity of mind
and warmth of human understanding,
that a nation may heal an old wound
and honour those whose land it was.
Lord, we need wisdom.
Grant us your spirit of healing
that, before what is expedient
or what is economic,

we may seek what is honourable
and generous and the seed of hope.

Bernard Thorogood
London/Sydney

Don't Call Me a Stranger: The Cry Of a Migrant

Don't call me a stranger:
the language I speak sounds different
but the feelings it expresses are the same.

Don't call me a stranger:
I need to communicate,
specially when language is not understood.

Don't call me a stranger:
I need to be together,
specially when loneliness cools my heart.

Don't call me a stranger:
I need to feel at home,
specially when mine is very far away from yours.

Don't call me a stranger:
I need a family because mine I've
left to work for yours.

Don't call me a stranger:
the soil we step on is the same
but mine is not 'the promised land'.

Don't call me a stranger:
the colour of my passport is different
but the colour of our blood is the same.

Don't call me a stranger:
I toil and struggle in your land
and the sweat of our brows is the same.

Don't call me a stranger:
borders, we created them
and the separation that results is the same.

Don't call me a stranger:
I am just your friend
but you do not know yet.

Don't call me a stranger:
we cry for justice and peace in different ways
but our God is the same.

Don't call me a stranger:
Yes! I am a migrant
but our God is the same.

National Council of Churches
India

For Oppressed People

I have heard . . . Exodus 3:7

Saving God,
since time immemorial
your people have believed you heard their cries.
We believe you suffer
in your people's anguish;
and that you delight in their joy.

Hear our prayers
for your people living in
dark and difficult circumstances.

We pray:

> For those living as minorities
> surrounded by hostility
> and suspicion.
> Lord, hear their cry,
> be their peace.
>
> For those living
> with racial prejudice
> and hatred.
> Lord, hear their cry,
> be their peace.
>
> For those living
> in poverty
> and oppression.
> Lord, hear their cry,
> be their liberator.

National Commission for Mission
Uniting Church in Australia

Pray for People

For people in poverty,
a state of illiteracy and ignorance.

For people whose labour is less estimated and exploited
because they are unskilled.

For people who have migrated to cities,
other countries and continents
in search of jobs to improve the economic conditions of their
    families
but they are landed in the most strenuous
the dirtiest and lowest paid jobs.

For people who become the victims of well planned tourism
which is a source of joy
and satisfaction for many people.

For people who suffer at the hands of
their in-laws, because of dowry
and other cultural and family traditions.

For people who are suffering in pain and misery
because of illness and malnutrition
due to poverty.

For people who are deprived of mutual love
and close bonds of fellowship
because of separation and divorce.

For people who are struggling for dignity
and equality for all people.

For people working in affairs of policy and decision making.

Beulah Shakir
Pakistan

Our Lady of the Refugees

Mother, who heard the child whimper
Beneath the thin blue shawl,
Our aching hearts cry out to thee;
Mother, pray for them all.

A thousand Bethlehems mask dark to night,
The eyes of little friendly homes have lost their light.
Pathetic heaps of poor, dead things are laid aside . . .

A latched door swings,
A small bird sings.

Mother, whose sad Egyptian flight preceded all of these,
Guide them in faith beneath familiar stars,
Our Lady of the Refugees.

Source Unknown

Refugee

I am stood here –
Alone –
Surrounded by the sharpness
And the shattered edge of war . . .
For all around my young eyes see
The easiness of old familiarity
Wrecked . . .

The sky intrudes upon the attic stair,
Exposing all,
And endless water drips incessantly –
Wasted;
Conscious of my thirst
I taste the dust amongst the taste of fear,
And, from somewhere, hear the hiss of gas.

There is a sort of deathly stillness here,
Surrounding me,
Distilled amongst the ruins of my place;
I wait for some small sound of other life
Within this broken space
That was my home . . .
But there is none.

And in the outside street
I see a flood of all humanity –
Weeping and streaming
In its flight from fear
From here to where?

Their tears may lay the blood and dust of war,
But not allay the cost –
For all are lost, and flow directionless.

I join the flood, and hope
That in its tired momentum
I may find again the small illusion
Of belonging.

Would there ever be another place
That I could know as home,
With constancy of water for my thirst,
And bread for my small hunger?
May I sleep some future night once more
In fearlessness?
And will there be warm arms
To hold me through the darkness of my dreams,
To understand my childish pain?
To let me rage again, again,
And quietly comprehend the awfulness
Of my life's dispossession?

If this shall be,
Then there is hope for me;
And finally
I'll understand, with childlike surety,
That in the sweetness of security
The purpose of my life shall be regained . . .

And with my childhood agonies contained –
I shall be healed.

Margot Arthurton
England

She Had Come from Afar

Roasted grains offered
into open hands;
water shared; bread broken
. . . in harmony with each other
and with God's good earth
which fed them all
in this man's
fertile land.

She had come from afar
seeking this place of refuge,
carrying her own suffering,
her hunger . . . and her story
deep inside her.

'Why,' she asked the good man
from Bethlehem
'are you so kind
as to notice me
a stranger in your land?'

'Come,' he said 'I have heard
your story; you are stranger
no longer; come and eat
the fruit of my fields.
There is bread between us.'

Story in her;
story in him;
difference joyfully shared,
. . . pieces picked up
like broken grain
and kneaded gently

to make a new story
to change the world.

Joy Mead
England

Stranger, Standing At My Door

Leviticus 19:33–34; Luke 11:5; Matthew 25:35

Stranger, standing at my door,
you disturb me in the night:
you have needs I can't ignore,
you have eyes that speak your plight.
        Do I know you, nameless face,
        battered woman, detainee,
        hungry youth or sickness case,
        jobless parent, refugee?

        Do I know you, nameless face?

You are strange in speech and dress,
you have children at your side,
you are not like one of us –
you have begged away your pride.
        If you passed across my screen
        I might switch you out of sight,
        worlds away you might have been,
        yet you stand here in the night.

        Do I know you, nameless face?

I am fearful of your claim,
yet I cannot turn away.

Stranger with the foreign name,
are you angel come to stay?
   You are messenger and guest,
   you the Christ I can't ignore,
   you my own compassion's test,
   stranger, standing at my door,

You, the Christ I can't ignore.

Shirley Erena Murray
Aotearoa New Zealand

I Am a Southern Sudanese

My name is *Dusman.*
Translated: feud, war, conflict, these are my names . . .
I have never known *Salam.*
Translated: peace, tranquillity . . .
But I know many sisters and brothers called
Glaba, *Bazuka*, Comrade, *Maja'ah.*
Translated; forest, bazuka gun, comrade-in-arms, famine.

Over forty years I have experienced refugee,
displacement, uprootedness,
scorn, all unending.
I am the epitome of poverty, hunger,
nakedness marks me out.

Illiteracy is my crown
since they destroyed all the mission places of learning.
To get food I must convert to Islam,
to be clothed I must accept circumcision,
reciting the Koran is the only gate to school
and Arabic language and culture are my way of life.
For a job I must become a slave!
So humanity watches me wearing out!

My God-given land is a battlefield.
The greenness is wasted like the rain that waters it.
Instead of planting maize, beans, potatoes and rice,
land mines, bombs, bullets and
of course, corpses and bones littered it.

Instead of building roads, houses, churches
there was the destruction of houses and bridges
seemingly to eliminate rebellion.

Our village homes have become wild-life reserves
and their caves and dens have become
my hiding place.

In all this I have not lost Hope
because I believe in the Living God of Hope.
The God known to stand for the cause
of the oppressed, the deprived,
the persecuted . . .

Some day I shall be baptized.
I may even receive a new name,
a new identity
Salam Dusman – Peaceful Conflict,
or just Shalom.

Clement Janda
Zambia

A New Dawn

The land was dry as dust –
Gibeon, a place to break the heart of the farmer.
Water an absent commodity – precious water.

In the north the river flowed untapped.
Troops moved in the border areas.
The people suffered injury and death by land mines
as they went about their lawful business.

In this land oppressed by drought and apartheid
war claimed its victims year by year
as people prayed for justice and for peace.

Came the day when the people danced and laughed.
South West Africa ended.
Namibia is born. Its people are free.
Gone the oppression of apartheid;
gone the suffering caused by occupying soldiers;
gone the lack of resources to irrigate the land.
Namibia is born; its people are free.

A Responsive Prayer for Southern Africa

Leader: The people who walked in darkness

Response: have seen a great light.

Leader: The people who suffered oppression

Response: have seen their burdens lifted.

Leader: The people who were made to carry Pass Books

Response: joyfully accept the responsibility of voting.

Leader: The people whose children were deprived of
                their rights

Response: now have their schools and resources.

Leader: The people who were restricted to homeland
                areas

Response: now have the right to move freely.

Leader: The people who walked in darkness
have seen a great light.

Response: **They lived in a land of shadows**
but now light is shining on them.

More precious than gold
more treasured than silver
the right to free movement,
the right to vote,
the right to religious expression,
human rights,
more precious than fine jewels.

John Johansen-Berg
England

Children

There was a weeping on the hillsides and wailing in the
streets
in David's town of Bethlehem.
A king and his army had slaughtered the babies
out of fear and suspicion and love of power.

There is weeping in the forests and wailing in the camps
across this world of hunger.
Ten thousand children suffer daily
through savagery and neglect and greed.

There is sorrow in the city and shame in the slum
where children are taken into slavery.
Tourists pay their money and innocence is sold
as sex becomes a market trade.

Our Lord hears the cry;
he weeps for the children;
he gathers them in his arms
and calls to us,
Were you at Bethlehem too?

We pray, let our thoughts and our work,
our church, our homes and our nation
bring security and health and laughter,
for the children of your world.

Bernard Thorogood
London/Sydney

A Human Being

Tamoina, aged twelve years, used to beg with other homeless children who lived on the streets at a popular café in Antananarivo, the capital city of Madagascar. From her infancy she had to earn a living. Then she had the opportunity to be a member of the Malagasy team who attended an international conference on children, held in Oslo, Norway. She returned changed, not physically because she still wore the usual unhealthy clothing but she had changed her mind about life. Tamoina was more confident for a better future. The unique experience helped her know that she has many friends around the world; friends who can help each other. She has left the streets and thanks to the help of a social Christian non-governmental organization she now attends courses at a French Cultural Centre. She is learning sewing and other handicrafts. There is one less child on the street; there is one more child as a human being.

Naliranto Ranaivoson
Madagascar

The Slaughter of the Innocents

It was Rachel weeping for her children and refusing to be comforted
because they were no more. Matthew 2:18

Do not talk to me of wise men.
I have had enough of the wisdom
which sanctions abuse
and denies protection
to my child.

Do not tell me of stars and journeys.
I am moving on and on
driven, homeless, a refugee
looking for a place to rest
with my child.

Do not offer me precious gifts.
What use are gold, frankincense and myrrh
when all I want is food, water
and something to stop the wailing
of my child?

Do not speak to me of kings and armies.
Men's lust for power
has burned my village, destroyed the crops
left us desolate
and killed
my child.

You tell me God is with me
here in this messy world
of blood and politics.
I tell you
'Keep your God
and give me back
my child.'

Jan Berry
England

203

For a Young Man and His Mothers

In the crowded room he found me.
'Good evening, Mrs Schwab. How are you tonight? Your son
    performed well in the play didn't he?'
Relaxed. Well groomed. Confident. Polite.
Thus you stand before me. I am impressed.
'Yes, my son did well tonight. I am well also. Thank you. And
    you? How is it going?'
I want to add 'really' but the word sticks in my throat.
I dare not.
We are not yet friends. Some kids know and speak so openly
    about it.
While they have one mother and a father or perhaps one
    mother alone, you, you alone have two mothers.
While some are kind, do you hear the others mock and jeer?
Born of a mother and a father yet raised by two women who
    love deeply, who are committed.
What to a one and three year old seems so natural because it
    simply is, to a seven and ten year old is obviously different
    and to an older teen demands explanation.
How did you handle it?
With what sharp pain did that first vicious cut thrust deep
    into your heart and soul?
How do you speak of it now in your own most inner self?
    With your friends? With your too often cruel peers?
Taunting, bullying, has it ever ceased?
Was either mother a ghost parent because you just preferred
    she not come? Or that they not come together? 'This is my
    Mom. This is my Mom. '
Lesbigay youth – fourteen times more likely to commit
    suicide; thirty per cent of high school dropouts; forty per
    cent of kids selling their bodies on our streets; kicked out of
    their homes; discrimination; put downs; homophobic slurs
    and lies. How does one unsure youth ever answer them all
    other than with death?
Was that their life and struggle, your mothers?
How can those youth find safe people like your mothers?

What stories could they tell each other if truth were their
     focus and sharing their gentle means?
And you tonight, before me now, talking with a teacher not
     far from my quiet gaze.
You already so manly, so ready to begin your path through
     university and into a job. What do you hear? What do you
     see?
What will you hear? What will you see?
The law givers rule your mothers have rights – just like me.
But churches rally as to a battle cry and tell the government
     'Legislate not on their behalf! We don't want them.'
The Hatred. The Mockery. The Jeers. The Slurs. And the
     deaths of so many gentle, honest, gifted people.
Will you weep alone? Or with a loving wife/partner
     somewhere?
Will you live to see acceptance one day the norm?
Long after I'm gone I fear.
How deeply I admire you.
You stir nobility in me I never knew I had.
You evoke courage in me I never knew I had.
You awaken Christ in me.
Love not hate!
Thy Will be done, Oh Lord.

Betty Lynn Schwab
Canada

A Prayer for Homeless People

Loving God,
we pray for all who will try to sleep tonight
in cardboard boxes or shop doorways or on park benches
in hostels or night shelters or in DSS 'bed and breakfasts'
in rooms with too many people in them
in cold rooms with damp walls
in homes which they know they will soon have to leave
or in homes which they long to leave
if only there was somewhere else for them to go.

We pray for those who have the power and influence to help
    them –
for members of parliament and local councillors
for workers in building societies and Benefits Agency
for landlords and property developers and housing workers.
We pray for ourselves who have the right to choose
how our society will be governed
and ask for wisdom as we make our choices.

Loving God,
you have made it clear that we cannot love you
unless we show love for others.
Help us to see the need that stares us in the face
and not to shy away from it
but reach out to meet it
as Jesus did,
in whose name we pray.

Heather Pencavel
England

Sunday Morning

a slippered shadow
bent at the waist
but straight in the back
stitches from driveway
        to driveway
down Clergy Street

two pink barrettes pull
clipped grey hair back
from almond eyes
in a rice paper face
chopstick arms and legs
poke past the cuffs
of black-bleached-grey

tunic and slacks
and clenched in one hand
swings a clear plastic bag
      inside
an empty beer can

she turns into
another driveway
kneels before
a green plastic bag
untwists the tie
and one by one lifts out
boxes bottles and cans
making only muffled metal sounds
– sounds that the gospel hymn
blaring from steeple speakers
around the corner
      cannot quite
wipe out

Norm S D Esdon
Canada

Our Responsibility

'Buy The Big Issue!'
cried the homeless one.
'The Big Issue!'

But <u>is</u> it?
Is the cold reality
of people
with nowhere to live
<u>the</u> big issue
for many of us?

Or is it
just one more thing
we accept
as unfortunate
but inevitable?

Do we
'buy it'
and
'own it'
as our
responsibility –

Or,
do we
pass by
on the other side?

Susan Hardwick
England

So Cold

I'm cold – I'm so cold. I have no home, I have no hope. My heart is empty. My life seems spent. And I sit here, with my goods in two bags, on the pavement outside a very grand house. And I look over at a church – locked and lightless. And I wonder if anyone will come.

And he comes – driven by the undertaker at full speed. He had forgotten some hymn sheets for the funeral he was conducting at the crematorium. He dived out of the car and started running for the church door – gown flowing. And then,

'Father, father!'

The minister stopped and looked round.

'Father, I'm sitting here because I've got nowhere to go.'

And the minister was caught in a confusion of feelings. He

had barely enough time to photocopy the sheets and rush back to the car and speed off to the crematorium and this man needed some sort of help. The man was pleading from his heart. And it pierced the heart of the minister, troubled that time just wouldn't permit him to seem anything other than rushing past on the other side. 'I'll see you when I get back. I will be back. I won't be so very long,' the minister called across. But part of the minister rather hoped that the man would not be there when he returned. He wasn't. And the minister's heart was pierced even deeper.

I might have come for baptism or confirmation. I might have wanted to be married, doubtless a funeral would have been possible; but all I wanted was some hope, all I wanted was some soup, all I wanted was some sense in my distress, all I wanted was some love, all I wanted was to find a home. I'm so cold.

Stephen Brown
England

The Squatters' Prayer

Foxes have holes and the birds of the air have nests,
but the Son of Man has nowhere to lay his head. Matthew 8:20

Lord Jesus,
you did not have a house to call your own,
you stayed in homes that were not yours,
you know what it's like for us to be squatters,
to fear angry grunting bulldozers ready to raze our houses
standing on land we cannot call our own.

You fasted in the wilderness as the vultures circled,
you felt the pangs of hunger as days turned into weeks,
you know how we feel when our stomachs groan,
not knowing when our next meal will come,
as we watch our children grow underweight.

You walked under the relentless desert sun,
you felt the scorching heat down your back,
you know how hot it gets as the sun beats down,
making us dizzy as our metal roofs burn,
the sweat trickling down our brows.

And yet, you are somehow present in our midst,
you are among us amidst the squalor and filth,
you know how we live – in despair and in suffering
as the sun rises, another hard day unfolds
and we toil to earn our daily bread.

Lord Jesus, who shall we go to?
Do not forsake us.
You are the bread of life, our shining star.
In the darkness of our hopeless lives
won't you light up a ray of hope?

Anil Netto
Malaysia

Home Is Home and Bush Is Bush

You may be in another country,
a country that is very rich
but if you can't return to your homeland,
you're still in the bush.

Away from your homeland
    anyone can treat you as if you're worthless.
        You endure life as a vagrant.
            You meet prejudice and misunderstanding.
              Your integrity is ruined.
Away from your homeland
    people see you as useless.

Your kinfolk faint away,
          the respected elder as well as the child.
               You persevere amidst disaster.
Away from your homeland
   you're like a baby that's been weaned too soon.
          You're disowned by your friends.
               You're devoured by a toothless animal.
                    You're made into a docile creature.
Away from your homeland
          your soul knows deep sorrow.
               Life seems useless, useless, useless, too useless.

Bartholomayo Bol-Mawut Deng
Kakuma Refugee Camp, Kenya
(adapted)

I Am Dirty

I am dirty:
not just under my fingernails
but under my skin.
I have nowhere to wash,
so I am dirty.
I lie on concrete
trodden by city-stained shoes,
so I am dirty.

Sometimes the dirt
seems to have pierced my heart
and my mind:
in the anger troubling my dreams;
in the dragging weariness
when all striving seems
futile;
in the clinging despair which craves any means
of escape:
drug induced joy
or oblivion.

Because I am dirty
some pass me by in disgust;
others feel that they must
share what they have.
I hear the kind word,
take the blanket, the food . . .
I have learned to say
'Thank you', look grateful . . .
I am in a way;
but I know that few,
very few,
would want me
in their clean homes:
because I am dirty.

After Jesus had washed their feet,
he put on his outer garment
and returned to his place at the table.
'Do you understand . . . ?
 Do you understand . . . ?'

Sue Brown
England

Gypsies Are Your Creation

O God, we pray for Gypsies, for the Roma:
They frighten us because they don't quite fit into our way of
    life;
We find them anarchic, untidy, they leave rubbish around;
Some of them (like us) may steal and cheat;
They live by their wits instead of having proper jobs.

So they are refused permission to park their vans;
We shift them from county to county,
We don't like them as neighbours,

We don't want their children in our schools.
The National Front finds them convenient targets.

But Gypsies are your creation just as much as we are;
You gave them the wits they survive by;
You enjoy their gaudy flamboyance,
Their craving for freedom;
You made them handsome and wilful;
And you know it's good for us
To have our middle-class self-satisfaction punctured.

Now persecuted Gypsies have arrived here
Trying to find refuge.
Give us grace to be decent to them and to treat them fairly,
Even to love them as our neighbours.

Louise Pirouet
England

Who Are These Strangers?

Tune: Goma

Who are these strangers? Why do they throng,
crowding the place where we belong?
Why do they haunt us with their pain,
eyes that have seen so many slain?
We do not know them, yet we kneel
and bring them to this holy place
where bread is broken, wine is shared,
suffering met by love and grace.

Nameless they raged against the world,
burning to break and kill and tear.
Nameless they passed and in their path
the sounds of weeping filled the air.
We cannot change them, yet we kneel

213

and bring them to this holy place
where broken bread and wine declare
suffering born, an offered peace.

Nameless they stand in endless lines,
waiting for what will not be theirs:
shelter and food and peace of mind,
places to rest, an end to tears.
We cannot help them, yet we kneel
and bring them to this holy place
where bread is broken, wine is shared,
suffering known, a sign of grace.

Nameless they fall beside the road,
passed by a thousand dusty feet,
nameless they lie – no friend to mourn –
wrapped in a ragged winding sheet.
We cannot name them, yet we kneel
and bring them to this holy place
where broken bread and wine must speak
suffering shared, a wordless grace.

Colin Gibson
Aotearoa New Zealand

Prisoners of Conscience

For those who grasp their prison bars
helplessly, that we may walk free –
    a thought.
For those who rot in the dark so that
we may walk in the sun –
    a thought.
For those whose ribs have been broken
so that we may breathe our fill –
    a thought.
For those whose backs have been broken

so that we may walk erect –
     a thought.
For those whose mouths have been
gagged so that we may speak out –
     a thought.
For those whose pride lies in rags on
the slabs of their jails so that we may
proudly walk –
     a thought.
For those whose wives live in anguish
so that our wives may live happy –
     a thought.
And for their jailers and for their
torturers –
     a thought.
The saddest of all, they are the most maimed
and the day of reckoning is bound to come.

Salvador de Madariaga
Country of Origin Unknown

Prayers for Detained Asylum Seekers

O Lord, strengthen and sustain those who are placed in
     chains when seeking refuge from their oppressors.
Grant them the courage to continue their fight against evil,
the faith to endure the onslaughts of tyranny
and the love to care for those who imprison them.
Through Jesus Christ our Lord.

Anonymous

O God who sent your Son to set the prisoner free,
we pray for asylum seekers detained in our country
after fleeing persecution in their own.

They have committed no crime
and cannot understand why they are imprisoned.
Be with them in their despair and anger and bewilderment;
be with prison officers, chaplains and probation officers who
  care for them;
give your wisdom to all who work for their release
and campaign to bring this injustice to an end.
We ask this through Jesus Christ our Lord,
who with his parents was forced to flee from Herod's
  persecution
to seek safety in another country.

Louise Pirouet
England

Jean's Story

Jean left Zaire (as it was then) in central Africa in March 1993 to seek asylum in Britain. He was a member of an opposition party and had received death threats. When he arrived in Britain he was put into detention and despite having committed no crime, either in Zaire or the United Kingdom, he was moved eight times through five different prisons and detention centres in the next sixteen months. Here is a summary of Jean's experience.

When I arrived at Stansted Airport I told the immigration officer I wanted to seek asylum. I was asked my name, date of birth and reason for fleeing Zaire. I was then left for five days in a small room in the airport detention centre. I did not realize I had been detained and asked the attendant in my minimal English if I could go for a walk. An African woman who spoke some French explained to me I was in detention but nobody could tell me why.

A few days later I was moved to Heathrow, then to Harmondsworth Detention Centre nearby. You have to get up at 06.00, eat breakfast and clear out of your room by 09.00. I became unwell and was moved again, to Haslar, a former prison near Portsmouth. I learned English and computer studies there. Then they moved me to Winchester prison. I later discovered this was because of my mental condition.

I kept asking why I was detained. I wrote to the authorities in my 'Franglais' asking to be released. So did my solicitor. I got three replies, in November 1993 and January and July 1994. They said things like 'we cannot agree to your request as we are not satisfied you would comply with the terms of temporary admission' and (to my solicitor) 'we have taken your representations into account but regret to inform you we have decided not to release your client.' Does this explain why I was detained?

I was ill most of the time I was in detention. I had headaches, diarrhoea, stomach acidity and an abscess in my back passage where the Zairean security forces had inserted pens and other things. When I could not sleep the doctor said I was showing signs of post traumatic stress disorder. I was given paracetamol and other painkillers. I took about 2,000 paracetamols while I was detained plus 500 Iboprufen and another 500 anti-depressants and sleeping tablets. Detention has permanently damaged my mental health. I still see scenes of my detention – like films – passing in front of my mind.

After initially being refused, after an appeal in October 1995, Jean was given full refugee status. He prefers not to have his full name revealed in print because 'you never know with the Home Office what they will think.'

David Haslam
England

The Ogunwobi Family

Sunday Ogunwobi arrived in the United Kingdom from Nigeria in 1982 to study. He achieved a number of qualifications, including university degrees. He also linked up with Cherubim and Seraphim Church and undertook some work for them. Before completing his studies he met Bunmi; they fell in love and married, and in 1986 their first child Deborah was born.

Deborah was born prematurely and was worryingly underweight for some time. Their second child, Tunde, began to experience behavioural problems, perhaps because of the uncertainty the family were now facing. By the early 1990s, the Home Office were saying the Ogunwobis should return to Nigeria. Sunday was still studying, Bunmi was helping to support the family and Deborah and Tunde were both receiving treatment for their health problems.

After ten years away from Nigeria, links with family and friends had been broken. Sunday had joined a Baptist church in Hackney, London and become a church elder and a school governor. In late 1993, he was offered work on a project to reach out to young people who had dropped out of school. The Home Office had decided on a Deportation Order but delayed further action as Bunmi was pregnant with Phoebe.

The family appealed against the Deportation Order on the compassionate grounds of the children's health but this was refused and they were given a date to leave the country. They sought the advice of friends and decided to take sanctuary in the Hackney Downs Baptist Church to avoid deportation to a Nigeria where few of their family remained and they had no guarantee of a home, a job, education or health care for their British-born children.

Home Office officials, many supporters and several church leaders, including the present Bishop of London and the Baptist Union President, visited them. A campaign committee was set up which began to produce leaflets about their situation, collect help and take the children each day to school. Sunday said he would never leave the church until he was carried out, as he felt his family was being treated so harshly.

The family held vigils outside the Home Office on 15 March each year, the date Sunday first went into sanctuary. Phoebe grew up in the church, the only home she knew. The third anniversary came and went. All representations to the Conservative government were in vain, but there was new hope when Labour won the 1997 election. The support committee stepped up the campaigning and pressed the local Member of Parliament, Diane Abbott, to persuade the government to change its mind. Finally, in June 1997 the Home Office announced the Ogunwobis were being given exceptional leave to remain on compassionate grounds. It was an overwhelming experience for them to come out of the church, celebrate with friends and get back to normal living. Later, Sunday was offered a part-time job with the Hackney Churches Refugee Network which his experience has admirably fitted him to fulfil.

David Haslam
England

Share Together

Leader: As they face this day, O God,
find those who are lost,
separated from those they love,
crossing unknown borders,
without a country or home,
not knowing where to turn:

People: **Find them, God who always seeks for the lost,
and cover them safely as a hen covers her
chickens.**

Leader: As they face this day, O God,
stand among the ones in refugee camps around
the world,
in the hunger and despair,
in the crowds and the emptiness,
in the wet and the thirstiness:

People: **Be their hope and their strength
in the crying out for justice
and open the ears of the world to hear their
cries.**

Leader:	As they face this day, O God, may those who live with us, uprooted from their homelands, find a new home where their history is respected, their gifts and graces celebrated and their fear departed from them.
People:	**May we be their home, may we be the ones who open our hearts in welcome.**
Leader:	As we face this day, O God, sing to us your song of encouragement, paint for us your bright pictures of a new world where people need not flee from wars and oppression, where no one lacks a country or a home, and where we are all part of your new creation.
People:	**For we long to be your people, in spirit and in truth. We pray in the name of Jesus the Christ, who knew the life of a refugee.**

Christian Conference of Asia, Hong Kong
Uniting Church in Australia

Uprising Is Christianity

The Sunday before I met him in Jerusalem, Bishop Kamal Bathish, Auxiliary Bishop in the Latin (Catholic) Patriarchate in the Diocese of Jerusalem, went to Nablus, a town in the West Bank, for a routine Confirmation. The local people there, all Palestinians, had organized a street protest that day against the continued incarceration of political prisoners in the town's jail. The unarmed protest got out of hand and the Israeli military responded with tear gas, rubber bullets and live ammunition from automatic weapons. Two young Palestinian men were killed and many were hospitalized from the effects of tear gas.

Bishop Hamal arrived in Nablus two hours after the event. He had seen the burning tyres on the streets and realized a protest had gone wrong. He dropped the Confirmation sermon and said this to the people:

> Today you have two new martyrs, in a long and noble line of martyrs right back to St Justin, who in this town opposed the Roman might, refusing to deny the Mass and to deny Christ and he was killed for it. Intifada is Christianity and Christianity is Intifada.

I knew that Intifada was the Arabic word for uprising but that in the Palestinian areas it stood for nonviolent protest against Israeli occupation of their lands. I looked surprised when he told me that story. I thought the identification of Intifada with Christianity was maybe too stark, too political.

He explained: 'I was doing what Jesus did, applying the gospel to the events that happened.' I reflected that this was the essence of spiritual courage and risk-taking. He risked being misunderstood as having made a political statement when he was making a spiritual statement about liberation theology. The uprising is within us and it is for justice and righteousness. This *must* reflect the character of God.

Alan Nichols
Australia

The Newspapers Say It All . . .

'Churches send delegation to seek exemption from human
    rights legislation.'

God said, 'Let us make human beings in our own image after
    our likeness.'

Men and women.
Able and disabled.
Black and white.
Young and old.
Gay and straight – the wonderful variegated image of God.

But No.

> No gays here. No women bishops.
> No blacks we might say but we dare not.
> No children to interrupt our holy meditation.
> No human rights here.
> > After all we are the Church!

> The Church – the body of Christ.
> Christ who dined with tax gatherers and prostitutes.
> Christ who affirmed women and respected them.
> Christ who praised the Samaritan and the Roman.
> Christ who stretched out his hand to the lame.

> Two thousand years later when will we learn?

Jean Mayland
England

Who's Right?

A reading for five voices

One	Right!
Two	Right!
Three	Rights!
Four	Rights!
One	All right!
Two	I'm right!
Three	My rights!
Four	What rights?
One	My world's fine!
Two	My world's the right one!
Three	My world belongs to me!
Four	My world is hopeless!
One	I don't have problems!
Two	I have all the answers!
Three	I don't take 'no' for an answer!
Four	I don't ask questions!
One	I've got a good lifestyle.
Two	I've got the right attitude.
Three	I get everything that's due to me.
Four	I've got nothing.
One	My life is comfortable.
Two	My life is fulfilling.
Three	My life is my own.
Four	My life's not worth living.
One	Religion means nothing to me.
Two	Religion is for good people.
Three	Religion would cramp my style.
Four	Religion doesn't apply to me.

One	God? Not necessary!
Two	God? He knows I'm right!
Three	God? Only if he's on my side!
Four	God? Where are you ?

One	Right!
Two	Right!
Three	Rights!
Four	Rights!

One	I am all right.
Two	I am always right.
Three	I demand my rights.
Four	I have no rights.

Questioner	Who is right?
	What are rights?
	And who will face a righteous God
	without fear?

Marjorie Dobson
England

Become the Church for the Stranger

I cry every night when I go to bed ... no woman should be forced with such a choice ... Parents don't know how lucky they are to be able to kiss and hug their children every day. My employers don't even know that I am a mother ...

Domestic worker
Hong Kong

A Cambodian boy uprooted by the civil war says: 'We returned to our land and house which had been destroyed by the bombs. I hoped that we would again have a happy life and

I would play with my friends. But after my leg was blown off by a land mine when I collected water at the river, my family had to return to the Red Cross camp for food.'

Source Unknown
Cambodia

An internally displaced woman in Sri Lanka says: 'Now I have to return to the North and stay with my other children. We can't see any future. We have no house, the schools are occupied by armed forces and there seems no end to the fighting'.

Source Unknown
Sri Lanka

Thoughts

based on Psalm 137

How can we sing the Lord's song in a strange land?
How can we sing the Lord's song where children are thrown
    out of home, ill-prepared to fend alone?
How can we sing the Lord's song where street children are
    rounded up as vermin and shot?
How can we song the Lord's song where children are abused,
    used as objects of lust by angry, uncaring adults?
How can we sing the Lord's song where women are raped
    and discarded as worthless?
How can we sing the Lord's song where those who flee
    torture and persecution are turned away yet again?
How can we sing the Lord's song where land mines maim
    and destroy?
How can we sing the Lord's song where rivers flow with
    blood and hands are stained?

But it is there, there that we *must* sing the Lord's song.
Not in quiet, holy temples where peace reigns:
But there, out there, where people weep and shout and
   scream.

And You, O Lord, are in the midst of us.

Jenny Spouge
England

Speak to Me in the Body

And the Word became flesh and dwelt among us. John 1:14

Words are no longer enough:
speak to me in the body.

Speak to me, God,
in the body of the woman
shamed and abused
torn with pain in bearing life
longing for the gladness of morning.

Speak to me, God,
in the body of the watcher
waiting for the disappeared
weary with deferred hope
strong and enduring in her faithfulness.

Speak to me, God,
in the body of the stranger
severed from her roots
made other in her own land
longing for the place she can claim as home.

Speak to me, God,
in my body:
the body of a woman

waiting for redemption
searching for my salvation.
Speak to me:
hear me into speech
and make me
hearer
and
word.

Jan Berry
England

We Are Called to Be the Church

We are called to be the Church
the witness of Christ in the world.
The disciples who follow in the steps
of the one who lived within and for the marginalized
– those kept to the outside of society.
We are called to welcome the stranger in our midst.
But our hospitality is hindered by our anxieties.
Our open arms are closed by our fears.
Stir within us the flame of Solidarity
so that we will commit ourselves to action.
That by our thoughts, our words, our dreams
the stranger in our midst will find their home.

Christian Conference of Asia
Hong Kong

Let There Be Shalom

Leader: In the stillness of worship with the stories of
                  people
              who are suffering taking seed in our hearts –
                  we affirm that we are the people of God:

| People: | Called to listen to the voices of others. |
| | Called to action on behalf of those who suffer. |

| Leader: | We affirm that it is Jesus of Nazareth who shows us the path we should follow: |

| People: | 'If anyone wants to come with me, that person must forget self, carry the cross and follow me', |

| Leader: | This is not always easy to do. |

| People: | Empower us through your Holy Spirit to be People of Shalom. |

| Leader: | To build communities committed to the needs of others: |

| People: | People who invest in the dignity of others, people who walk and live in partnership with others. |

| All: | Let there be Shalom! |
| | Let Hope shine in the faces of all people! |

Silence

Christian Conference of Asia
Hong Kong

The Whereabouts of Peace

Being on the Side of the Angels

When the *New Dictionary of Christian Theology* came out in 1983, I immediately ordered a copy and the first entry I looked up was 'peace'. It was not there . . .

Where is peace to be found if not in theology and especially in the *doing* of theology? And where can theology more tangibly be seen to be done than in the doctrine of God in creation – 'a God not of disorder but of peace' (1 Corinthians 14:33; – note the word to define the opposite of peace!) – and in the doctrine of the incarnation, of God's identification with flesh-and-blood human beings, individually and in society?

The Bible tells us that both these events – creation and incarnation – were embedded in angels' song (cf. Job 38 and Luke 2). We don't know anything about the libretto of the former but we are familiar with the latter: 'Glory to God in the highest heaven and peace on earth . . .'

If the seemingly unconnected Palm Sunday story is put alongside this, in Luke's version, we make the startling discovery that, unlike the other Gospel writers who say that it was the general public – the people of Jerusalem, Jewish pilgrims and religious holiday makers – who welcomed Jesus into the city, Luke says that 'the whole multitude of his disciples' began to praise God: 'Blessed is the king who comes in the name of the Lord.' So far, so good, perfectly respectable and traditionally correct, but then, after their hosannas, Jesus' *own* disciples began to sing: 'Peace in heaven . . .'

It is a completely crazy and a total misrepresentation of what God had in mind from the beginning. The angels sang 'peace on earth'. The followers of Jesus sang 'peace in heaven'

– many of them still do, whereas we should be on the side of the angels. Peace in heaven is none of our business. As earthly disciples we should not waste our imagination and emotions on envisaging peace in heaven, because we are human beings inhabiting what everybody nowadays calls 'the real world', which *we* are called to 'fill with the Father's glory'.

When Christ wept over the city, he was not deploring the absence of peace in some imaginary 'heavenly Salem' but in the harsh reality of an earthly city – *Yerushalayim* in Hebrew, which is plural, a divided city, up-town and down-town, leafy suburbs and tree-less housing estates. *Yerushalayim*, where even the temple had become a sad symbol of division, with foreigners only allowed so far, women literally kept in their place and the clergy having all the best seats.

The whereabouts of peace and the need of it are pin-pointed by the living presence of women, men and children in our own time. May God redeem us from the blasphemy of praying for peace 'with lazy hands and unintending feet'. Being on the side of the angels on the only earth we know is not an optional extra. It is an integral part of a life of love that has its origin in worship and its logical sequence in service.

Glory to God in the highest heaven and in the real world: peace!

Fred Kaan
England

Spirit of Peace

John 20:19b

Jesus –
'Peace be with you!'
you said to your disciples
when you came
and stood among them –
locked as they were
into their bewilderment
and their fear.

Breathe your Spirit of Peace
into *our* troubled hearts,
our full-of-fear world.
Enter into
our turbulence,
our disorder and our discord.

Bring your peace,
your serenity
and your harmony.
Calm us,
still us,
open us up,
in order that we may be
channels of your peace
to those in need
of that Life-giving river.

Amen.

Susan Hardwick
England

Everyone Will Live In Peace

Call to Worship

Leader:
In Jesus' day
war was always present.
Rome occupied the Promised Land.
Jewish kings were corrupt.
And religious leaders, pawns of the
powerful,
cried 'Peace' where there was none.

All:
**Today the military absorbs
a large portion of every nation's
budget.**

Terrorism is a part of life;
'ethnic cleansing' – a new phrase in
our daily speech.

Leader: Yet God unfolds within us
a sacred vision of peace and integrity
of people living in harmony
honouring the Sacred in us all.

All: **For the sake of God's peace in our**
day
and in answer to Christ's call
to love those whom we hate,
come, now, let us worship God!

Call to Worship

Leader: Jesus came to bring Peace –

People on the sides: *not Peace as an absence of war*

People in the centre: *but Peace as the coming of God's dream.*

Leader: We enter God's dream

People on the sides: *when we listen and understand,*

People in the centre: *when we forgive and care.*

Leader: We enter God's dream

People on the sides: *when we remember those who die for*
Peace

People in the centre: *and those who work for Peace today.*

Leader: As we worship God,

| All: | let us commit ourselves to Jesus' Peace. |
| | May we bring His Peace to people everywhere. |

| Leader: | Amen! |

Betty Lynn Schwab
Canada

God of Peace

God of peace, we pray for those
who feel hostility
towards society
because of their dispossession
and the violence their people have suffered.
We pray for those who blame the victims.
Holy Spirit grant us the will and the courage
to establish justice as a basis for reconciliation in Australia.*
Sustain with courage those who suffer racism
and bring to an end all racist oppression.

We pray for energy, courage and wisdom
for all of us who are committed to the Covenant
and to do those things which build
a more just, caring and respectful society in this land.

John P Brown
Australia

* *Name your own country*

Peace is . . .

Peace is not the product of terror or fear.
Peace is not the silence of cemeteries.
Peace is not the silent result of violent repression.
Peace is the generous, tranquil contribution
                    of all to the good of all.
Peace is dynamism.
Peace is generosity.
It is right and it is duty.

Oscar Romero
El Salvador

Repentance Speaks Simply

'Tis a simple word
of two syllables
– word of power.
If spoken from the heart,
if called forth by the Holy One
via the deepest recesses of the soul,
if offered appropriately
before witnesses
in true repentance
this word can act as a salve,
be ointment to wounds of the spirit,
become an anointing
leading to healing, restoration,
reconciliation, deliverance.

The word is pure, straight-on;
its implications and consequences immense.

The word is 'sorry'.

Discernment of wrong – a raised consciousness.
Deep regrets. Painful sorrow. Heartfelt grief.
A flow of lamentation.
Shame.
These create the 'sorry' factor.

'Sorry' said by nations, public figures
can begin the healing process
following outrage, injustice, violation especially on a grand
    scale,
following official neglect and the continued practice of evil.
No matter that it was a different generation who did or
    allowed
the evil deeds. The responsibility
for making amends
initiated by saying 'Sorry!'
belongs to the *now* generation
as part of the continuum of selfhood,
as part of the communion of saints and sinners.

> I am sorry for any evil
> that my bloodline has been associated with or
>   perpetrated.
> I am sorry for those things which I have done
> which were unholy, unjust, unloving, neglectful, wrong.

> I am sorry for not acting, not saying, not caring enough
> about certain things – when my silence meant
> a condoning of evil, a refusal to get involved,
> a dismissal of personal responsibility.
> As Martin Luther King said, 'The appalling silence
> of good people (needs repentance).'

> I am sorry. I messed up.
> I didn't make the grade. I sinned.
> Truly I am sorry.
> Is 'sorry' enough?

Only when my lifestyle signals transformation
and a steady application against evil
towards the highest ideal of good.
Help me God!
Yes! Yes! Yes!

Glenn Jetta Barclay
Aotearoa New Zealand

Repentance

Tune: Bunessan

Lives have been broken,
Peace has been shattered.
Words have been spoken
Best left unsaid.
Lying around us
Remnants of loving.
Joy out of focus,
Happiness dead.

Careless of feeling
We trample onwards,
Barely concealing
Lack of concern.
Hurting and bleeding
We leave behind us.
Where is it leading?
When will we learn?

Stark and revealing
Then comes a moment
When broken feeling
Makes us aware.

All we have shattered,
All we have broken,
Loving that mattered
No longer there.

Then comes the sorrow
Of realization.
What of tomorrow?
Torment, remorse!
Lord, grant us healing
In our awareness,
Your love revealing
Compassion's source.

Yours was the dying.
Yours was the suffering.
On you relying
We see the way.
In your forgiving
Those who destroyed you,
You offered living
In a new way.

Lord take our sadness.
Grant us renewal.
Out of this madness
Help us to see,
As we restore love
And beg forgiveness,
May we feel your love
Setting us free.

Marjorie Dobson
England

Reconciliation

Lord, you reached out to us in spite of our rejection of you
  – deliver us from false pride and help us to welcome
    those who
  disdain, despise or fear us.
Lord, you called us to love our enemies
  – remove hate-filled memories from us and help us to
    embrace
  those at odds with us, yesterday, today or tomorrow.
Lord, you made peace with those who threatened you
  – in that peace which you and not the world gives us,
    help us
  not to be ruled by fear of others but to find mutual
    understanding.
Lord, you challenge us to go beyond merely loving those who
  love us
  – recognizing that you loved us before we loved you,
    help us to
  reach out to those to whom we do not warm readily.
Lord, you continue to love despite the desertions and denials
  of your disciples
  – free us from paralysing guilt and resentment and help
    us to
  accept the reconciliation offered to us by others.

All this we pray in the awareness that you sent Jesus to make
  peace
between you and us and that he has given us the work of
  making peace.

Ian Gillman
Australia

Reconciliation Prayer for Australia

Holy Father, God of love, You are the Creator of this land
and of all good things.
We acknowledge the pain and shame of our history
and the sufferings of our peoples and we ask your
forgiveness.
We thank you for the survival of indigenous cultures.
Our hope is in you because you gave your son Jesus to
reconcile the world to you.
We pray for strength and grace to forgive, accept and love
one another,
as you love us and forgive and accept us in the sacrifice of
your Son.
Give us the courage to accept the realities of our history
so that we may build a better future for our nation.
Teach us to respect all cultures.
Teach us to care for our land and waters.
Help us to share justly the resources of this land.
Help us to bring about spiritual and social change
to improve the quality of life for all groups in our
communities, especially the disadvantaged.
Help young people to find true dignity and self-esteem by
your Spirit.
May your power and love be the foundations on which we
build our families, our communities
and our nation.

Aboriginal People
Australia

Let There Be Peace

In a dimly lit room sixteen women from many different countries sat around a table. The long day of business was ended and they gathered to worship at the close of the day. The only light in the room came from moonlight shining through the window and the light of the Christ candle burning in the centre of the table. The women, strangers in many ways, but united in their faith, listened in silence to the quiet yet strong voice of Mary from Beirut.

Mary told of her life in that city of strife. She lived in fear and deprivation. It was a life of bomb shelters and darkened homes and streets. She spoke passionately of her country, once beautiful to live in, now torn and ripped apart by bombs.

Children had forgotten how to play. Their eyes were wide with fear, their hearts broken by loss of family. She shared the longing for peace in her land. Hearts ached to return to ordinary days of routine chores and tasks done in the sun without fear. Nights of peaceful sleep and mornings that came gently to the city were a cherished memory that needed to be given new life. She wanted to see bright lights at night and hear laughter by day.

Each woman had been given a small hand-made pottery lamp. Silently they lit them from the Christ candle. The feeble flames added a little light to the darkness. But each flickering light glowed as a symbol of the hope for peace.

They sang, softly, Let There Be Peace On Earth.

They prayed:

God of peace, send your light
to the darkened corners of our world.
Let swords be beaten into ploughs
and guns be turned to useful goods.

God of light, send your hope
to all the world's oppressed.

Let the chains be broken
and the prison doors opened.

God of love, fill the hearts
of men and women with compassion.
Give us the will to create a world
of justice for all your people.

Betty Radford Turcott
Canada

A Prayer of Peace

Loving God,
we thank you that
whatever we face
whatever befalls us
however we feel
you will not desert us.

Loving God,
we thank you that
you never forget us
you are always near us
you always embrace us
you never decline.

Loving God,
we thank you that
in the storms you are like sunshine,
in the noise a still, small voice,
in the bitter wind a haven,
in the swirling tides our choice –
our firm and steadfast and sure anchor:

holding us, healing us,
till peace is breathed and calm comes.

Loving God,
we thank you,
in Jesus' name.

Stephen Brown
England

At Times of Trouble or Catastrophe

Bread of Affliction

At the celebration of the Eucharist or Lord's Supper in church or in a worship group.

Read Isaiah 30: 15–26, then repeat verse 20: 'The Lord may give you bread of adversity and water of affliction but He who teaches you shall no longer be hidden out of sight but with your own eyes you shall see Him . . .' (NEB).

Use this verse to introduce a symbolic act in which – in sorrow and repentance – bread and water are brought forward and placed on a black cloth on a small table in front of the white-clad communion table. Appropriate sombre music may be played whilst the bread is rendered inedible with soil and the water undrinkable with vinegar, so that they represent 'bread of adversity and water of affliction'.

Then, in silence, or with a change to joyful music, move to the communion table and uncover and/or raise the bread and wine. One way in which God becomes visible, 'no longer hidden' for us, is in the bread/body and wine/blood of Christ, the incarnate Son.

Although present events call for our sorrow and repentance, God has not deserted us – and this we can celebrate even in and through our sadness. God is fulfilling the promise to bring us a feast very different from the 'bread of adversity and water of affliction': the Eucharist symbols of bread and wine are a foretaste of this feast in the kingdom of shalom, as well as a recollection of Christ's complete self-giving for a broken world. They thus signify a re-membering in both senses of that word.

Kate Compston
England

In the Face of Violence and Terrorism

Turn to the way of peace the minds of those who seek to strike terror into the hearts of individuals and communities,

>those who share our common humanity
>but would have us live diminished lives entrapped in fear;

>those who have despaired of other ways to reach their goal;

Give us all, terrorist and terrorized, the love to seek reconciliation, the courage to forgive and the boldness to hope.

Philip Freier
Australia

Pitch-dark World

>In the pitch-dark world
>Peace is going to disappear.
>I am afraid in boiling blood and
>With fiery greed for victory,
>Human beings wage a war against each other.

God and gospel in the world –
If everyone lives by it,
The world will be beautiful.
Make their world beautiful singing hymns,
Do unto others as you want to be done unto.

Dove of peace with its wings spread,
While gliding in the sky and composing a song,
Has vanished into thin air.

Naing ye Kaung
Myanmar

Support My Dreams

I am a youth.
There are many dreams I have had,
Many I have reached,
Many I have to wait for.

A nightmare came so suddenly –
No time for me to think, just run.

In a foreign land,
I buried my head in my hands,
Cried for Rwanda, my sweet motherland.
I am a refugee.

As days went by,
I realized the nightmare had broken my dream into
    thousands of pieces.
How can life go on without a dream?

I am a refugee but I am a youth;
I want to set my spirit on fire,
To keep my hopes alive.
I painfully wait, struggling for transformation.

246

Oh friends, support my dreams,
Strengthen my struggles,
Reach out your hand across the land.

'Urakoze' is the word of thanks I say.
'Amahoro' is God's peace for you I pray.

Uwamaholo Lekheng
Rwanda

Hope for Rwanda

The world is at war
but the people long for peace.
Tribes are in conflict
but families search for reconciliation.
Will the Lord of love
bring peace to his people?
Is there hope in this despairing society?

Here is a church that stands as a stark reminder;
the decaying rags, the dry bones,
the rows of skulls tell their terrible story.
These were God's children
seeking sanctuary in his house,
hacked by machete to an agonizing death,
women, men and children.

This might well remain a place of darkness
but the Lord of love brings light through his people;
with faith, courage and vision
they pray and work for a just peace,
for reconciliation, one with another.
May the Holy Spirit bless their work
with spiritual fruit.

Responsive Prayer

Leader: All of us were like sheep that were lost,
            each of us going our own way.

            Lord, for the times when we have been
            neglectful of our neighbours,

Response: **Forgive us, for like sheep we have gone astray.**

Leader: Lord, for the times when we have spoken bitter
                words
            and made angry accusations,

Response: **Forgive us, for like sheep we have gone astray.**

Leader: Lord, for the times when we have had malicious
                thoughts
            and planned wicked actions,

Response: **Forgive us, for like sheep we have gone astray.**

Leader: Lord, for the times when we have been in
                conflict
            and have harmed others by thought, word or
                action,

Response: **Forgive us, for like sheep we have gone astray.**

Leader: Lord God, because of our wickedness Jesus was
                wounded;
            because of the evil we did he has been beaten.

Response: **We are healed by the punishment he suffered,
            made whole by the blows he received.**

Peace is like a delicate bowl of glass,
multicoloured and lovely to look at.
I carry it in my hand with loving care.
If I become distracted or if someone with malice
puts an obstruction in my way
I may trip and fall, letting go my precious burden.
It will shatter; then who will have the wisdom
to remake that broken bowl?

John Johansen-Berg
England

An Ordinary Man

Before the war
I used to be a teacher of mathematics
Respected in my way –
Teaching the young
Life's complicated mysteries.
Some would listen close and well,
Some would watch the sky
(Longing for football)
Some would watch the girls, I know,
And some, uncomprehending, found mathematics
Hell . . . but now they know
It s not maths, but war, that's Hell.

Before the war
I used to be a happy, loving husband
To my young heart's delight.
Together we faced
Life's curious joys and miseries.
We did the things young couples do,
Enjoyed our many friends,
Lived just as we'd expected to
Until the war, destructive, tore our lives apart,
And, by my sweet wife's random death,
It broke my heart.

Before the war
I used to be a fond indulgent father
To our small firstborn son,
Learning each day
With his bright wide-eyed wonderment.
We loved him well, he made us laugh,
He sometimes made us cry –
I little thought, that awful day, held closely in his mother's
    arms,
That he would also die.

Before the war
I used to be a local well-known face
In my familiar town –
An ordinary man –
A teacher, husband, father, friend . . .
Today, I find, few friendships show,
And most my feelings shatter –
'A Serb!' they sneer, although they know
I was a Serb before the war,
– It never seemed to matter.

So I went to join the army,
To be busy and forget,
And there I learned of hatred,
And to twist a bayonet . . .

Before the war
I used to be a teacher of mathematics,
A husband, father, friend . . .
Before the war
I used to be
Me . . .
Now I am
Nothing –
For war has . . . diminished me . . . finished me.

Margot Arthurton
England

At the Ceasefire

Children emerge –
Creviced blooms at the ruin's edge,
Warmed by the sun,
Astonished by silence –
Small fusions of victim and hope . . .
Suffused by light,
In birdsong they play;
The unconscious future –

Tomorrow's Peace.

Margot Arthurton
England

Sweet Peace

How sweet is peace, even in the rain –
Nature's turmoil is a balm
Upon the wastes of war . . .
Wind bends the trees in graceful dance,
And lightning pierces darkening cloud –
Illuminating earth without malevolence.
Wild thunder imitates the sound of guns
In threatless mockery,
Whilst tumbling torrents cool the feverish fields,
And to the hate-baked land
Bring Resurrection.

How sweet the soothing sun that follows rain,
Reflecting light in every glistening drop;
How sweet the silence when the great guns stop,
Hope-held and wondering at the cease of strife –
Sweet peace encapsulates the breath of life.

Margot Arthurton
England

Wash Hands – Be Clean?

Not mine the hands that fashioned
Cluster bombs providing jobs
In some suburban park

                                   'Yet it is one

Not mine the fingers keying codes
Of laser-guided death on helpless
Cowering conscripts

                            of you who dips

Not mine the fear or hate that spills
A nation's blood and anvil-hammers
Ploughs to pangas

                                    a hand in

Not mine the empty bowl held high
In trembling hand that pleads enough
For just another day

                            the dish with me

Not mine the stocks and shares, or power,
The throne, the mitre or the Mace
To sway a different destiny

                        who will betray me'

Edgar Ruddock
England

God of Our Contemporaries

Based on Psalm 90 for Remembrance Sunday

God of our ancestors,
God of our contemporaries,
God of our children and children yet unborn,
We worship you.
God of our land,
God of all the earth,
God of the whole created universe,
We worship you.
God of ages past,
God of now,
God of years to come,
We worship you.
God of all people,
God of all places,
God of all time and eternity,
whose love cannot be limited,
whose peace passes understanding,
we remember your grace,
we celebrate your promises,
we rejoice in giving you thanks today.

Peter Trow
Wales/England

Peacemakers' Prayer *

This was written for and prayed in a multifaith service during the Gulf War on February 24, 1991. This service was produced and presented for the general public by an ad hoc group of people calling themselves 'The Companions' whose members were from Jewish, Islamic, Hindu, Baha'i and Christian (various denominations) religions. Each faith represented at the service brought its traditional 'bread' and after the service everyone was invited to break bread together. The prayer is still relevant today.

God of us all,
    you are with us
    in the valley of darkness
    as well as in mountaintop light.
You would have us follow
    your down to earth human way
    which Jesus of Nazareth pointed to.
Yet sometimes, God,
    it's like walking a tightrope:
    You challenge us to balance
    liberating the oppressed
    with loving our enemies.
You call us
    to loose the bonds of injustice
    without lifting the sword,
    to stand for the oppressed
    without becoming oppressors ourselves.

God of us all,
grant that we may find the courage to beat
    our swords into ploughshares – not
    our enemies into submission;
grant that we may abandon
    the way of the sword
    for your better way –
the way that leads
    out of self-serving pride
    into mutual understanding,
    out of our valley of darkness
    into your mountaintop light.

Norm S D Esdon
Canada

254

Cross Makers

Into his hands he took an axe
and felled a living tree.
He stripped its bark and smelled its blood:
the sap of Calvary.

Into his hands he took the tree;
two heavy planks he sawed.
Rough hewn he shaped them, top and tail;
carpenter of the Lord.

To beam, and boom he took his tape,
the width of outstretched hands.
And in the centre carved a notch
to hold the Son of man.

With hammer blows on iron nails
not once a strike he missed.
And, rising, dirty from his work,
the finished cross he kissed.

Instrumental music

And still today we crucify
our Lord, but not with planks,
but radar-guided missiles
and armour-plated tanks.

In factories across the land
cross makers we employ,
who shape today's weapons of death;
new Christs to crucify.

Will God forgive us cross makers?
Do we know what they do?
Not 'til we banish cross and mine,
the risen Lord we choose.

Ed Cox
England

255

Living with Self and Others

A dialogue with God in the tradition of Job

Lord, you said blessed are the peacemakers. Bless means to bow the knee, so how does bowing the knee help me to be a peacemaker?

And the Lord replied, 'It always takes two to argue. When someone is angry with you, you have a choice of arguing back or bowing the knee.'

It sounds like bowing the knee means much the same as kneeling down to be a doormat. My assertiveness class would not agree.

And the Lord replied, 'Doormats are passive – they just lie there. I am not suggesting that at all. By all means take an active role. Tell the person you are offended by their anger but do not argue back. Arguments breed arguments.'

I suppose that means that if I am a peacemaker I should never be angry.

And the Lord replied, 'You suppose wrong. Did you not hear me say, "Be angry and sin not?" Some things, like injustice for instance, should always make you angry. Peacemaking does not mean peace at any price. Sometimes you might have to show anger to procure peace.'

Now I am confused. So far you have told me that I am to be an active angry doormat. Weird.

And the Lord replied, 'You are not listening very well. The first rule of peacemaking is to listen. Most arguments are caused by people talking past each other. Listen carefully and make sure you hear what the other person is saying. Then you will probably find that person is not too different from you.'

Les A Howard
Aotearoa New Zealand

I AM

take off your shoes –
    where you stand
    is holy ground
be still
    and know that
    I am God
be still and hear
    in your laced-up soul
    the name of the holy
    I-AM-WHO-I-AM
be still and know that
    I-AM sends you
    to be who you are
    to be the
    I-AM in you
unlace your soul –
    wherever you stand
    wherever you are the
    I-AM in you
is holy ground

be still and know
    that I-AM God.

Norm S D Esdon
Canada

The Tangled Thicket

Lord, who calmed the raging sea,
Still the images
Within me;
The complex images
Which flash
Across the hectic forefront of my mind –

A busy thoroughfare
Where future plans
Collide and jostle
With action replays of the past;
Where guilts and fears,
Dreams and hopes,
Intertwine so powerfully
With memories and regrets.

Lord, still my mind.

Accept this complex jumble of my thoughts
And make each one
A prayer
As I consciously, tenderly,
Lift them up,
Entrust each thought
To You.

Create a clearing, Lord,
Within the tangled thicket of my thoughts.
Prune out a space where I can grow.
Create a sacred space
Where there can be
Just You
And Me.

Create a space within me, Lord,
And flood it with your peace.

Pat Marsh
England

Peniel

Genesis 32: 22–32

Wrestling God,
meet us when we are complacent,
when we hide from reality.
Grab hold of us and do not let us go
until we have faced up
to who we really are
and who you really are.
Even at the cost of wounds,
change us,
so that we can make the courageous decision
and go forward,
even limp forward
into the possibility you create
for forgiveness, reconciliation and peace.

Peter Trow
Wales/England

Getting My Pages Straight

Author of the Universe
you have written your Word
in the pages of my heart –
    your morning star
    in my starless gloom;
    your freshening breeze
    in my stagnating fear;
    your living water
    in my parched resolve;
    your still small voice
    in my earthquake wind and fire.

Author of the Universe
you have penned your Word
in my heart's pages – but

I keep getting my pages mixed up –
    I weep
    when I would laugh
    – laugh
    when I would weep;
    I hang on
    when I would let go
    – let go
    when I would hang on;
    I speak
    when I would be silent
    – am silent
    when I would speak;
    I bend
    when I would be firm
    – am firm
    when I would bend;

Author of the Universe
    writer of your Word
    in the pages of my heart
help me acquire the wisdom
    to get my pages
    straight.

Norm S D Esdon
Canada

A Calling to Faith

Dear God, we look out into our world
and we wonder if it is possible to have faith.

We see the powerful oppressors
run rough-shod over the suffering people.
We see the refugees fleeing their borders
year after year.
We see the might of violence win

in the face of peacefulness and love.
We see our own small efforts for change
apparently come to less than nothing.

Dear God, we believe.
Help us in our unbelief.

Sometimes we would rather not know any more
about the pain of the world,
in case it stretches our faith to breaking point.
And then, we remember those who live the suffering,
who cannot escape the oppression,
whose bodies bear the violence
and who have less power than we do.
We are called to faith again,
because they, our sisters and brothers,
cry out to us and call us on.

Dear God, we believe.
Help us in our unbelief.

Dorothy McRae-McMahon
Australia

Patience

Patience is a virtue
I think, until
it becomes martyrdom.
Until waiting gnaws
deep down to my core
and begins slowly
to devour me.

Patience is a virtue?
Then I want to be unvirtuous.
I want to be angry.
But anger is not the
opposite of patience,

just as doubt is not the
opposite of faith.

In patience there is room
for hard questions and gut feelings, just as
in faith there is room
for uncertainty, insecurity, ambiguity.

For we are never complete beings.
We are only made in the image.

Ruth Harvey
England

Nothing Else

The old master told this story to his young disciple who was
also his son. Once my great-grandfather, in order to rid his village of the sickness, went with his son into the forest. There he
performed the ritual, he made the gestures, he spoke the
sacred words and then in fatherly love, embraced his son. And
the sickness fled. Then my grandfather, to save his people
from their enemies, went into the forest with his son.
Although he had forgotten the sacred words, he performed
the ritual, made the gestures and then in fatherly love,
embraced his son. And the enemy passed by. Then my father,
to save our people from oppression, took me with him into the
forest. Although he did not know the sacred words and had
forgotten the gestures, he performed the ritual and then in
fatherly love, embraced me. And the oppression was eased.
Now you and I are in the forest seeking to remove the yoke
laid upon our people. I do not know the sacred words or the
gestures and I have forgotten the ritual. All I know is the
embrace of love.

Then they embraced and it was enough. Always the
embrace of love is enough – for really there is nothing else.

Traditional Jewish story, & source unknown
Adapted by Derek H Webster
England

262

Kindness

Kindness is the spontaneous expression of love in small
  things,
    the unconscious revelation of God at work in all of us.
Kindness is easing the awkward moment,
    smoothing the rough pathways and rounding the sharp
      corners.
Kindness is the deflater of anger, the neutralizer of enmity,
    the scattering of modest seeds of reconciliation.
Kindness is helping in small ways to restore lost trust
    and heal broken relationships.

Alan Litherland
England

I Want to Soar High

Yes, I am an Indian woman,
The crown of God's creation,
Unequalled handiwork of his art,
I want to break free from the chains.

So understand me, please.
Accept me as I am.
I also want to fly into
The open blue skies.
Don't clip my wings when
I want to soar high.
Let me wake into a dawn of freedom.

Beena Thomas
India

Blessed Are the People Who . . .

Blessed are the poor . . .
    not the penniless, but those whose hearts are free.
Blessed are those who mourn . . .
    not those who whimper but those who raise their voices.

Blessed are the meek . . .
    not the soft but those who are patient and tolerant.
Blessed are those who hunger and thirst for justice . . .
    not those who whine but those who struggle.
Blessed are the merciful . . .
    not those who forget but those who forgive.
Blessed are the pure of heart . . .
    not those who act like angels but those whose life is
        transparent.
Blessed are the peacemakers . . .
    not those who shun conflict but those who face it
        squarely.
Blessed are those who are persecuted for justice . . .
    not because they suffer but because they love.

P Jacob
Chile

A Prayer for Our Pilgrimage

You call us, O God, to travel into the risk and opportunity of
    your future.
We pray for the nations and peoples of the world as together
    we seek new ways of shaping our lives.

Heal us of the hurts we have experienced on the road.
Forgive us the pain we have caused those who travel with us,
bind up our old wounds, that out of reconciliation may burst
    forth endless possibilities for peace and harmony.

Draw us into a closer unity of respect and understanding,
that justice may be fostered,
that life may be cherished,
that the gifts of creation may be used wisely.

    And give us grace to recognize Christ
    in the faces of those who walk beside us.

O God, source of our journey and our journey's goal,
lead us on our pilgrimage
through Christ the true and living way.

Peter Trow
Wales/England

A Prayer for the Travellers

God, we ask that you be with those who travel:

the tourists,
who spend and collect and then forget –
that they might remember
what is real of what they live;

the refugees and migrants,
who save and lose but always remember –
that they might forget
what is inhuman of what they experience;

the sojourners,
who flee from injustice,
who wander,
who search for guidance,
who seek to serve others –
that they might find
your voice,
your touch,
your love and presence.

May we pay attention to the world around us,
take the risks of change and hope,
follow the call –
always knowing
that you travel with us.

Raúl Fernández-Calienes
Cuba/Australia

Shalom

Shalom.
Shalom.
May God's peace
rest here with you.
Shalom.
Shalom.
Wherever you go,
whatever you do.
Shalom.
Shalom.
True peace
of mind
and heart.
Shalom.
Shalom.
A word
of greeting,
a word
for parting.
Shalom.
Shalom.
A word
of beginning . . .
a whisper
of eternity.
Shalom.
Shalom.
Shalom . . .

Susan Hardwick
England

Light for the World

Science and Technology

A Contribution of Vital Significance

At the beginning of the second millennium, Arabic numerals were just beginning to spread into Europe, replacing the clumsy Roman system of arithmetic notation. At the beginning of the third millennium, every year seems to bring into use ever more powerful and sophisticated computers. At the beginning of the second millennium, childbirth was a hazard bringing death to many women. At the beginning of the third millennium, advances in genetic engineering have given us the power to intervene in the structure of DNA, the stuff of life itself. The pace of scientific and technological change is breathtakingly rapid and it seems to be continually accelerating.

Every discovery of this kind brings with it new possibilities both for good and for ill. Science grants us knowledge but if we are to choose the good and refuse the bad we shall have to add wisdom to knowledge. Not everything that can be done should be done. The technological imperative ('If we can do it let's go ahead and see what happens') must be tempered by the moral imperative (means are only used in an ethical manner for morally desirable ends). The advice of experts is indispensable for only they can say what the possibilities and consequences are likely to be. Yet the scientists and technologists have no special privilege when it comes to ethical insight. They are not to be made judges in their own cause, not least because the excitement of doing research can so easily tilt the balance of judgement in favour of just going ahead. The participation of society as a whole in the decisions to be made is also indispensable if wise choices are to result. The experts need to have put to them the question, 'Have you really thought about the moral significance of what it is that you are doing?'

The world faith traditions are the reservoirs of wisdom accumulated over centuries. They have much to offer in the quest for the ethical and beneficial use of scientific discoveries in the course of the third millennium. To enable society to steer its course between unthinking refusal of new opportunity and unthinking acceptance of every proffered novelty, meeting places have to be established in which the experts and the general public can together seek wise ways ahead involving morally acceptable decisions and a just sharing of the fruits of human discovery. The tone of discourse must be exploratory and not confrontational. Very few, if any, technological advances are wholly good or wholly bad; almost all have some degree of ambiguity in the character of their consequences. Only careful discussion by people of goodwill can enable us to make the right decisions about when to exploit and when to refrain from exploiting some new technological possibility.

At the beginning of the second millennium the world already had lands which human activity had turned into areas of infertility. Roman exploitation of the agricultural resources of North Africa had played a major role in the desertification of the region. At the beginning of the third millennium we are in a situation in which human exploitation has consequences that are global in impact and no longer confined to a particular region. The problems of pollution and global warming must receive an adequate response early in the third millennium. Science can help, not only through advice and assessment but also through possible further discoveries. For example, the world's energy needs would find an accessible and non-contaminating solution if the problem of nuclear fusion energy were to be solved in a commercially viable way.

We face a future which contains much promise and many threats. Scientific and technological insights are essential in decision making for which knowledge is a better basis than ignorance. Yet wisdom is also badly needed. Religion can make a contribution here of vital significance, testifying to the values of justice and generosity and maintaining the ethical constraints that are due to a respect for life understood as the gift of the Creator.

John Polkinghorne FRS
England

Let Your True Light Shine

We are brighter than a thousand suns,
cleverer than two thousand years:
all power belongs to us,
except the power to make peace:
except that there is an ancient darkness of our hearts
and a rage that steals our sanity.
God forgive us
and let true light shine on us
and your world.

Bob Warwicker
England

You Are Like a Light for the Whole World

Matthew 5:14

A Call to Worship

Leader: Flashlights and fluorescent tubes
candles and sunlight –
what need do we have
for more light?

All: **In our work there is much darkness:
ignorance and self-centredness
love of power and
fear of the unknown.**

Leader:	Jesus is the Light of Life. He calls us to be like light for all the world.
All:	**So, let us not hide! Rather let our faith shine boldly in our living – so that all may see Jesus Christ and draw near to Him.**

Betty Lynn Schwab
Canada

Celebrate Wisely

A church of the common place will embrace new knowledge gladly, will reflect on it critically and celebrate those who use it wisely. There is nothing to be gained from obscurantism or suspicion. Neither should we leap too soon to moralize about new knowledge before understanding it. This will be particularly the case in the burgeoning field of genetics and in the exploration of human consciousness, both of which so directly affect us all. Therefore, we need to encourage the scientists amongst us not to be too easily silenced by the language of faith which the church uses in its hymns and prayers, and which sometimes suggests a pre-modern age. Neither should they be discouraged from saying to us, 'This is how it is, difficult though it may be for you to come to terms with.' The alternative is a discreet silence and a widening gap between faith and reality.

Nigel Collinson
England

Newborn

Fragile shadow of a child
Too soon arrived –
Transparent you lie,
Suspended on a thread
Between technology
And infinity . . .
Do you know
Who you are?
Do we?
Will you stay?

Margot Arthurton
England

God of Computer and Test-tube

Isaiah 40: 13–14 and 28–31

God of space-ship and satellite,
of computer and test-tube,
we marvel at the complexity of the world
in which we live.
We thank you for the knowledge
you unfold before us.
We pray for all who make knowledge available to others,
for teachers and librarians
and those involved in literacy programmes and skills
    training.
We pray for researchers and developers,
that the discoveries they make may be used
for good and not for evil.
We pray for all who work in medical research that disease
and ill-health may be combated.

We pray for all who work with technology
and for all frightened by the speed of change.

Lord, in your mercy

People: **Hear our prayer.**

Jenny Spouge
England

Copyrighting Genes . . .

. . . is grand theft on a huge scale!
To claim the ownership of life's designs
is arrogance, like fleshing out
a tower blotting out the sun
that raised up human names high over God.

He acted once to show His power
and won't be slow to prove again
the gifts that He has freely given
must never dispossess the poor,
must not be rigged to make us each more poor!

Peter Comaish
England

An Errant Engineer

God created humankind, men and women
and blessed us with the bounty of nature,
giving into our care the earth and the animal creation.

Our human family was keen to taste
the fruit of the tree of knowledge
and too ready to neglect worship of the true God.

Human pride conquered the world,
by bow and arrow, by spear and shield,
by musket and cannon, by guns and bombs.
We surveyed the battlefield
and saw that it was bad.

Human pride advanced into technology,
inventing the wheel and the spindle,
the combustion engine,
the telephone and television,
the microchip and computer.
We surveyed the world in its complexity
and thought it was not so bad.

But pride reached further
and we began genetic engineering
and forays into cloning.
If we can clone a sheep
why not a human being?
We stepped back to survey the world,
with the result of drugs and profiteering,
the families wrecked and grieving
and we saw that it was bad.

We have wandered in the wilderness
and not found the promised land.
It is time to lay aside our pride
and find in the guidance of our Creator
the way back to a garden of Eden.

Litany of Confession
led by Leader or alternating group

Leader: Lord of heaven and earth,
           you created your people
           to live in peace together
           on the face of the earth.

We have failed
because we have loved ourselves

and neglected the poor and needy.
We have caused conflict.

Are we our brother's keeper?

Response: **The Lord God replies:**
You are called to take care
of your sisters and your brothers.

Leader: We have failed because
we prefer to manufacture weapons of war
rather than instruments of peace.
We have caused conflict.

Are we our sister's keeper?

Response: **The Lord God replies:**
You are called to take care
of your brothers and your sisters.

Leader: We have failed because
God gave us a garden in its beauty;
we have polluted the earth
and poisoned the seas.

Are we the earth's protector?

Response: **The Lord God replies:**
You are called to take care
of the planet I entrusted to you.

Leader: We have failed because
we thought we could be as God,
making animals by technology,
creating people by cloning.

Are we to be held responsible?

Response: The Lord God replies:
You are called to worship your Creator,
not to create what you desire to worship.

All: Lord God, forgive us for our pride
which pretends to have your power
yet fails to show your love.

John Johansen-Berg
England

The Fruit of Knowledge

It is dazzling – that power
of science and technology;
to create and clone life in the laboratory,
send words and pictures thousands of miles
with the touch of a button.

We are god-like in our achievements,
with power to create or destroy;
yet child-like in our curiosity,
pushing every discovery to its limits.

Yet sometimes
we long to return
to the dreamed-of simplicity of a lost garden.
But we have stretched out our hands
and taken the fruit:

now we must live with the knowledge,
good or evil,
struggling to hide our nakedness,
our vulnerability,
our fear
of our own mortality.

Jan Berry
England

A Reflection on Parenthood

Inspired by Psalm 139

Pregnancy and childbirth are becoming increasingly 'high tech'.

Medical progress has prevented many maternal and infant deaths. As the millennium approaches advances in medical intervention are racing ahead; babies are being born and kept alive at an earlier gestational age; women are conceiving against all odds and at a later age. Within all this there is a movement towards more gentle and natural non-invasive pregnancy and childbirth. More babies are being born in the quiet and calm of home. Women are more aware of the need for respect of their pregnant bodies and campaign for a different view of pregnancy where it is not seen as an illness to be managed solely by medical staff. Perhaps we are beginning to appreciate again the wonder and miracle of conception, pregnancy and childbirth.

The quietness and the darkness
wait to receive new life;
and you, God, are there –
watching
waiting
hoping,
calling life into being,
making and mothering it,
shaping and fathering it.

Nothing can separate us from your love.
Even in the womb,
where life is received
and grows in secret,
your love is there,
warm and brooding.

You keep watch
as life unfolds.

Butterfly movements
as webbed fingers stretch and reach
to touch the watery darkness;
sudden kicks and squirms
as limbs move and flex
in new-found strength;
all are seen by you.

And as the watching and waiting draw to an end
you are there
bearing the pain and the joy
as our bodies and our resilience are stretched to the limit
and new life is thrust into the world.

You are with us
bearing the pain and the joy
as nurturing love flows from our breasts
and our hearts.

Creator God
you know the exhilaration and the hurt
of bringing forth new life.
You know the joys and struggles of creation.

Give us strength
to hold on to the knowledge of your love
and your presence with us,
when the nurturing becomes a burden,
when we are weary and worn and tired
from doing too many things.

Refresh us and renew us,
when we have poured out love and care,
when we have given of our very selves
to nourish others.

Give us glimpses of the joys of parenthood
and help us to hold on to them
through pain, frustration and weariness.

Help us to hold on to you,
to be nourished by you,
to receive tenderness and mercy from you
so that we are strengthened
to give life to others.

Sarah Brewerton
England

For Benjamin

who lived for one day.

Medical advances save lives. However, these can raise serious ethical dilemmas such as whether or not to continue life-support for a premature and very sick baby. There is still much to learn about prematurity and its treatment. Some babies still die.

Benjamin
'son of my right hand'
our first born.

Through you I learnt how precious life is
and yet how fragile.

Tiny, fragile, precious
I loved you.

I ached for you
in your struggle to live.
You lost the battle,
and, in a way, so did I.
For you were part of me once.
You and I, completely one.

280

The parting came too soon for you
and for me.
The parting which should have been a beginning
was but an end.

Tiny, fragile, precious
I loved you.

You lost the earthly battle;
but the parting, though an end for me,
was but a beginning for you –
a beginning of love,
far greater and deeper than any love
I could have given you.

Through you I learnt how precious life is.
Through you I knew joy,
complete and un-utterable joy,
welling up inside me,
causing me to proclaim your beauty
as I held you for the first and last time.

For that joy
there is no end,
only a beginning

Sarah Brewerton
England

Heaven and Earth

God of the great heavens above
and the earth beneath,
the endless universe of stars and planets
and our home here of oceans, seas and land:
we gather in awe and wonder to worship you.

We gaze at the sky on crisp starlit nights
and think on the beauty of all that we see,
and we wonder why we are so special to you.

Yet we know that you do love us
wholeheartedly:
sending Jesus to show us
the Prince of Peace to our world;
sending your Spirit here among us
to breathe wisdom and light for our ways.

Great God of heaven and earth,
we worship and adore you.

Stephen Brown
England

Space

Dear Lord,
I get inspired each time I see
new coverage of space probes primed to find
the nuances of your holistic dreams
that give fresh glimpses of your majesty.
There is such vastness,
    vision,
    diversity
in the far unfolding spaces of your thoughts
that I'm longing to uncover more and more.
I pray that those who get the chance
to travel further from our sun
will go with awe, humility
and recognize the maker's mark
upon the splendour all around
not trying to impose a human span
on gorgeous galaxies you've set in place.
Teach us new insights on your power
your order, your sufficiency

so that today in all we do
we don't have faith in flawed desires,
but in your expertise to lead
us on to where we need to go
to grapple with great sights and sounds
you wish us to confront
to raise our hopes.

Peter Comaish
England

God Help Us to Use Technology Right

Leader:	Lift up our hearts.
Congregation:	**We lift them to the Lord.**
Leader:	Let us give thanks to the Lord our God.
Congregation:	**It is right to give our thanks and praise.**
Leader:	Yes God, it is good to thank you and praise you because the world you have given us is so good. You have put in this world all we need to live on, food and drink, clothing and shelter, the ability to love and be loved. You have given us the gift of life itself: and with life you have given us creative power, power to invent and build, minds to discover.

Congregation: **We praise and thank you**
for science and technology.

Leader: It is amazing
that people can travel to the moon,
see inside the atom,
understand the secrets
of human inheritance.
It is wonderful
that we can talk to people on the
    other side of the world
as if they were in the same room.
There is so much light and colour and
    joy in our lives
because of the creative abilities you
    gave to us
as people made in your image,
people of your soul.

Congregation: **God help us**
to use technology right.

Leader: God forgive us
when we use technology to destroy
    and exploit,
to express hatred and to do harm.
And we thank you God,
that when we do wrong with
    technology,
and we, the human race
sit crying among the broken dreams
and shattered lives:
that you are the one who forgives us
and offers us a new start,
and in Jesus Christ you forgive us;
on the cross you share our
    desperation;
and give us hope because of

the glory of your love.
And so we praise you for that glory.
We join our voices with people
everywhere and say . . .

All: **Holy, holy, holy Lord,**
God of power and might,
heaven and earth are full of your
glory.
Hosanna in the highest.

Leader: Blessed is the one who comes in the
name of the Lord.

All: **Hosanna in the highest.**

Leader: Living God
in the silence we
remember Jesus . . .
expect the Holy Spirit . . .
and praise and thank you for creating
this world,
the wonders of this century,
and the glories of the next.

All: **And so, One God, Creator, Sustainer**
and Redeemer,
we give you praise and glory, now
and for ever . . .
Amen.

Bob Warwicker
England

Basic Questions

Of
what use is it,
and how will it
benefit us,
to discover
the ultimate secrets
of the universe,
if it does not help us
to answer
the truly important
questions
of why
we are here,
or how
we can solve
such problems
as feeding
the starving peoples
of the world
???

Susan Hardwick
England

Widen Our Vision

Eternal Wisdom –
not caught into space and time,
but seeing the story
of the world
in its entirety,
and filling in the gaps
between past,
present and future
so they become one.
You have given us human wisdom

286

to discover
and to comprehend
the mysteries of your creation
so the world may become
a better place:
your kingdom here
on earth.
May our increasing knowledge
widen our vision of you.
Help our hearts to keep pace
with our learning,
and to beat out constantly
your rhythm of
universal and eternal
love.
Amen.

Susan Hardwick
England

The Barrier

Last night I told myself a dream.
I dreamed of the day when science creates a machine,
to eradicate war.
I dreamed of a box of tubes and wires
with a button to press.
Instead of a mushroom, there are flowers.
Instead of a flash, a gentle hum.
Instead of death, the sight of birds and smiles.

I told myself this dream.

The machine warmed, power flowed.
A barrier grew.
Not against the weak, but against the strong.
Not to trade, but to evil.
That all can pass through
and all will be well.

I told myself this dream.

And, as I dreamed, the barrier grew,
to slowly cover the land.
It did not kill one for the sake of another.
It did not stop black for the benefit of white.
Never did it ruin crops,
or poison rivers,
or spread disease,
in order to make a profit.
It simply grew.
And people rejoiced.

I told myself this dream.

Scientists declared it successful.
Politicians proclaimed their backing.
Financiers smiled at a brighter world.
It was a dream.
And the barrier had its effect.
People could enter but guns could not.
Water could flow but poison stayed out.
Tools could be swung in labour, but never in hatred.

I told myself this dream.

All weapons vanished.
A blow struck in rancour removed the striker.
A fist thrown in anger transported the thrower.
And all who lived,
with evil in heart or mind,
never could enter.
Instead, they needed to act:
Shaking hands instead of fists.
Kicking footballs instead of neighbours.
Shouting encouragement instead of abuse.
Then they could enter.

I told myself this dream.

I told myself this world could be such a place.

Then I stopped telling.
And I thought of today.
I thought of the abused and exploited.
I thought of the confused and alone.
I thought of the selfish, with cool drinks,
when, in factories,
the helpless sweat more than a glassful.
And I thought of those whose hearts were hard,
gnarled and lifeless,
living off other people's fear.

I dreamed of a day when science
would create a peace machine.

I told myself this dream.

And I wondered.

Duncan L Tuck
England

A Guided Rocket

Technology may be a rocket in the skies
or a comet in the heavens,
a symbol of destruction
or a sign of hope.
Like Janus, it has two faces
and sometimes it is hard to determine
which way it looks and what direction it takes.

Through technology
we have devised weapons of greater accuracy,
protecting property whilst killing people.

Through technology
we have brought the human family closer together,
reducing travel time and reaching other planets.

By the ingenuity of the human brain
we can vastly improve the quality of human life
and sometimes deliver new-born children from early death.
Through technology a person restricted and confined
by disease or handicap can be given mobility
and released to play a fuller part in society.

How can we be sure that technology
will take this creative path
and not become the trojan horse
that releases death and destruction in our city?
For technology to be life-giving
human intelligence needs to be informed and guided
by the wisdom and compassion of the divine Creator.

A Cup of Butter

Ours is a scientific generation
which seeks answers in the laboratory,
where the laws of physics and chemistry
can be demonstrated with accuracy and skill.
By careful weighing and assessment
the technician can give a list of all the parts
that make up a human being,
in muscles, bones, blood and water.
What is missed out is the mind that cannot be weighed
and the soul that cannot be itemised.
As the definition of a cup of butter
cannot adequately portray a buttercup,
so the list of physical parts falls far short
of the glory of this man or woman,
made in the image of God.

John Johansen-Berg
England

God of Money and Machine

Deuteronomy 15: 1–11; Matthew 20: 1–16; 1 Corinthians 15:58

God of gear-wheel and machine,
we thank you for the benefits we gain,
for machines which make our lives easier,
for developments that enable us to live comfortably,
for the wealth that pays
for our hospitals and schools.
We pray for those who work in industry and commerce,
for those whose work seems dull and monotonous,
for those whose jobs are insecure,
for those who have to make decisions
affecting the lives of others,
for those who hold on to ethical beliefs
and work with integrity,
for those who attempt to work
for change in the power structures,
for those who appreciate the work of colleagues
and enable employees to develop their potential.

Lord, in your mercy

People: Hear our prayer.

Jenny Spouge
England

Obsession

0–60 in 7.2 seconds.
200 yards in London in 10 minutes.
Across the road in 6 minutes.
Into hospital sooner than you think.
200 micrograms of Salbutamol twice a day.
A bypass in 2 years.
A tree in a century, if ever.

An hateful oppressive din 24 hours a day.
Acceleration on impact, 2000m^{-2}.
Deaths in the millennium year, 3,000.
Why?

God forgive us
our obsession with the car.
God comfort those who mourn
as nobody else can;
comfort the families and lovers
of the pedestrians, cyclists,
drivers and passengers
who will be killed in the millennium year
on the roads.

Bob Warwicker
England

Progress

So many years ago that Child was born.
The world was different then.
No science – of the kind we know.
Technology was primitive,
medicine based on herbs and folk-lore
and charity chiefly given at the discretion of the rich,
or in obedience to the Jewish law.
Poor people had so little to give.

Now, in our time, the world has changed.
Science has broken down barriers,
given us a space programme and weapons
and pesticides and pollution, along with its benefits.
Technology can speak to the world in micro-seconds
and make life easier for those who can afford it.
Medicine brings wonder drugs with unknown side-effects,
or, alternatively still relies on herbs and folk-lore

and charity is occasionally given at the discretion of the rich,
or extracted from the poor with promises of riches of their
   own,
or two seconds of television fame in a fund-raising marathon.

How many years before we learn
the lessons that the Christ Child came to bring?
Or will our progress always be tainted
and obstructed by self-interest?

Marjorie Dobson
England

Thanksgiving for Our Computer Age

Creating God, our own age
caught many of us unaware.
Suddenly computers are everywhere
in shops, offices, homes and schools.
Artists and astronauts. Publishers and doctors.
Musicians and accountants. Every corner store clerk.
Pre-schoolers, teens and retirees.
Drudgery gone. Curiosity explodes.
Information at the ready for everyone.
All at the click of a mouse.
Key pals to chat with.
Alphabet and number games to learn and play.
Calculations made easy.
New cities to build.

Creating God, our age is an exciting time.
We give you thanks and praise:
for the wonder of the human mind
   so able to dream and create;
for the gifts of industry
   able to produce, distribute and repair;
for churches and retirees delivering
   recycled computers to inner city schools;

for bridges of communication built within our homes;
  and questions quickly answered;
  and a young student's first book so neatly printed out.
For our computer age, Creating God,
we give you thanks and praise.

Yet we rightfully worry
and sometimes fear.
The ignoble among us use it
  for their ugly gains: mass distribution
  of pornography and false information
  internet stalking and virus spreading.
Other people lose their jobs because
  they are too slow to learn or to keep up.
Still others find computers are an escape
  from daily life and the messy
  problem of human interaction.
Outdated computers fill our landsites
  and boxes still unopened pile up in dumps everywhere.
We confess, Creating God,
  this is our age too.

Creating God, come and help us in our times.
If war could be globally legislated
  into virtual reality only
and if medical computer research
  could be financed like our sports
what a beautiful age ours could be!

Creating God,
Guide as we create
  and as we acknowledge and solve
  the problems we uncover.

May we, with your loving grace
  be open
  and unafraid
  yet wise in all our ways.

So may our age be blessed
by you, Creating God.
And may the wonder of your Creative Life
flood even our computer screens.

Betty Lynn Schwab
Canada

Healing in Our Computer Age

'Computers, Mom, they're doing God's work! They're not Jesus, Mom, but they're doing God's work.' David Schwab – aged 17.

Surprising, life-giving God,
when Jesus walked among us
He cured the lame
made the blind to see
healed the wounded
and ended epileptic seizures in the young.

Today in Britain,
a brilliant physicist writes and talks
with a speech synthesizer.

Today in America,
a computer bypasses the optic nerve and eye
and a blind teenager sees.

Today in Canada
micro surgery repairs a foetal hernia
before his birth into our world.

Today around the world
focused radiation shrinks tumours
medical imaging reveals it's just a cyst
an implanted electrode enables the brain injured to walk
and delicate robotic surgery

repairs an elderly man's heart
with a piece of vein from his leg.

Ours is not a perfect world.
Risk is part of every choice and act.
Not all tumours shrink.
A solution is found too late.
Life support must be shut off.
Unforeseen damage comes.

Yet we have much for which to give you thanks and praise:
our growing knowledge of the human body,
computer technology increasingly able to restore and give
    back life,
medical research pushing back frontiers of disease,
new medical procedures,
successful new drugs,
dedicated nurses, technicians and doctors,
patients willing to try,
people living in hope,
people working hard.

Like Lazarus and the woman with the flow
like the centurion's daughter and Tabitha,
we bow in gratitude before you.
Surprising, life-giving God, we pray for your Wisdom
and your help:
help us in our sickness and our health,
in our living and our dying;
inspire those working on our frontiers.
Guide us all in hopes and fears.
May your vision of a healing world be born.
In the name of the One who healed
and whose Spirit heals today, Jesus Christ.

Betty Lynn Schwab
Canada

The Web

The web can give us a way to new places
or it can entrap us in its silky embrace.
Open the channels
and you find them used for good and ill.
The same power of communication
which can help spread the gospel
can also release a tide of filth.
It is our responsibility to ensure
that the God-given technology
which makes our world a global village
is used for creative purposes.

Values are important in any civilized society.
When two communities have different values
they can exist with mutual respect
though there may be hostility.
When the same society has different values
expressed by various leaders carrying equal respect
there is a great danger of division and conflict.
In such societies it is vital to look carefully
at history and tradition and to seek consensus
in any changes that are made.
Sometimes new knowledge enables creative change;
at other times vested interest demands destructive
change;
the survival of a civilized society depends on right
choices.

Responsive Prayer

Leader: Holy God, in the beginning of time
you spoke through your Word
and the Word brought life.
The light shines in the darkness

Response: and the darkness has not overcome it.

Leader: Lord, we pray for all whose work is word,
           those who teach in schools and preach in
               churches
           that they may seek to proclaim true wisdom.
           The light shines in the darkness

Response: **and the darkness has not overcome it.**

Leader: We pray for all those whose work is writing
           and those involved in broadcasting
           that they may produce what is worthwhile and
               wholesome.
           The light shines in the darkness

Response: **and the darkness has not overcome it.**

Leader: We pray for those working with computers
           and those involved in the world-wide web,
           that information technology may contribute to
               wisdom and truth.
           The light shines in the darkness

Response: **and the darkness has not overcome it.**

Leader: Lord God, grace and truth came through Jesus
               Christ;
           grant us the grace to proclaim the truth in word
               and action.
           The light shines in the darkness.

Response: **This is the true light that shines on everyone.**

From a spacecraft riding far out in space
the earth shines in multicoloured splendour.
The space traveller sees it with a sense of awe
and wonders what undiscovered secrets lie hidden in it.
What new knowledge will be given to earth's inhabitants?
What glorious experiences await them in a new age?

When will the new dawn come
when across the globe there will be justice, peace and
harmony?

John Johansen-Berg
England

Communication

The pace of technology
Exhausts us.
The speed of interaction
Drains us.
Video screens, keyboards,
Silicon chips
Flash messages around the globe
In a hazy World Wide Web
Of speed.

Information
At our fingertips
So fast
We can't absorb the mass of data
Flashing at us
From the powerful imagery on our screens.
We live with the illusion
That we are masters of
Communication.

But come,
Come and sit quietly
By the side of one who's hurting.
Hold hands
With one whose needs
Run deeper than they have the words to say.
Look gently
Into the eyes

Of one whose heart is full of tears.
Be with the hurting.
In the silence of your loving presence,
Embrace them.
Let them rest their weary head
Upon your shoulder.
Give them space.
Give them time.

Then you will begin
To know.

Communication.

Pat Marsh
England

Connections

I can talk to you
through the Internet,
and we can share;
we can learn the vastness
of a shrinking world.

From far apart,
we can embrace,
speak in love,
in joy, in harmony,
and
in one moment,
own together
the whole of our world,
forever.

Connecting to a thousand things,
we can combine
what never was combined before

and linking to
a thousand others,
recognize more sisters,
more brothers.

So stretch communications' limbs,
explore these new horizons,
ecstatic with the knowledge
new understanding brings.

Miriam Bennett
England

Jubilee Hymn

Tune: Woodlands

Creating God, we bring our song of praise
For life and work that celebrate your ways:
The skill of hands, our living with the earth,
The joy that comes from knowing our own worth.

Forgiving God, we bring our cries of pain,
For all that shames us in our search for gain;
The hidden wounds, the angry scars of strife,
The emptiness that saps and weakens life.

Redeeming God, we bring our trust in you,
Our fragile hope that all may be made new;
Our dreams of truth, of wealth that all may share,
Of work and service rooted deep in prayer.

Renewing God, we offer what shall be
A world that lives and works in harmony;
When peace and justice, once so long denied,
Restore to all their dignity and pride.

Jan Berry
England

There Is One Voice That Matters

It never stops;
humming, buzzing, fans,
the traffic roar,
the modem screaming and gurgling,
voices, insistent voices,
catch-your-eye pictures;
stuff, head-stuff, too much stuff.
Oh God!
O God,
there is one voice that matters,
small and still,
speaking to our stillness,
speaking to the almost-vanished kernel
of quiet:
let us hear you.

Bob Warwicker
England

Drawing Energy

God, make my prayers like a candle-flame,
always aspiring, hoping, stretching for heaven.
God make my prayers like a light-bulb,
drawing energy from a network
that extends far beyond my sight.
Thank you for the vision you give us;
and for the world-wide community of sisters and brothers
in which you place us.

Bob Warwicker
England

Wisdom is Calling

Worship and Spirituality

Listen!

'Listen! Wisdom is calling out in the streets and market places, calling loudly at the city gates and wherever people come together.'
Proverbs 1:20

A strange thing has happened to modern peoples. In becoming literate they have lost the ability to read the world around them: in amassing so much learning they are losing out on wisdom. A world that can read the word but not the world is in imminent danger. Wisdom is not the sole possession of any religion or group of people: wisdom can often be hidden from the learned and yet available to the simplest of peoples. Wisdom is that which dances through all creation, it is not even unique to humankind, yet certain groups have 'acquired' it over the ages. Wisdom is found in many traditions and all main religions. Primal peoples understood that wisdom was to be met in all of creation: wisdom was the 'word' to be read in the world before any words were committed to paper. In the same way they saw creation as the 'primary scriptures'. If you do not understand the world, you will not understand its creator; if you are out of tune with the world you will be out of tune with yourself and your life. If your relationship to the world is wrong, it affects your faith and your theology. The Celtic Christians talked of three Scriptures: the New Testament that is understood through the Old Testament and the Old Testament that is understood through the Primary Scripture, which is the world. We all need more than book learning, we need a deep sensitivity and an awareness of all that is going on around us. We need to be open to the mystery and wisdom all about us and within us. Too much education has been head stuff alone, we need to develop our gut reaction and our heart response, we need to develop each of our senses and to hear what the earth says to us.

Today the ecological crises we face and the crises of our world are crises of the human soul. Its lack of wisdom is being projected on to the earth itself. In seeking to possess things we have lost out on wisdom. In making ourselves the centre of the world we have failed to see how important the rest of the world is to us. We are using short-term methods to our immediate advantage and this is not wise, for it is to the detriment of the future of our planet and all life upon it.

It was said by the American Indians that, when the white man came to America, he did not look with awe and wonder on that great land but took an inventory. Instead of being filled with wonder he wanted to possess. Our conquering attitude to other creatures shows a lack of wisdom, a lack of understanding of our relationship to, and interdependence with, the rest of creation. We need wisdom in all our dealings.

In looking at the wisdom of the past there is a desire for a new wisdom, a new response to the Power that dances through the universe. We have discovered new worlds; we have seen the earth from space, we have looked into the atom and it has increased the mystery and wonder of all that is around us. Much of modern science is quite mystical in its statements. We are on the edge of not just a new learning but a new wisdom. We need to walk with awe and wonder, we need to be aware of the deep mystery and power that flows through all things. We need to listen and to be open to the glory of the world, to be sensitive to the inter-connectedness of all things. We need to discover again that there is an adventure to be lived in our world, a personal discovery to be made of the presence and the life that dances in all things.

To help us in this we look to the primal peoples and to those who lived, and do live, close to the earth. We need to discover that we share this world with brother sun and sister moon, that all created things are our cousins – and not too distant cousins at that. To help us in this quest we look back to those who have gone before us, and to those who have responded in wisdom to the world around them. Whatever our religion, we should travel this road in joy and let it enrich our faith. Heed the words from Fyodor Dostoyevsky:

Love all of God's creation, the whole and every grain of sand in it, love every leaf, every ray of God's light. Love the animals, love the plants, love everything. If you love everything, you will perceive the divine mystery in things.

The Brothers Karamazov

David Adam
England
Vicar of Holy Island
and author of many books
on Celtic spirituality

Entrance

Pause at the threshold
Of the sacred space;
Bow low.
Prepare for fresh
Encounter
With the Holy One.

Ann Lewin
England

A Morning Psalm

Mysterious Friend, You gladden my heart with:

Scent of
Herbs and drying streets,
Children's laughing breath;

Touch of
>   Feathers and spike's sharp,
>   Lovers' warm embrace;

Sound of
>   Rhymes and sparrows' quarrels,
>   Life's longing song;

Sight of
>   Arches and silent spiders,
>   Friends kneeling, seeking;

Taste of
>   Wine and broken bread,
>   Grace-giving gifts.

Mysterious Friend, as day breathes afresh,
>   Stay with me.

Derek H Webster
England

With Drums and Trumpets

Let the trumpet sound
and voices blend with melody
in a song of celebration
for a new era of freedom and of love,
for a new era of freedom and of love.

Celebrate the new millennium
in which both old and young
receive a home to live in.

Celebrate a loving partnership
of women and of men
respecting one another.

Celebrate our global family
where all are welcomed in,
moving from state to nation.

Celebrate the precious gift of youth
who give by trust and love
a sign of hope and new life.

Let the bass drums beat
and voices join in harmony
in a song of celebration
for a new era of justice and of peace,
for a new era of justice and of peace.

John Johansen-Berg
England

Christ Is Living in Our World

Through human lips
    Christ has spoken
Through human hands
    Christ has healed
Through our hearts
    Christ is loving
Through us all
    Christ is working
So, behold the truth
    Christ is living in our world.

Richard Becher
England

Jubilee Song

Sound the horn!
Sound the trumpet!
Declare the year of Jubilee!
Let's celebrate with songs of hope
of living, loving unity.

Bang the drum!
Yell and cry!
Declare the year of Jubilee!
Let's demonstrate with shouts of 'No'
to modern forms of slavery.

Strum the harp!
Pluck the lyre!
Declare the year of Jubilee!
Let's weep together, you and I,
and seek again God's sov'reignty.

Sound the horn!
Sound the trumpet!
Declare the year of Jubilee!
Let's celebrate with songs of joy
for Christ the Lord has set us free.

Ed Cox
England

Hymn for the Millennium

Tune: Reconciliation by Jillian M Bray

Where the love of God is guiding
there is now another way:
new awareness of compassion
learned from one another;

love, the face of God in Jesus,
new creation's thrust,
love, transforming tears and terror
into health and trust.

Where the truth of God is driving
there is now another way,
shining through our times' confusion,
sharp with revelation:
    words that stifle sense or spirit
    changed and redefined,
    crosses raised to teach division
    lowered, left behind.

Where the life on earth is dying,
there is now another way,
where a child may grow in safety,
where there's peace and shelter,
    when we hold the fragile planet
    in our conscious care,
    when we see again as sacred
    all we are and share.

God will lead us on this mission,
God, the flight path and the power,
lifting all who grasp the vision
into understanding:
    so the heart and hope within us
    sets each other free,
    where the love of God is guiding,
    this shall come to be.

Shirley Erena Murray
Aotearoa New Zealand

Spirituality

Spirituality is a curious word. When some hear it they think of musty churches and shadowy aisles. Others think of ancient monasteries and chanting monks. Practical people often think the world of spirituality is not for them; it belongs to those who spend much time on their knees at prayer or to those whose mystic meditation reaches out to another world.

Spirituality is not a curious state. It is what holds our faith and life together. It is the substance of the insubstantial. It brings Christ into the factory and the office. It brings the glory of God into the ordinariness of the classroom and the kitchen.

Spirituality is a yearning and an enabling. It glimpses the glory of the kingdom and then spares no effort in seeking to work for the Kingdom of God on earth. It seeks to walk alongside the Christ of the lakeside and to wash feet in the upper room.

Spirituality is a dove's flight and the vigil by the side of a wounded victim. It is the vulnerable, offering to be an instrument of healing. It is rooted in the earthliness of daily work and service; it is reaching up to the glory of God's presence.

Spirituality is the song of the soul; it is the voice of the voiceless. It is the link between the word and the silence. It is light in darkness and life in death. It is re-awakening and resurrection.

The bowl of the valley
slopes down from the hills;
above, a low straight cloud,
like the gash in the Saviour's side.
Five birds fly gracefully
against the darkening sky,
each a reminder of a book of the Torah.
Down below the outer settlements
of the bustling city,
some in curving avenues
of comfortable living;
some in high rise flats

which stretch up in a scream of pain,
sheltering the lonely and the overcrowded.
From these hills, dotted with trees,
humanity funnels down to the city's heart.
Lights begin to glint, orange, white and red,
as the city's night life prepares
for celebration and terror,
whilst the suburbs settle for a televised drama
to induce a night of sleep.
Over it all, brooding like a mother dove,
the divine Creator looks in compassion
into the homes and lives, the hopes and fears,
of humanity in all its variety.

John Johansen-Berg
England

A Spirituality for Women

The three pillars of a woman's spirituality are love for God, love for herself and love for others. These may seem to be the same as the pillars upon which all spirituality is based but for women they are different.

The God we were introduced to by Christian preachers is a God who does not like women. It is a God who does not want them to be in positions of leadership because they menstruate and become pregnant and because they are inferior. It is a God who created them to be like Eve, tempters, the devil's gateway and unredeemable beasts. It is a God who actually hates them for being who they are.

It is these traditional beliefs which make it impossible for women to love God and themselves at the same time. They cannot connect with such a God, let alone believe that this is the God who created them.

And yet women do still want to claim Christianity as their inheritance too. But they believe that the God of Christianity is the God of all, not a patriarchal God who favours men. The

God women yearn for is the God who gives them support precisely as women, who loves them and who is satisfied with the way they have been created. The God who will look at them and say: 'It is good.'

Loving Ourselves

Just as it is hypocritical for us to confess love for God while we hate our neighbour, so also it is hypocritical to confess love for others while we hate or look down upon ourselves. Women have been socialized into treating themselves as inferior, neglecting themselves, suppressing what is in them and accepting things that conflict with their own experience – to the point of hating themselves and all other women too.

A healthy spirituality is a spirituality which affirms us as persons who are important and loved by God. Once we learn to love ourselves as women and to believe that God loves us, we can learn to love God and other people too.

Love for others is a dimension in our lives where we as women become God's feet, eyes, ears and hands. Women's spirituality has to do with the mind, the soul and the body. It is a spirituality of connectedness to oneself, to others, to nature and to God.

For women to have healthy spirituality they must critique any understanding of Christianity that destroys or denies life. Jesus came that we might have life and have it in abundance. Women today are defining for themselves who they are in defiance of the negative images given them by the early fathers of the church and by some contemporary fathers too. That is a liberating and life-giving spiritual experience.

Libuseng Lebaka-Ketshabile
South Africa

An Increasing Hunger

Today there is an increasing hunger for spiritual involvement which religion appears to be unable to deal with. Due to its

314

own limitations of inclusiveness and its narrowness and its fears, the Church as an institution has severely weakened the Christian Movement's mission. Fear, escapism, moralism, domination and control have led to a lessening of church attendance. Clearly, the religious, moral and spiritual breakdown has to do with religion itself and not with spirituality. This is why so many no longer look to religious institutions, or persons associated with them, for guidance.

Working and listening with many who feel themselves not only outcasts of society but also of the Church institution, I have become acutely aware that most persons are spiritual rather than religious – they feel the latter inhibits them, while the former releases them. Many recognize the aesthetic value of old churches (when open or not) but they are no longer essential for the purposes of the Christian Movement. People are.

The ministry of the Christian Movement today is seen as emanating from within the workplace, the shop front, and the converted coal-bunker. In my own situation, while being associated with the local parish church, my coal-bunker chapel is available to anyone. In this small space prayers are said, the Eucharist is celebrated and at other times people visit it to 'simply be' in the mystery of silence.

Such initiatives throughout the Christian Movement can be seen as the spirituality of today unfolding: daring to be the 'passion of God' by meeting and evoking the passion of others through the gift of ourselves. Nurtured by the empathy of compassion towards all, we dare to grasp the vision of the absolute uniqueness of each person. It is this passionate spirituality that allows us to be merciful towards others as well as ourselves. Together we evolve towards the mystery which is calling us forth with our 'wounds and all' to be the powerful passion of God who initiated the Christian Movement through the person and the spirituality of Jesus the Christ.

Bill Kirkpatrick
Canada/England

Prayer of an Old Chief

An Aboriginal Psalm based on Psalm 42

Like a deer running from the hunter,
my heart gallops.
Like the hart longing for the flowing stream,
my soul burns.

> Our streams have dried up
> and the mountain springs disappeared.
> The tourists leave behind their empty soda cans
> on the dry riverbeds.
> How the sight pains me!
> My heart mourns for the waterless river.
> My soul thirsts for Him who is my Redeemer.
> My eyes long to behold the moment of salvation.

My tears have been my food, day and night,
while people constantly ask,
'Where is your God?'
They sing happy songs
in their vacation houses.
They force us to bow down
for their money.
Once, I sang and danced
with my own people,
joyful songs of praise
for your wonderful blessings.
Today, we have to sing for the tourists.

> How my soul is cast down
> as I remember the past,
> how my tears flow unbidden
> when I recall those former days.
> Where are those happy girls who sang with me?
> Where are those exuberant, leaping youths?
> And where did the places we gathered disappear to?

Oh God, how heavy is my soul!
Like a tribe that has lost
its life-giving spring,
my soul is parched,
it thirsts for the eternal spring
that only you can give.
Oh my Lord, have mercy on these people,
please give us back our life!

>The waterfalls have long been silent,
>the songs of praise no longer echo
>in the mountains,
>only your love and mercy
>still overwhelm me in my moment of prayers.
>I recall your great deeds of the past.
>Those things you did in the light of day,
>I remember in my hour of darkness.
>I have not forgotten, Lord,
>how you were the God of my Life.

My soul is tormented
as I witness the indignities of my people.
My soul is consumed by fire
as those who trample and abuse our land
mock my indignation, saying,
'Is your God still alive?'

Oh God, look upon this sorrowful heart
whose life is about to go out;
please rekindle my hope
so I can tell it once again,
lift thine eyes on the God of Life,
because He will give us
our spring of life,
He will chase the clouds away
and make the sun shine forever.

Jen-wen Wang
Translated by Vivian T Su
Taiwan

Is This God Really Wise?

There is a God,
who comes to us as wisdom,
but is this God really wise?

Here we are, O God,
down in this deep dark pit of struggle,
of lack of hope and faith as we look at our life,
and there you are beside us, among us and around us,
joining our weeping, our angry protest
and the burden of our journeying.
Is this wise?

This, our God, joins us
with arms wide open and bleeding hands
and wounded side,
nailed to a cross.

What sort of wisdom do you offer to us, O Jesus Christ?

(Silent reflection)

How can it be that your pain
absorbs our own?
And yet it might,
if we wait upon the moment in hope.

Dorothy McRae-McMahon
Australia

The View from the Mountain

In the silence and solitude of this mountain
I sit still surveying the scene.
I see no burning bush
nor do I hear a thundering voice.

From this vantage I look at the sight below.
I see the fire raging across the land.
I hear the ascending cry
of millions of anguished voices.

In the silence and solitude of the mountain
I gaze intently at your reality
no longer with a myopic vision
but with a higher, wider, deeper eye view.

The purge goes on within.
I am emptying myself completely
to allow you to penetrate
the deepest part of me.

The more I become one with you
the more I fathom your liberating will,
the more I see with your eyes,
hear with your ears,
feel with your heart,
and walk with your strength.

In the silence and communion of this mountain
I see no beatific vision,
only the sight below:
our people enslaved and starving.
I feel no ecstasy,
only the agony of seeing them
exploited and dehumanized.

I cannot levitate.
I cannot go up another higher storey.
I have to go down and meet you on level ground
so that I may walk with you and other people
in their exodus from this no man's land
towards the promised land.

How I wish I could pitch my tent
or build my mansion on this beautiful mountain.
But my true home is somewhere down below
where the people are
and where they are going.
This mountain can only be a place of rendezvous
with my deeper self and with the absolute you,
so that I can sharpen my vision
and clarify my mission.

There will be other mountains to climb
along the way.

Amado L Picardal
Philippines

These I Want

1 Thessalonians 5: 23–24

I want every child in this world to be happy
I want fathers to nurture their children and mothers to bring
them up
to be strong and gentle.
I want my eyes opened to the reality of other people, to hear
what they
are not able to articulate.
I want to add to an atmosphere of trust where people who
were
deeply hurt when they were young can heal, recuperate and
recover.
I want to see justice run like a river bringing healing
and peace to the nations.
I want to sing the songs of my sisters and brothers.
I want to tell their stories, dance their dances and recite their
poetry.

I want to add my voice to the resonance that conveys what
each person
on the face of the earth
wants the rest of the world to know . . .
Her vision. His dreams. Her strength. His gifts. Her hope.
His yearning. Her anxiety. His fears. Her grief.
His sadness. Her indignation. His anger.
Her determination. His striving. Her joys. His excitement.
Her discoveries. His dawnings.
I want the eyes of my heart to see the grace of God that is
present to me
in every child, woman and man I meet.
I want to be able to see differently, to think differently, to live
kindly,
to walk humbly, to serve graciously and gratefully.
Come, Lord Jesus. Come always and save me –
that I may want what you want, that I may live in you,
that I may be completely holy.

Romeo L del Rosario
Malaysia

The Water of Life

Three people were searching for the water of life, hoping to drink from it and live forever.

The first was a *warrior:* he reckoned the water of life must be very mighty – a torrent or rapid – so he went in full armour with all his weapons, believing he could *force* the water to yield to him.

The second was an *enchantress*: she reckoned the water of life would be something very magic . . . perhaps a whirlpool or geyser – something she would need to manipulate with spells; so she went in her long star-spangled robe, hoping to *outwit* the water.

The third was a *trader*: he reckoned the water of life would be very costly – a fountain of pearl-drops or diamonds, perhaps – so he loaded his clothes and purses with money – hoping to be able to *buy* the water.

When the travellers reached their destination, they found they had all been quite wrong about the water of life.

It wasn't a torrent to be intimidated by force;
it wasn't a whirlpool to be charmed by spells;
and it wasn't a fountain of pearl-drops or diamonds to be
    bought for money.

It was just a tiny, sparkling spring – its benefits were
absolutely free – but of course you had to *kneel* to drink from
    it.

This caused the seekers great consternation.

The warrior was in full armour and couldn't bend.
The enchantress had on her long magic robe and if that
    became soiled it would lose its power.
The trader was so loaded with money that if he did no more
    than incline his head, coins started rolling away into
    corners and crevices.

All dressed up, the three could not lower themselves to drink from the spring of the water of life.

There was only one solution.
So, the warrior laid aside his armour,
the enchantress laid aside her magic robe
and the trader laid aside the clothes he had stuffed with
    money.

And then each of them – naked – could kneel to drink from
the water of life and receive its sweet,
   cool,
       startling
           benefits.

Kate Compston
England

The Poet and the Elder

'Tell me about your creative work,' said the Elder.
The poet replied, 'My work is a rainbow of five hues.

   Its first hue is *seeing*.
   Creators find patterns
      In sea's sound, moon's light and
         cornflowers' wreath;
      Find values in children's tears,
         and nature's rules;
      Discover meaning.

Its second hue is *awareness*.
   Creators awaken their eyes,
      Catch fire and weep
         at Spring's colours;
      Sight begets insight, rejoice for the
         manifold is One;
      Embrace all.

Its third hue is *intimacy*.
Creators are friends
      Equally to dark and light, height and depth,
         inner and outer;
      Joining the living to the dry, knitting
         beyond to within;
      Commingling contraries.

Its fourth hue is *birth.*
Creators unlatch doors,
        Bring the night's bud to blossom,
           allow to be;
        Smother the stars with kisses,
           and ride the sun;
        Fix no boundaries.

Its fifth hue is *mystery.*
Creators grow silent,
    Walk in trackless meadows,
        Smell coloured grasses;
        Find lost islands where shearwaters fly,
        dwell in paradox
    Astonished by truth.'

'This is the fulfilment of God's secret will for them,' said the
   Elder.
'No,' said the poet, 'it is the pondering of who I am.'

Derek H Webster
England

Lord, Teach Us

Lord, teach us to be strong,
but with compassion;
teach us to be just,
but with insight;
teach us to be active in the cause of what is right,
but with patience.

Nigel Collinson
England

The Sound of God

Remain receptive to the sound of God,
 deep in drumbeat, song and symphony;
 explore it in sea, forest, mountain and meadow,
 feel how it falls through green, yellow and blue.
Its echo reverberates in a craftsman's skill,
 is captured and carried
 in sculptures, paintings and poems.
It is woven into the patterns
 of the myriad forces of life,
 breathes softly wherever there is peace,
 a voice for the just in discord or tumult.
Enlarge your heart to receive the sound
 and hear it
 everywhere.

Miriam Bennett
England

New Light

A morning prayer for people with busy schedules

In the shelter of new light
Before day's weight begins
O God, hear my prayer.

As earth charts her course towards night
So may I chart mine:
with quiet clarity,
with visible compassion,
with clear integrity.

May the scope of this created journey
Run broad with recognition:
for each subtle miracle,
for each transparent mercy,
for each tender joy.

May the sweep of this day be steadied
By your gestures of presence:
Infectious grace,
Persistent love,
Outrageous vision;
Until an iridescence grows within
Marking my course with peaceful certainty.

Keri K Wehlander
Canada

A Highway Shall Be There

The most serious challenge that lies ahead of us is our ability
to maintain the reality of human beings living in society with
a sense of obligation and mutuality. There are increasing pressures that pull us apart. There are the fragmentation of working patterns into smaller units, the narrower horizons of
individualism – what is good and right for me and my family
– the insistence on rights, which often leads to single issue politics, the tendency to live behind security fences. There is an
anxiety that new technology which ought to bring us all much
closer together and open up a way for greater inter-depen-
dence and communication, might lead to increasing isolation.
Are we being sold another form of reality which will turn out
to be fantasy? Will the ultimate division in a technologically
rich world be the opting out by communities of the wealthy
across the world, controlling their wealth digitally and fortify-
ing their homes with electronic hardware and private police
forces against depredations of the have-nots at their gates?

Other more hopeful values are on offer with a larger vision
of what it is to be a human being. The shape of morality is
changing. For younger people morality now includes care for
the planet; racism and sexism are becoming unacceptable to
most thinking people although both still flourish in places and
will die hard. University computer departments look closely
at the ethics of their subject; business schools offer courses on

ethics and leadership; in the finance world, green investments are increasingly seen as a profitable option. All of this is not the preserve of Christianity, but it is the sort of territory upon which faith has always operated. It is not the whole of faith, but it will be seen by many as its cutting edge; faith will want to say more, but it cannot say less. It will best communicate its essence not from the exclusivist position of fundamentalism but as a community of faith which offers a common place to all, a place which nurtures a critical, contemporary Christianity.

Nigel Collinson
England
adapted

Stillness

I believe in the sun
even when it isn't shining.
I believe in love
even when I cannot feel it.
I believe in God
even when I cannot see him.

I believe.
I believe that I am never alone.
God is with me. He is my Father.
He has made all things, including me.
I believe that I can never stray so far away from God
that there can be no way of return.
I believe that God wills life for me, not death,
joy for me, not misery
and that he is with me today and to all eternity.

We thank you that today and tomorrow,
as yesterday and always,
we receive life by your grace, O Lord,

from this earth, from bread, from light
and from all around us.
We thank you for our life in the here and now,
with its difficulties and delights
and we pray that neither the future nor death
may separate us from Jesus Christ
who is your love for all mankind
and for the whole creation.

Hauptkirche St Michaelis, Hamburg
Germany

Circles

Stones a million years old
link us with prehistory.
As the candle burns
the circle of stones around it links us
with God's creation.

Circles speak to us of God,
without beginning or ending.
God's love is endless
and he created the world to express his love.
So the circle represents his world
and his eternal nature.

God reveals himself to us as our Father,
who created the heavens and the earth.
God comes amongst us as the baby
born in Bethlehem, the child of Nazareth,
the Saviour on the cross outside Jerusalem.
God is with us as the Holy Spirit,
the gift of Jesus to his people,
the enabler, guide and comforter.
Morning, noon and night it is our delight
to worship God, Father, Son and Holy Spirit.

Responsive Prayer

Leader: The world and all that is in it belongs to God;

Response: The earth and all its people belong to the Lord.

Leader: When I rise to greet a new day,

Response: Lord, be with me in my coming and going.

Leader: When I go out and begin my work,

Response: Lord, be with me in the day's tasks.

Leader: When I set out on a long journey,

Response: Lord, go with me as I travel.

Leader: When I experience pain or sickness,

Response: Lord, heal me by your sacred touch.

Leader: When I go to bed at night,

**Response: Lord, grant me the rest of sleep
and refresh me for the beginning of a new day.**

Two streams of Christianity flowed across Europe
and met in turbulent cross currents in the British Isles.
The Roman flow cascaded from the centre of imperial power;
the Celtic river rising in ancient places rushed freely through
the land.
What joy there might have been if both streams
had been allowed to flow together, to mingle in creative
torrents.
But some were not content until one river was blocked
and redirected

and the other allowed to flow with increased strength across
the land.
The Spirit bides his time and now it seems
the Celtic river flows again.

John Johansen-Berg
England

True Riches

In our wealth is our poverty;
in their poverty is their wealth.
In their spirituality is our hope;
in our aridity is their challenge.
In a time of oppression people learn to trust God;
in a time of power people neglect their Maker.
May Europe learn from the Exodus faith of Africa;
may the west learn from the liberation message of the east.
May we share the jubilation
of those who have trusted God for liberation.

Responsive Prayer

Leader: Once more God will send us his Spirit

Response: The waste land will become fertile.

Leader: Lord, hear the prayer of your people

Response: Rescue them from injustice.

Leader: Lord, hear the prayer of your people

Response: Deliver them from cruel oppression.

Leader: Lord, hear the prayer of your people

Response: May their hunger be relieved.

Leader: Once more God will send us his Spirit

Response: **Everywhere there will be peace and security.**

Every day the sun rises
and shines on the field where I labour.
Every noon the sun is hot
on the building plots where I work.
Every evening the sun sets
over the deep mines where I dig.
Mine is the effort, the sweat of the brow,
but others reap the reward of my work.
But one day justice will dawn
as a brighter sun throughout the land.

John Johansen-Berg
England

On the Third Day

On the first day I saw the messenger of the passing millennium. He recounted his story of hunger and want, of violence and oppression, of war and killing. A thousand years passed before my eyes with sounds of fury and conflict. Empires rose and fell; the rich trampled on the poor. There was wealth in palaces, abbeys and cathedrals but stark poverty in huts, houses and hovels. Famine and terror stalked through these cruel centuries. I saw that the messenger was sad and asked the cause. He replied that he was sad because his millennium was coming to an end. I was sad that so much time had been wasted, so many people had been harmed and oppressed. No doubt in the darkness there had been many hidden occasions of light but I was not sorry to see this messenger depart.

On the second day I saw the messenger of the new millennium. He spoke of the promise of peace and described the many people who longed to share what they had with those who lacked this world's goods. He recounted the visions of those who dreamed of a new world, a planet of justice and harmony, where people of all races and colours would respect and love each other. In this new world every child would be cared for, every family would be comfortably housed and no person would be hungry. The messenger was full of joy and ready to celebrate and I asked the cause. He replied that he was happy because a new millennium was coming and it was an opportunity for God's people to experience God's blessing and to delight the Father's heart by their care of one another. No doubt in the new millennium there will be some causes of darkness but I was glad to hear this messenger of hope.

On the third day promises were fulfilled, because on the third day Jesus rose from the dead; he overcame the darkness and brought light into the world. He calls us to be his messengers. He commissions us to announce the acceptable year of the Lord.

John Johansen-Berg
England

God of All Love

Voice One: We have need of vision and imagination;
                     that we may see the beauty of the earth
                         as a finite whole;
                     that we may be aware of inter-
                         dependence and the sacred integrity
                         of each part of creation;
                     that we may celebrate diversity while
                         valuing wholeness.

Response   **God of all love and every truth**
                   help us to look with open eyes,
                       to see with open hearts.

Voice Two: We have need of awe and wonder;
                    that we may see eternity in a grain of
                        sand;
                    that we may see the understanding of all
                        in the fall of a sparrow;
                    that we may see greatness in two pennies
                        on a plate;
                        life in a seed that seems to die;
                        trust in a baby's reaching hands;
                    that we may see how Christ the Lord of
                        all
                        smiles from the small.

Response   **God of all love and every truth**
                    help us to look with open eyes,
                        to see with open hearts.

Voice Three: We have need of compassion and
                    commitment;
                    that people may be put in the picture;
                    people: unique, solitary in nature,
                        created good, but capable of evil
                            choices;
                    people with powers to create or destroy;
                    people in all their mystery, depth and
                        ordinariness;
                    people often hungry, thirsty, strangers,
                        naked, sick or in prison;
                    people suffering; people without hope;
                        people who deserve something better.
                    people hidden; indigenous peoples,
                        native peoples,
                    whose long and earthy memories
                    whose ancient wisdom for survival and
                        celebration,
                    could even now be our hope and our
                        salvation.

Response	God of all love and every truth
	help us to look with open eyes,
	to see with open hearts.

Voice Four: We have need of fire and vigour
that we may be angry at short-sighted
policies, cold-blooded economics
and heartless trading;
that we may protest at greed and the
misuse of the earth's resources;
that we may desire justice with all our
being and seek passionately
the use of our abundant knowledge,
skills and resources to
sustain and cherish all life.

Response   **God of all love and every truth**
help us to look with open eyes,
to see with open hearts.

Joy Mead
England

Living on the Edge

The edge is in fact always the centre of spiritual renewal.

*

The Christian Church has always been renewed
by those it placed on the edge,
such as St Francis and John Wesley.

*

Jesus was edged out of the synagogue, out of the temples,
out of the city, out of society and out of life –
yet remained totally in touch with the heart of life.

334

*

Any Christian movement that becomes respectable risks
being brought from the edge to the centre –
and so is given the kiss of death.

Martin Wallace
England

A Litany for the Millennium

Spirit of God, life-giving, life-enhancing
Enliven us in your love.

Word of God, sharing our earth, our blood, brain, bone and
guts
Renew us in your love.

God, our eternal parent and creator
Complete us in your love.

Holy and Blessed Trinity
May we share your life more fully, may your kingdom come.

From pride, vainglory and millennial triumphalism
Good Lord, deliver us.

From greed, self-satisfaction and millennial
blindness
Good Lord, deliver us.

From the delusion that more can only be better
Good Lord, deliver us.

From the destruction of this planet
and the destitution of our descendants,
Good Lord, deliver us.

From the abuse of all you have entrusted us
Good Lord, deliver us.

When we refuse to repent
and would much rather celebrate
Good Lord, deliver us.

When we refuse to reflect critically
on what most people take for granted
Good Lord, deliver us.

> By the wonder of your creation groaning in
>   travail
> **Word of God, deliver us.**
>
> By your life in poverty on earth,
> by the pure water of baptism,
> by the fruits of the earth become your body
>   and your blood
> **Word of God, deliver us.**
>
> By your rigged trial and squalid death,
> by your risen human life
> and by the Spirit sharing
>   your self-giving love
> **Word of God, deliver us.**

At the end of a century
when more people have been killed by Christianized nations
than have been slaughtered in all human history
Lord, have mercy.

When more people than ever before,
who could have received food,
have been malnourished
Lord, have mercy.

When more people than ever before,
who could have been fed and lived,
have starved to death
Lord, have mercy.

When more foetuses have miscarried among the poorer
and been aborted among the wealthier
and more infants have died in childhood
Lord, have mercy.

When more people have died in prison camps,
under torture
and in communal violence
Lord, have mercy.

When still greater burdens have been placed
on nine tenths or more of women
Lord, have mercy.

When the poor are getting poorer and we rich, richer
and still more destructive
Lord, have mercy.

When more species of mammals, birds, fish, reptiles,
insects and plants
have been humanly destroyed
than in a hundred millennia before
Lord, have mercy.

When more of the planet's resources have been raped
and squandered
and more life-destroying pollution amassed
Lord, have mercy.

When the tedium of affluence leads to drug dependency
Lord, have mercy.

When we your people care little for all of this
and do less
Lord, have mercy.

May your Spirit breathe life into our faithless
    prayers,
O Lord our God
Hear us, Good Lord.

May your Church be the living body of the Christ,
filled with his love and truth
and united to serve you
and this precious speck of your creation
Hear us, Good Lord.

Give your people grace to hear and receive your
    word
and to bring forth the fruit of the Spirit in costly
and effective discipleship
Hear us, Good Lord.

Guide the leaders of the nations into the ways of
    just sharing,
of peace and sustainable life for all
Hear us, Good Lord.

Strengthen those who stand, comfort and help the
    fainthearted,
stir up the complacently pious,
re-kindle cold love
and beat down Mammon under our feet,
Hear us, Good Lord.

May we share your life more fully,
may your kingdom come
Even so, Come, Lord Jesus.

F Gerald Downing
England

Prayer and Mission

Prayer feeds mission and mission feeds prayer.

*

Prayer is work and work is prayer.

*

Prayer without mission can be self-indulgence.
Mission without prayer is merely human activism.

Martin Wallace
England

Incarnation

The Inescapable,
    Present in a broken jig-saw of hopes and fears:
        Connecting.
The Incalculable,
    Here in a sly wilderness of loves and hates:
        Reconciling.
The Incomparable,
    Nigh in thistle stings of failure and victory:
        Reminding.
The Incandescent,
    Alive in Nature's manifold and human nakedness:
        Pointing.
The Incognito,
    Nigh in grey enigmatic sand, a labyrinth's pale shadows:
        Naming.
The Infinite,
    Here in splinters of freedom and love:
        Striving.
The Inconceivable,

Present in him and her, you and me:
Incarnate.

Derek H Webster
England

Becoming a Child

'. . . unless you turn and become like children' Jesus of Nazareth

What is it to become like children? There is a childhood when in tender years, we play with computer games and trains, Barbie dolls and bikes. There is another childhood which can remain within us as we mature or it can be lost. If it stays it represents, not what is subtle or sophisticated but what is simple and pure. It is the affection of an undivided heart which sees all life as valuable – caterpillars and beetles, bats and cats. It is the love which is uncompromising – for CDs and TVs, kin and friends.

This other childhood is an openness to what is encountered in living. It allows everything to be sacrament: the woollen sweater, the loaf of bread, the burning bush. It is blind to distinctions: black and white, friend and foe, sinner and redeemed. It draws a circle of love so wide that no-one is excluded: neither Muslim nor Jew, neither handicapped nor elderly, neither me nor you.

This adventure of remaining a child as we grow is the real task of our maturity. It is the task of retaining an infinite openness to God. This is done by so living that the seeds of a community of love are sown each day. For our true childhood is measured in our response to the call made in the lives of our neighbours; to the call of creation for liberation; to the call of a young man who walked by the sea-shore and said, 'Follow Me.'

Derek H Webster
England

A Psalm of Salvation

Your Spirit spills over, paints the world
   And our eyes are drenched with:

Orange
     Flock of marigolds and burning sun:
Blue
     Cornflower wreath and empty sky;
Green
     Stalk and pod, stretching tree:
Purple
     Crocus, thistle and king's gown;
Brown
     Earth and wood, sour vinegar;
Red
     Berries, lips, blood and death;
Yellow
     Ripe grain, bread, newly risen sun.

     Newly risen Son,
   Rainbow crowned and shining:
     Rise in me to-day
       AMEN.

Derek H Webster
England

I Rise to This Day

I rise to this day
    in confidence
    of the Father's protecting me
    of the Son's love for me
    of the Spirit's filling me.

I walk out today
    with the Father above me
    with the Son beside me
    with the Spirit within me.

So as I walk
        let the joy of others touch me
        let sorrow not hide from me
        let life and death meet with me.

For I rise and walk today
        with God the Holy Trinity.

Bob Commin
South Africa

A Prayer for Twenty-four Hours

Creator God
Father and Mother,
you brought into being
all that breathes and moves,
all that changes and grows.
Give us wisdom
to be good custodians of our inheritance.

At the dawn of this day
We praise and worship you.

Diligent Christ,
carpenter, teacher, healer,
son, brother, friend,
you channelled your gifts and skills
into love and service for all.
Give us discernment to recognize our talents
and use them in our work and our relationships.

During this working day
We praise and worship you.

Encompassing Spirit,
friend and comforter,

you are able to lift us
from weariness of body
and apathy of spirit.
Give us vitality and enthusiasm
to enjoy our hours of leisure.

In the evening of this day
We praise and worship you.

Mysterious Trinity,
three in one, one in three,
constant as the phases of the moon,
ceaseless as the ebb and flow of the tide,
ever beginning, yet never ending.
Give us restful bodies and quiet minds
as we enter healing sleep.

At the end of this day
We praise and worship you.

Heather Johnston
England

An Evening Psalm

Now the crane flies homeward to her mate,
The fizz of bees is stilled and locust wings.
With a thousand eyes, in black apparel
You watch to guard Your creatures.
Entrap the thief in his own snare,
Shadow the sight of snake.
Bathe Your children
In quietness
And peace,
Darkling
God.

Derek H Webster
England

Homemakers

Keeper of the hearth, birth giver to home
Warming rooms, warming lives.

Keeper of the hearth, nourishing the body,
Making fire, making bread.

Keeper of the hearth, living in community,
Loving hands, loving heart.

Keeper of the hearth, wise woman of the earth,
Teaching truth, teaching faith.

Keeper of the hearth, daughter of God.
Mothering hope, mothering life.

Betty Radford Turcott
Canada

A Mother's Prayer

Lord you are in my baby's awakening
Your Spirit is filling her
Your Spirit is Peace.

Lord you are in this playful washing
Your Spirit splashes her
Your Spirit is Peace.

Lord you are in the way I feed her
Your Spirit satisfies her
Your Spirit is Peace.

Lord you are in the games I play with her
Your Spirit delights in her
Your Spirit is Peace.

Lord you are in the song I sing to her
Your Spirit soothes her
Your Spirit is Peace.

Lord you are in her time of sleep
Your Spirit keeps her
Your Spirit is Peace

Bob Commin
South Africa

Wisdom, Grace and Favour

And Jesus increased in wisdom and in years and in divine and human favour. Luke 2:52

Leader: Visualize the child Jesus, experiencing, testing human interaction, hearing faith and folk stories, being given advice, being taught formally and informally while absorbing lessons from the world of nature. This human side to Jesus means that his relatives had immense impact. How did Jesus increase in wisdom? What part did his father Joseph play?

Picture possible scenarios – Silence

God of Wisdom, we link Joseph as a vital source of Jesus' wisdom to the fathering ones of today –
the daily dads, the foster dads, the male carers and guardians
especially those known to us.

All: **We give thanks for Joseph and for all wholesome, masculine goodness which nurtures children. Increase male wisdom and grace.**

Leader: From where did Jesus' wisdom gain its increase? Surely, it was strengthened by mother Mary?

Picture possible scenarios – Silence

God, Lady Wisdom. We link Mary as a resource of
Jesus' wisdom with the mothering ones of today –
the daily mothers, foster mums,
female carers and guardians
especially those known to us.

All: **We give thanks for feminine wisdom and intuition
which nurtures children healthily. Increase female
wisdom and grace.**

Leader: How did the young Jesus tap wisdom?
Was it deepened by the blunt simplicity
of his siblings and playmates telling it 'like it is'?

Picture possible scenarios – Silence

Wise God. We link Jesus' peers with children today
especially those whom we know.

All: **Thank you for all children who challenge
foolishness and injustice, as they offer raw
wisdom. May this continue and increase.
Thank you for Jesus whose legacy of Wisdom is
ours to use.**

**May all who relate to children and youth – older
people and young adults too – tap into your Holy
Wisdom and Goodness
while continuing to grow in grace and truth
through Christ's Holy, Wise Spirit.**

*Glenn Jetta Barclay
Aotearoa New Zealand*

A Thanksgiving for Australia

God of holy dreaming, Great Creator Spirit,
from the dawn of creation you have given your children
    the good things of Mother Earth.
You spoke and the gum tree grew.
    In the vast desert and dense forest,
    and in cities at the water's edge,
    creation sings your praise.
Your presence endures
as the rock at the heart of our Land.
When Jesus hung on the tree
    you heard the cries of all your people
    and became one with your wounded ones:
    the convicts, the hunted and the dispossessed.
The sunrise of your Son coloured the earth anew
    and bathed it in glorious hope.
In Jesus we have been reconciled to you,
    to each other and to your whole creation.
Lead us on, Great Spirit,
    as we gather from the four corners of the earth;
enable us to walk together in trust
    from the hurt and shame of the past
into the full day which has dawned in Jesus Christ.

Lenore Parker
Australia

347

A Prayer for Australia

Australia is often described as a land of extremes. Australians of European descent have sought to use their two hundred year habitation of this ancient continent to smooth over these extremes. Dams have been built to limit river flooding and to provide irrigation water for agriculture, trees have been cleared and the native flora and fauna exposed to introduced new species. Aboriginal Australians (known as Murri people in north-eastern Australia) thrived in the continent for millennia with all its extremes and have faced genocide and indifference during Australia's European history.

Draw us to an understanding of the spiritual heritage which is strong and familiar to this land.

Lead us to a repentance for past wrongs and present injustice.

Give courage to all who work and live for reconciliation.

Develop in your people an appreciation for all that shows your care across ancient aeons in this place.

Just as you guided the Murri people to a richness and diversity of culture, guide us all, in all our diversity, to the richness of understanding which sees us discover our common humanity in you. Help us to affirm these things in each other.

Take from your Australian people the fear that leads to domination and the insecurity that leads to oppression. We have known these evils too often.

Give to your Christian people a spirit that delights to discover Christ in neighbour and stranger. By a miracle of your grace help us to see with new eyes that are unclouded by the divisions and injuries of the past. Save us from the forgetfulness that prevents us from acknowledging the injustices which are so familiar as to be unrecognized.

Show us the way to live more lightly on this land so that its distinctiveness will always be part of the richness of creation.

Philip Freier
Australia

Ash Wednesday Liturgy

In the Australian bush, fire often consumes the trees and grass leaving the landscape charred. Several days after the fire, shoots sprout from the grass roots as well as the stumps and branches and make a brilliant cover of green over the fire-blackened bark and earth.

We come to be united with the blackened earth as we receive the mark of ash on our skin. Just as new growth surely follows the fire so new things await us as we make this journey of repentance.

Because we have covered ourselves with pride and arrogance:
Cleanse and set us free.

Since we have been content with the empty and the superficial:
Fill us from the depths of love.

When we become trapped in old patterns and struggles:
Lift our eyes in hope.

Even though we are broken and far short of perfection:
Form us for loving service.

After our best efforts have met with rejection and discouragement:
Encourage us still to trust.

So we bring before God all that is in our life, knowing that we can hold nothing back from the fire of love which consumes even those faults which we dearly cherish.

Let us then share these ashes from each other's hands and know that God will surely fulfil the promise of newness within our life.

Philip Freier
Australia

Good Friday

No longer do sun and moon, ritual clocks for day and night;
No longer do folded mountains and uneasy, white seas;
No longer do plovers' eggs and mulberry's bud;
Shine with Your Radiance.
No more do lissom limbs
And keen eyes,
Honey breath,
Ivory skin,
Glorify
You.
Now
The earth's
All frowning.
Its paths crooked,
Blocked with hewn stone.
The grapes are sour, the corn decayed.
I ponder the Holy Words to find You in them,
I recite prayers to lay my head on Your Shoulder,
But You have fled from me, turned Your Back, left me.
My joy has gone: life is without meaning,
    tinged with my death.

Derek H Webster
England

Litany of the Lord's Prayer

Leader: Our Father who art in heaven.

People: And in the hearts of all those who love you.

Leader: Hallowed be Thy name,

**People: Especially among those who are weak in
faith and those who have been kept away
from their Saviour by their circumstances.**

Leader:	May your kingdom come,
People:	**Among those who have denied their Christian values out of fear or because of a greater dependence on material things.**
Leader:	On earth as it in heaven,
People:	**Especially among those who are oppressed and deprived of their human rights and dignity.**
Leader:	Give us this day our daily bread,
People:	**Especially among those who will go to bed hungry today, to those who are starving to death, to those caught in earthquakes, storms and accidents.**
Leader:	Forgive us our trespasses.
People:	**Our laziness and lack of commitment, our mistrust of one another, the lies we sometimes tell to preserve our position and pride, the selfishness which sometimes motivates our actions.**
Leader:	As we forgive those who trespass against us.
People:	**All those who have oppressed us and taken advantage of the poor; who have denied their freedom because of the inconvenience they may cause them.**
Leader:	And lead us not into temptation,
People:	**Into either too great or too small an estimation of ourselves, into a complacency based**

on a false sense of security, into pointless anger which leads us to treat others in a way we would not want to be treated ourselves.

Leader: But deliver us from evil.

People: **From all those things which threaten our faith in ourselves, our hope in the final revelation of your kingdom, our love for every part of your beautiful creation.**

Leader: For yours is the kingdom, and the power and the glory.

People: **And so we pledge again to you this day our bodies, minds, souls and spirits.**

Leader: Now and forever.

People: **In this world and the next, you are our God – the one and only and we are your handmaidens.**

Beulah Shakir
Pakistan

The Lord's Prayer

Four variations

Father,
Heaven's Keeper,
Your Grace crushes.
Pitch Your tent here.
Give light to our paths,

Let them mirror a holy Way.
Set bread to nourish, wine to quench.
Score out what has gone awry,
Likewise we for evil doers.
Keep us from temptation,
Untie sin's thongs.
Glory's Yours
Always
Amen.

*

You, Who fathered here
    Wood violets, untidy finches, puzzled snails:
And there in that other place outside time's arch,
    Yarrow that does not wither:

A cloudburst of glory
    Pours down to drench the earth,
Giving it name and purpose. This little life
    Pulses with eternity.

The profusion is breathless –
    Sunflower seed, pomegranates' pip,
Sperm from ram and skate. As there is earthly meat,
    May there be heavenly bread.

Others have brewed
    A bitter drink to bring us to harm.
And we have repeated their faults.
    Forgive us and them.

The sirens of the night pursue us.
    Silence them
Before they drag us to that place
    From which we will not escape.

Muddy potatoes, squadgy earth
   All that is here;
Canticles and crowns, all that is There;
  Are everlastingly for You.
Amen.

                         *

          Trinity in Unity,
We turn to find You in others' eyes –
             In ourselves.
Your Name is mysterious islands
             In distant seas of mists and suns.
Rest in all that is in this place,
             Wait to stir it with Your glory.
Imbue all that is in this place
             With your design, intent.
Give rice and barley to feed our neighbours,
             Fill their wells, pipes and channels.
Weave no reins to draw us to sin.
             Drag us from its mire.
Absolve our iniquities, as we absolve from theirs,
             Those who have wronged us.
All is yours, aconites and moons,
             All is yours, in an eternal Now.
          Trinity in Unity
          May all this be.
          Amen.

                      *

We who know the pain of broken ties may say,
   Our Father.
We who inhabit the ghettoes affirm of You,
   Who art in Heaven.
We whose names are remembered for abuse, of Yours say,
   Hallowed be thy Name.
We who suffer brutality, discrimination and death, cry to
  You,

Thy will be done on earth as it is in Heaven.
We who are refused the harvest of Your land and sea plead,
   Give us this day our daily bread.
We give and seek compassion appealing
   Forgive us our trespasses,
   As we forgive those who trespass against us.
We ask to be kept from what brings others into subjection to us,
   And lead us not into temptation but deliver us from evil.
We, without power, await the restoration of all things and say,
   For thine is the Kingdom, the power and the glory.
Amen.

Derek H Webster
England

Wild Strawberries

They shared astonishment at his death, But their task was to shape a liturgy which would celebrate a life. It was to be for themselves and the rest of the school. But what was appropriate for such occasions? Conversation bubbled quickly. (Yet it could not disguise their surprise as they became aware of the wound of mortality which each bore.) The deputy-head, glancing at the vicar, wondered if they should look at those ancient rites whose hallowed prayers still served their own time. The students decided that these were too heavy and ornate a brocade to speak of Andy. It was a mature decision – though not one of the committee of three boys and two girls was yet seventeen. They wished instead to tell his stories.

The teacher and the priest understood that they were in the midst of 'the tears of things' and accepted intuitively that silence was their shared role. They listened as five young people tried to shape a liturgy which whispered of the integrity of Andrew Smith's life. A rite emerged seeking to span the thin space between time and no time. Its myths bequeathed to the students a space in which the death from leukaemia of their geography teacher could be contemplated. Its images took words from their place to no place, and reminded them of the uniqueness of this brief career spent wholly at Woodfleet Comprehensive School.* His death at twenty-eight was an intimation that each life is an enigma. And it seemed to be this thought which uncovered a path for them.

They each remembered his haunting insistence that a dream can be the highest point of a life. So this would be the focus of their liturgy – Andy's dreams for them and for all his pupils as they moved towards the millennium. It must be a vision of what he strove for and what they might become. Beginning to discuss his idea it was obvious they needed to integrate three themes:

> he had always pressed them to think globally and act locally. So their first theme would be *the earth and its place in the universe*,

> he had made them laugh as he told them of a Bedouin he met who wore Levis beneath his traditional robes. So their second theme would be *joy at cultural diversity*,

> he had made them weep within when he had set before them the annual holocaust of fourteen million children dying from preventable diseases. Then he had reminded them of the miracle of who they were and of their task to unclench the fist of not-being from the heart of love. So their third theme would be *the search for the soul of the world and its new life – their life.*

Like a poem, a liturgy is a form which embraces vision. So the stories these five young people told their fellow pupils about Andy were about a man and his gods. Their half-hour liturgy was a crucible for transformation, for his vision enshrined values which encouraged a response through action and attitude. Five students then, on a warm and still July morning, tried to express for hundreds of their peers what begins before all words and ends beyond them. Perhaps it is true that we know ourselves in our mortality. This seems to be the case with the students who composed their liturgy for a popular school teacher and then planted a small bed of wild strawberries in the school grounds in his memory.

The paths and the time of this world I cannot escape.
They offer an infinite landscape of possibilities.
So let me plant seed where I happen to be.
Let me hope for a harvest from them,
Though it be beyond the span of my life.

Life is a journey which is older than thought,
and some deeper than death.
Its possibilities – which are my possibilities – are
bequeathed by others.
They are re-inscribed as tasks for my energy and thought when
their energy and thought has moved away.
I vow to commit myself to my own possibilities.
(From *A Rite for Andrew Smith*)

Derek H Webster
England

* *The incident is true: the name is fictitious.*

Unconditional Love

Wisdom is calling us
to cancel debt
to risk in faith
to give
unconditional love.

Wisdom whispers
in the rubbish dumps
of South America,
in the arid wastes

of suburban jungles,
in the gay bars
and the desolate home.
Wisdom whispers words of comfort
words of hope.

Spirit of Wisdom,
breath of God
awaken in us
understanding and forgiveness
insight and commitment
as we try to follow
in the footsteps
of Jesus.

Kate McIlhagga
England

Wisdom Without Compassion

Wisdom
without compassion
is the worst form
of ignorance;
for it robs the world
of its humanity
and of its
Godliness

Susan Hardwick
England

Wisdom Is Calling

I hear you calling
 in the whisper of the wind
 in the rising sap of the trees
 in the storm-waves of the sea
  and the reddening of the earth.

I hear you calling
 in the summons of the drum
 in the buzz of the shopping-mall
 in the protest meeting's march
  and the rage of the oppressed.

I hear you calling
 in the coursing of my blood
 in the singing of my heart
 in the silence of my soul
  and the tears that scald the night.

  Yes, I hear you!
  I hear you unfolding.
  I hear you laughing.
  I hear your lament.
  Wisdom is coming!
  Listen! Listen!
  What does she say?

'I undergird creation in the dance of the Earth:
 Step more gently.
 Attend to all that is.
 Celebrate what this world might become
  in the vibrant hands of God!

'I beckon all into the community of love:
 Hear one another's stories.
 Seek to understand the hurts.

Walk often in your neighbour's shoes.
Be the healing hands of Christ!

'I am the grail of every questing soul:
Simplify your living.
Run barefoot: be poor.
Be profligate in sharing the gifts
which the Spirit pours into waiting hands.'

Wisdom is calling
to me and to you.
'This is the hour of opportunity:
"Ephphatha"! Open up!'
What might we hear?
How might we be led?
Where might the wind be blowing now?

Kate Compston
England

Wisdom Made Known

Praise to the Goddess, Holy Wisdom,
made known in the hidden certainty
which logic would silence or ignore
but which speaks the truth of body and soul.

Praise to the Goddess, Holy Wisdom,
made known in the spells and secrets
passed woman to woman through the ages,
the healing mysteries of life and death.

Praise to the Goddess, Holy Wisdom,
made known in the hard-learned lessons
wrought out of experience, pain and struggle
and the triumphant joy of life renewed.

Praise to the Goddess, Holy Wisdom,
made known in the creative spark
which dares to think differently
and defies convention with its foolish vision.

Praise to the Goddess, Holy Wisdom,
made known in the child-like simplicity
which finds the world a playground for innocence
and delights in all that is made.

Jan Berry
England

Be Near Us, Loving God

Loving God,
we would come close to you
in the worship of our work,
Be near to us and give us Wisdom.

We would speak peace
in the turbulent to and fro of church life,
Be near to us and give us Truth.

We would find joy
in shared faith and fellowship,
Be near to us and give us Love.

We would bear grace
to fractured and frail hearts,
Be near to us and give us Compassion.

We would listen for your voice
at the heart and on the margins,
Be near to us and give us Discernment.

We would do your will,
heart, soul, mind and strength,
Be near to us and embrace us on our Way.

Stephen Brown
England

I Have Heard Your Cries

A Litany of Affirmation for homosexual men and women.

Insert the names of the people concerned and encourage them to prepare their own stanzas appropriate to their experiences.

The Loving, Liberating God,
who holds a rainbow arch
of acceptance and hope
over your downcast head,
Says to you . . .

I have heard your cries;

When you longed to be able to tell someone
yet dared not name a love like yours.

When the one you loved has left you
to look for comfort in another's embrace.

When believers have berated you
as blasphemous and bent.

I have heard your cries;

When thugs have bashed and beaten you
or trampled you with hobnailed words.

When you have wept by an isolated bedside
and been the only one to hold death's hand.

I have heard your cries;

When your longing to parent children
has been dismissed as antisocial or unnatural.

When you have lost your job
your dignity or your self-respect,
because of other people's bigotry or fear.

The Loving, Suffering God,
who was hammered to a cross
Says to you . . .

I will stretch out my arms to defend you;

When the fist of fear is screwed up in rage against you;
When the finger of suspicion is pointed in scorn.

I will reach out my arms to support you;

When it seems like all the world is against you;
When you long to be accepted for what you are.

I will hold out my arms to welcome and embrace you;

When you are sick of being shunned
or told to stick together with your kind.

The Loving, Suffering, Liberating God
Says to you . . .

I will bring you through this sea of trials.
I will hold you in the hollow of my hand.
For you belong with all my people.
I have called you . . .
And my promise stands.

Jean Mortimer
England

Woman Wisdom

Woman Wisdom, Weep for Us.
Forgive us, Woman Wisdom, when we feel unworthy. Challenge us to speak up when the world calls us just home-makers, just secretaries, just nurses, or when we refer to ourselves as 'just' something.
Woman Wisdom, Weep for Us.
Many of us are disadvantaged because we are women. We are the poorest people in the world, we care for the old and the young and often feel that no one cares for us.
Woman Wisdom, Weep for Us.
Our bodies bear children, bear pain and struggles with our culture's ideas of worth and of beauty.
Our bodies age but the years do not take away our need for a loving touch.
Woman Wisdom, Weep for Us.
Woman Wisdom, you who are of God, pardon the sins we confess, affirm us in our faith,
accompany us as we journey.
Woman Wisdom, Awaken Us.
Awaken us, Woman Wisdom, to a new awareness of our bodies, stimulate us to become whatever we desire to be. Challenge us to stand up for ourselves and our sisters.
Woman Wisdom, Awaken Us.
Awaken us, we pray, to our own strengths. Our lives have made us strong for our families and friends, make us strong enough to change the world.
Woman Wisdom, Awaken Us.

Remind us, in your wisdom, that as a journey begins with a single step, any change can begin with any one of us, right where we are, just as we are. Remind us of the power of a single snowflake, the impact of one straw, the value of one life. We know this because of the One we call Jesus, the Christ. *Woman Wisdom, Empower Us.*

Dorothy MacNeill
Canada

Divine Wisdom

A Short Liturgy for Small Groups to take place out of doors.
Soft guitar music can be played in the background.
Let there be lighted candles and a flower arrangement.

Gathering:

At the sound of a gong, people gather in a circle; take off their shoes and with a smile on their faces become aware of the sacredness of the gathering, the place of the Divine Wisdom.

Call to Celebration:

Liturgist:	Listen! Wisdom is calling . . .
People:	**We are listening. Wisdom is calling.**
Liturgist:	Wisdom is calling out in the street and market places.
People:	**Calling loudly at the city gates . . .**
Liturgist:	And wherever people come together.

Song or hymn of praise: Free choice.

Give thanks around the circle:

Invite each person to say briefly what they are thankful for on that day.

Response: Thanks be to God.

Confessing, Reconciling, Renewing:

Put two kinds of flowers on a table in the centre of the gathering. One is fresh, the other is wilted or dried up. Place a bowl of water for cleansing and a white towel beside the bowl.

This is the time to confess sins against God, other people and oneself.

Silence:

Pass around the wilted flower(s) during the silence.

Words of Assurance from the Scriptures: Free choice.

Pass around the fresh flower(s).

Silence and Smiles

Music in the background

Two people at a time come to the table. They dip their fingers in the bowl of water, saying to one another: 'My friend, be strong, God loves You!'

Scripture Reading(s):   Free choice.

Short meditation or exhortation

Closing Prayer/Poem:

Blessed are You, O God,
who gave me the gift of life,
of breath, of a divine image in my womanist body.
Blessed are You, O Gracious and Compassionate Spirit
Who provides wisdom and compassion
to women and men
regardless of colour, creed contexts and choices.

Fill the earth with love and peace,
kindness and wholeness.
Fill my midlife years with passion and compassion.
Empty my heart of unhealthy emotions,
fill it with energizing ones.

Lead us to the paths of righteousness, openness, justice,
spirituality, sensuality and child-like joy!
Open our eyes to see the needy and the exploited.
And when we see them, become advocates for them,
struggling with them.

Bless our dreams, hopes, passions;
Bless our whole beings.
Bless Mother Earth and all that is within her and around
    her.
You are holy, O God. You are love.
You are beyond me and within me. Blessed be Your
    name!

You created us human beings, male and female, in Your
    image.
As we celebrate life in the midst of life's uncertainty,
Bless our lives with shalom and genuine security.

    We are alive! We are struggling. We are hoping!
    We are journeying in the new millennium.
    With fire in our bellies and compassion deep within
    We can change the world. So be it!

Response: Hallelujah, Amen !

Hymn of Commitment: Free choice.

Communal Benediction:

Liturgist: Take courage, sisters and brothers in
                    Christ. Go in Peace!

All:	**Take Wisdom, Experience Wisdom, Go in Wisdom!**
Liturgist:	May the Creator, Redeemer and Sustainer be with you always.
All:	**And also with you. Amen and Amen!**

Elizabeth S Tapia
Philippines

Greenwood of Wisdom

Leader:	When we let the seed fall Into the good soil of our spirits:
All:	**God's greenwood of wisdom rises once again.**
Leader:	When we receive God's banquet welcome Into the void of our uncertainties:
All:	**God's greenwood of wisdom rises once again.**
Leader:	When we gleam like a hillside city Into the sham of hidden tyrannies:
All:	**God's greenwood of wisdom rises once again.**
Leader:	When we bind the wounds of intolerance Into a balm of kind relations:
All:	**God's greenwood of wisdom rises once again.**

Bible Readings:

Proverbs 3:13 – 15, 17 – 18a
James 3:13

Wisdom: The Wisdom of Solomon 7: 22–28

Wisdom's Psalm

We scatter our decisions and days
With trifles and met expectations;
All the while, longing for the blaze and ember
Of bushes set on fire,
Or angels filling the sky with song.

We subdue the expanse of faith
Into prescribed meetings and lethargic institutions;
All the while, yearning for the spark and lustre
Of sunbeams flooding into empty tombs,
Or fiery pillars leading to liberation.

Even so, she is present.
All the wild reasonings of authority
Cannot quell her shining.
Like diamonds of lights
Dancing through the leaves
She beckons us to breathe Life in again.

Keri K Wehlander
Canada

Orthodoxy

Eternal God, re-awaken among Western Christians apprecia-
tion of Orthodoxy's stress on the necessity of union with
Christ, for in very truth apart from him we can do nothing!
May we understand afresh the union-with-Christ emphasis in
Baptism and Holy Communion.

Let us and our Orthodox sisters and brothers sit at each
other's feet, with a common readiness to be led by the Spirit
and to learn from each other new riches and understanding of
the Gospel.

Ian Gillman
Australia

Deep Silence

This was inspired by a visit to Abuna Elias Chacour's grotto. The grotto is a small chapel dug out of the hillside up in Galilee and we had a time of prayer there, which was largely a time of silence. Later in the evening I thanked him for it and he said one sentence, 'It's good to meet God in the deep silence'; and I thought that's what it had been – an encounter with God. I also refer to Christmas Eve in Bethlehem – the Greek Orthodox Christmas Eve, where I went to the Church of the Nativity and saw many ancient churches celebrating the birth of the Prince of Peace; and this song is a tribute to them.

Through the flickering light
Through the incense smell
Through the icon eyes
Through the crucifix sign
Through the bread and wine
Through the touch of time
I found you – I found you.

In a grotto or cave
On the side of a hill
Up in Galilee
By the olive trees
Through Abuna's words
Through the silence that I heard
I found you – I found you.

In the deep, deep silence – you were there
In the deep, deep silence.

It was Christmas Eve
Down in Manger Square
We were in Bethlehem
There were soldiers there
With their weapons of anger
They were mocking the peace
But I found you – I found you

Coptic Christians sang
And the Orthodox too
It was a timeless chant
Dedicated to you
On a night full of colour
On a night full of light
I found you – I found you

In the deep, deep silence – you were there
In the deep, deep silence.

Garth Hewitt
England

Ripples of Prophets

Bertolt Brecht of Germany
Chenua Achibi of Nigeria
Silenced by power
So was Tissa of Sri Lanka.
Tell tales of mitigation of Truth
Speech and freedom to speak
Write what one speaks
To create truth multi-dimensionally.
They surpassed restriction, interdiction and detention
People cannot be silenced though prophets
Be killed.
More sages, gurus and prophets killed
More are born
Replace them perennially
Ripples they become
Life and message.

Shanthi Hettiarachchi
Sri Lanka

Interfaith Dialogue

Interfaith dialogue is neither a miracle nor an overnight project of success. But a process of difficult steps with sensitive issues obviously by those strongly rooted in their faith, willing to enter-into-faiths, different to theirs. Interfaith relations, important and crucial in this land of many faiths, Abrahamic, Indic and Sino.

Each, migrated with traditions, cultures and customs, taken different paths in expressing them in the land they settled.

Such is reality of religions and faiths of contemporary Britain.

Differences make no enemies, though such, in relationships lead the parties to a critical harmony.

It creates an interface for interfaith dialogue.

Dialogue tells that they are different which is the very reason why they should converge further to dialogue.

Dialogue is the way to mutuality, cooperation and solidarity.

Perhaps the only way to be and sensible.

Shanthi Hettiarachchi
Sri Lanka

The Trunch Prayer

To God be glory, praise, honour, merit, power and rejoicing, giving thanks, love that never fails, through endless ages. Let all things say, Amen.

Trunch Church, Norfolk
England

Benefiting from Diversity

I believe that we are all more alike than we are different and that which makes us different is valuable. By the same token, I am convinced about the benefits of diversity. Moreover, valuing diversity is a critically important feature for the development and maintenance of a stable society.

If particular groups conclude that they have no stake in our society they are likely to believe that no matter what they do, however anti-social or unacceptable their behaviour might appear to others, it won't matter, because they have nothing to lose.

Valuing diversity and not simply tolerating it, and striving for greater diversity in our institutions and not simply learning how to manage it, will be the test of our belief in the possibility of achieving benefit from diversity.

Diversity

Simply put, diversity equals differences. Our differences include family background, education, geographical location, marital status, parental status, religious beliefs, work experience etc. as well as age ethnicity, gender, physical abilities or qualities, race, sexual or affectional orientation. For every individual, the mix of differences which we have and are, give us a unique range of attributes and characteristics and a distinctive 'world view' – and more often than not, it's that distinction that makes us valuable.

Diversity Brings Benefits

Benefiting from ethnic diversity is a reality, it is what is, now. It is already the case that we benefit from ethnic diversity. There are doubtless many ways in which we could increase the benefit we get from diversity but it is important to acknowledge the fact that we benefit already.

In a new millennium we should remember that the contributions made to the United Kingdom by countless individuals of African, Asian, Caribbean and Chinese origin during this century go right across the social, economic and artistic and cultural spectrum. It is easy to remark only on the more obvious areas of achievements like sport and entertainment.

Appreciating Diversity

To begin to appreciate the benefit of anything it is necessary to be aware of and acknowledge its existence. In the United Kingdom the largely positive liberal attitude towards visible minorities has tended to focus on similarities between people to the extent that we are often urged to be 'colour blind'. When it comes to benefiting from diversity a colour blind approach is rather like watching television in black and white instead of colour. When viewing in black and white it's very hard to appreciate and benefit from the sometimes striking, sometimes subtle differences in tone and texture.

To begin to benefit fully from diversity we have to recognize, acknowledge and appreciate difference. This might mean having to adjust our (mind)set and bring up the colour. And it will mean facing our past, or is it present? – thinking that different to us, means less than us.

A society which values diversity will be consistent and persistent in its efforts to create greater equality. Such a society will consist of individuals who recognize that they are more alike than they are different. More importantly, they will understand and appreciate the fact that that which makes them different is to be valued.

The Challenge

The challenge for our society is to create and sustain a culture which values human diversity and to develop institutions whose styles and approaches are compatible with that value.

Linbert Spencer
England

God

Your love is like a rock, firm and sure
which never falters.
It's liked a tree planted firm
roots deep and penetrating.
Your love is like a breeze
which coils the earth
and rocks the tree
disturbing all around.
My love is like a bird
carried by the wind
shaded by the tree
and resting on the rock
of you.

Valerie Shedden
England

The Wayward Spirit

Bind up the wayward spirit,
confine her heart
with treasures beyond measure,
call her home.

Become 'with-God',
answer only his voice.
Find in his immortality
your physical entirety.

I sang to the Lord, my words
were sincere but few.
I know only that he hears
the unspoken tune.

I am the wayward spirit
turning away from
a freedom which is love.

Valerie Shedden
England

The Light of the World

in its crown of glory the sun
empties itself – transforms
its self-giving heart into light
          the light of the world
this light-hearted sun
dies and lives again
          in grape and grain
to rise as the bread of life
to shine as the wine of life
          in all its yeasty fullness.

Norm S D Esdon
Canada

Like a Windchime

I raise a prayer to hear
          its crystalline phrases
          clink together
And in their brittle clarity
          the spirit speaks

Norm S D Esdon
Canada

May All Sentient Beings

May all sentient beings,
oneself and others,
find constant happiness through
love and compassion
associated with wisdom.

Tenzin Gyatso
The Fourteenth Dalai Lama
Tibet

Millennium

A thousand ages in Thy sight
    Are like an evening gone.
But in our sight the gulf is wide, a world away.
As we travel through the years
and meet the rifts and tensions
of the turning of an age;
grant us assurance that the years are yours,
that you are new every morning,
steadfast every night,
hopeful every dawn
and patient from beginning to end.

Bernard Thorogood
London/Sydney

For All the Saints

For all the saints who went before us
who have spoken to our hearts and touched us with fire,
we praise you, O God.

For all the saints who live beside us
whose weaknesses and strengths are woven with our own,
we praise you, O God.

For all the saints who live beyond us
who challenge us to change the world with them,
we praise you, O God.

Janet Morley
England

Hymn of Grateful Recall and Renewed Commitment

For all who have enriched our lives,
whom we have loved and known,
for saints alive among us still,
by whom our faith is honed,
we thank you, God, who came and comes
through women, children, men,
to share the highs and lows of life:
God-for-us, now as then.

For all who with disarming love
have led us to explore
the risk of reasoning and doubt,
new realms not known before,
we thank you, God, who came and comes
to free us from our past,
from ghettos of a rigid mind,
from truths unfit to last.

For all whose laughter has unnerved
tradition gone awry,
who with incisive gentleness
pursue each human 'why?',
we thank you, God, who came and comes
to those who probe and ask,
who seek to know the mind of Christ,
and take the church to task.

Now for each other and ourselves
we pray that, healed of fear,
we may re-live the love of Christ,
prepared in hope to err.
Then leave us, God, who comes and goes,
in human-ness to grow,
to care for people, tend the earth,
– the only earth we know!

Fred Kaan
England

In the Meantime

I am Advent
I watch and I wait
I am Mother expecting Child
> December expecting Christmas
> waning century expecting millennium

I savour time between
> blossom and apple
> I-want-you and I-have-you
> the Muse and the music
> I-wonder and I-know

I anticipate
> the rose
> in reddened thorn
> glory to God in the highest
> in the decree from Caesar Augustus
> eternity
> in the pendulum swing

I am Apotheosis of the Meantime
> between the slammed gates of Eden
> and New Jerusalem's opened door
> between the Baptist
> and the Messiah
> between cross taken up
> and stone rolled away
> between earth as it is
> and earth as it can be

I watch and I wait
I am Advent

Norm S D Esdon
Canada

The Holy Trinity for the Twenty-First Century

The Holy Trinity is born anew in us each day of our lives.

In all making: of beds, beer and babes; in all awakening: of music, rhyme and love; in all growing: of maize, pear and pine; in all understanding: of ice, energy and motion; and in all mothering, moulding and manufacturing, lies the breath of the Father. Only He is the creative Source of all.

In all bandaging boils, kissing cuts and sticking tape; in all giving to empty hands, signing cheques for refugees and daring daft stunts for charity; in each nodding 'Yes' for peace, each reconciling arm; in each kiss for a stranger; and in all compassion, mercy and sacrifice, lies the redemptive work of the Son. Only He makes atonement.

In all new toys for Christmas, each advance in philosophy and every novel birthday treat; in every poet's lines, every painter's daubs and each mechanic's solutions; in every movement of love from 'Thank you' to 'O my God!', each flash of fresh thought and all enriching wisdom; in all hopeful ideas and sentiments from the single to the complex, lies the inspiring work of the Spirit. Only It animates.

Christian life begins and ends with the Holy Trinity. The journey to God, which is true life, starts at baptism in the threefold Name. Journey's end is a communion in heaven with the Eternal Three. Between this beginning and end only one thing is important. It is this: that our lives reflect the pattern of the Life of the Holy Trinity in all of our creating, redeeming and energizing.

Derek H Webster
England

Pilgrim God

As you welcome us
may this place be a place of hospitality;

As you call us out
may this place be a place of challenge;

As you heal and strengthen us
may this place be a place of wholeness;

As you send us out
may this place be a place of departure;

that your love may be shared
wherever we pilgrim.

Kate McIlhagga
England

Magnificat for
a New Millennium

Magnificat for a New Millennium

Come! Sing and live a world Magnificat,
the new Millennium with hope embrace.
Now is the time for trust and taking sides:
say 'yes' in love to all the human race.

Reach out in faith to what is still unknown,
each day a first day, every dawn a birth,
new ground for sowing seeds and planting trees,
'Lest we forget' the future of the earth.

Praise all that makes the world a better place:
creative thought, invention and design,
the anvil and the plough of making peace,
of sharing land and shelter, bread and wine.

Risk to become all we are meant to be,
live out tomorrow's destiny today!
Let us unite to keep the dream alive:
a world at peace, the human race at play.

As past and future in the present meet
and we take stock of where we were and are,
may confidence inspire our forward way,
and love with justice be our guiding star.

Come! Sing and live a world Magnificat
for water, soil and air – the mystic trinity
of all that is today, of all that came to be,
created, sent evolving from the void of chaos
to the order of the day . . .

Water

water, giving rise to life, to earth, to birth,
cleansing water, quenching thirst,
streams of water, new beginnings.
Still water – as in lake – yet never still,
cascading from eternity to here;
heart-beating surf, pulsating moon-drawn sway
from oceans' farthest shore
to where you are, I am, with all the world . . .

Cry 'Kyrie' for pride and greed
in poisoned rivers manifest,
for waters, wasted unto death,
for streams imprisoned by prestigious dams;
for dying-crying seas
and oceans giving rise
to children's lives de-formed;
for mines and missiles poised
amid the grave of fish:

Kyrie eleison, Kyrie eleison, Kyrie eleison.

Come! Sing and live a world Magnificat
for water, soil and air – the mystic trinity
of all that is today, of all that came to be,
created, sent evolving from the void of chaos
to the order of the day . . .

Soil

earth-womb, shielding-yielding hope (world
without end!)
cradling ore and food for life,
scene of quest and exploration:
atomic power, the alphabet, the wheel,
technology and healing, music, art.
This island earth, one home for humankind,
where rights and tasks are shared
like bread and wine, enough for everyone . . .

Cry 'Kyrie' for pride and greed:
the politics of selfish gain,
oppressing those without a voice;
abuse of skills, inventiveness and power.
Cry for the death of trees,
research seduced for ill,
to cripple and to kill;
for arms refined and aimed
at ending life and birth:

Kyrie eleison, Kyrie eleison, Kyrie eleison.

Come! Sing and live a world Magnificat
for water, soil and air – the mystic trinity
of all that is today, of all that came to be,
created, sent evolving from the void of chaos
to the order of the day . . .

Air

oxygen, sustaining life, food for the heart,
air for breathing, yet unbound,
air pronouncing birds and fragrance,
day's backcloth for dialogue of souls,
blue playing-field for vapour trails and clouds,
for longings taking flight to see the world,
where love awaits, work is,
feet walk on air in freedom and delight . . .

Cry 'Kyrie' for pride and greed,
the shredding of the atmosphere
and lead that lines our city streets;
our peaceful valleys torn by screams of war –
dark bombers in the skies.
Shed tears for acrid smoke,
dioxin down the road,
as acid drizzle falls
on radio-active grass:

Kyrie eleison, Kyrie eleison, Kyrie eleison.

Come! Sing and live a world Magnificat
for water, soil and air – the mystic trinity
of all that is today, of all that came to be,
created, sent evolving from the void of chaos
to the order of the day . . .

So let every town and city,
every hamlet, every home
humbly, strongly meet the challenge
of the new millennium.

Let us bless the world around us
in our ways of thought and speech,
by our actions, our awareness
of the needs of all and each.

Reaching out to others, let us
vow to heal the hurt of earth,
seek the welfare of the nations,
human dignity and worth:

And now, my friends: all that is true,
all that is noble, all that is just and pure,
all that is loveable and attractive,
whatever is excellent and admirable –
fill your thoughts with these things . . .
and always be thankful!

Philippians 4:8 . . . Colossians 3:15

The Present Tense

Thank you, O God, for the time that is now,
for all the newness your minutes allow;
keep us alert with your presence of mind
to fears and longings that move humankind.

Thank you, O God, for the time that is past,
for all the values and thoughts that will last.
May we all stagnant tradition ignore,
leaving behind things that matter no more.

Thank you for hopes of the day that will come,
for all the change that will happen in time;
God! for the future our spirits prepare,
hallow our doubts and redeem us from fear.

Make us afraid of the thoughts that delay,
faithful in all the affairs of today;
keep us, Creator, from playing it safe,
thank you that now is the time of our life!

Fred Kaan
England

Index of Authors

Aboriginal People, Australia 241
Adam, David 305
Arthurton, Margot 21, 77, 114, 162, 194, 249, 251, 273

Babu, Jeevan 186
Barclay, Glenn Jetta 236, 345
Becher, Richard 117, 309
Bennett, Miriam 37, 300, 325
Berry, Jan 7, 203, 226, 277, 301, 360
Best, Marion 142
Boyle, Patricia 100
Brewerton, Sarah 278, 280
Brown, John P 235
Brown, Stephen 14, 105, 119, 147, 208, 243, 281, 361
Brown, Sue 211
Bryant, Audrey 35

Catholic Fund for Overseas Development 63
Christian Conference of Asia, Hong Kong 219, 227
Clutterbuck, Diane 5
Collinson, Nigel 8, 39, 72, 272, 324, 326
Comaish, Peter 78, 274, 282
Commin, Bob 146, 341, 344
Compston, Kate 244, 321, 359
Cox, Ed 12, 68, 73, 122, 255, 310
'Crosspoints', Sri Lanka 58

Dawson, Roger 92
de Madariaga, Salvador 215
del Rosario, Romeo L 320
Deng, Bartholomayo Bol-Mawut 210
Dobson, Marjorie 106, 124, 143, 223, 238, 292
Domestic worker, Hong Kong 224
Dove, Anthea 183
Downing, F Gerald 335
Duncan, Ruth 172, 173

Esdon, Norm S D 15, 18, 38, 80, 99, 157, 164, 206, 253, 257, 259, 376, 379

Fernández-Calienes, Rául 265
Freier, Philip 130, 245, 348, 349

Gibson, Colin 24, 213
Gillman, Harvey 148
Gillman, Ian 75, 151, 240, 369
Gledhill, Ruth 165
Gnanadason, Aruna 40
Gyatso, Tenzin – Fourteenth Dalai Lama 71, 376

Hardwick, Susan 48, 131, 178, 207, 232, 266, 286, 358
Harvey, Ruth 161, 261
Haslam, David 216, 217

Hauptkirche St Michaelis, Hamburg, Germany 327
Henderson, Stewart 51
Hettiarachchi, Shanthi 34, 78, 371, 372
Hewitt, Garth 25, 59, 133, 370
Howard, Les A 32, 167, 256
Hunt, Gillian 54
Hunt, John 60

Jacob, P 263
Janda, Clement 198
Jenkins, Jill 16
Johansen-Berg, John 9, 69, 120, 132, 159, 199, 247, 274, 289, 297, 308, 312, 328, 330, 331
Johnston, Heather 13, 27, 342

Kaan, Fred 107, 231, 378, 385
Kirkpatrick, Bill 149, 314

Lebaka-Ketshabile, Libuseng 313
Lees, Janet 95, 96, 139, 170, 171, 174
Lekheng, Uwamaholo 246
Lewin, Ann 5, 307
Litherland, Alan 263

Ma, Winnie 151
McCoy, Michael 50
McIlhagga, Kate 52, 97, 357, 381
Maclean, Katrina 18
McMullen, Vin 60
MacNeill, Dorothy 49, 260, 364
McRae-McMahon, Dorothy 49, 261, 318
Marsh, Pat 94, 98, 145, 257, 299
Mayland, Jean 16, 104, 222
Mead, Joy 36, 176, 196, 332
Millar, Peter W 45
Morley, Janet 377
Morris, Anne 118

Mortimer, Jean 362
Murray, Shirley Erena 185, 197, 311

National Council of Churches, India 190
Netto, Anil 209
Nichols, Alan 22, 220

Obbard, Elizabeth Ruth 168

Parker, Lenore 347
Pattel-Gray, Anne 187
Pearce, Brian Louis 53
Pencavel, Heather 20, 66, 130, 205
Phillips, Marlene 62
Picardal, Amado L 318
Pickard, Jan Sutch 155
Pirouet, Louise 212, 215
Plant, Stephen 84
Polkinghorne, John 269
Prance, Sir Ghillean T 3
Pulikal, Joseph 102

Ranaivoson, Naliranto 57, 202
Rebello, Cedric 86
Richmond, Helen 81
Romero, Oscar 236
Ruddock, Edgar 65, 143, 252

St Michael's Parish, Liverpool 57
Schwab, Betty Lynn 11, 49, 113, 127, 158, 204, 233, 271, 293, 295
Shakir, Beulah 192, 350
Shedden, Valerie 82, 375
Shomanah, Musa W Dube 153
Source Unknown, Cambodia 224
Source Unknown, Sri Lanka 225
Source Unknown, Traditional Jewish story 262

Spencer, Linbert 372
Spouge, Jenny 37, 62, 114, 225, 274, 291
Stacey, Viv 163
Stedman, Alison 115, 116
Steel, Lesley K 128, 175

Tapia, Elizabeth S 88, 89, 365
Taylor, Michael 111
Terrell, Vicki 144
Thomas, Beena 263
Thorogood, Bernard 23, 189, 201, 377
Trow, Peter 29, 102, 253, 259, 264
Trunch Church, Norfolk, England 372
Tuck, Duncan L 287
Turcott, Betty Radford 6, 242, 344

Uniting Church in Australia 30, 33, 76, 125, 129, 134, 150, 191, 219

ye Kaung, Naing 245

Wallace, Martin 71, 334, 339
Wang, Jen-wen 316
Warwicker, Bob 17, 271, 283, 291, 302
Wass, Rosemary 90
Webster, Derek H 67, 169, 307, 323, 339, 340, 341, 343, 350, 352, 353, 380
Webster, Rowena 55
Wehlander, Keri K 14, 28, 123, 126, 135, 141, 325, 368
Wiggett, Harry 19

Zainga, Goodwin 79

Index of Titles/First lines

A New Heaven and a New Earth

A Restless Star 16

All Creation Is Yours 8

An Urban Version of Isaiah 35 20

Back to Earth 18

Cathedral 19

Climate Change 30

Creation Song 7

Daybreak 5

Ecology-Theology 35

Enchantment in the Suburbs 22

For the Man and for the Woman 24

Fulfilment 23

God Give Me a Dream 17

I Saw a New Heaven and a New Earth 10

Intricate Wonders 14

Marking the Swallow's Fall 15

Mining and the Environment 33

Multi-coloured Glory 14

Next Year There Will Be No Nest 29

Pilgrim Bread 36

Rays of Hope 12

Rivers, Mountains and Trees 25

Simplistic? 21

Spirit of Creation 5

Spirit of God 6

Stargazing 16

Striding Out 37

The Land Is Holy 9

The Myth of Farming 32

Theoland 34

They Heal Their Bodies . . . They Heal the Earth 40

Tread Gently 37

Tree of Life 28

Trees 27

Trinity of Earth, Sky and Sea 13

We Are Responsible . . . 3

We Recycle 38

What Have We Done? 18

Your World 39

Love Is Made Perfect In Us . . .

A Creed of Commitment 63

A Malagasy Story 57

A New Village? 60

A Work of Love 45

An Ordinary Day 82

And What Is Love? 92

Birthing a New Creation 81

Bread and Wine 80

Children in the New Millennium 88

Christian People Sing Together 106

Community of Love 59

Confession 96

For Personal Meditation 71

God of Town and Village 62

I Saw You, Jesus 102

Illumined By Love 62

Inside Out 77

Into Egypt 97

Jesus Falls the First Time 86

Keziah, My Goddaughter 84

Lamentation and Dreams of a Streetchild 89

Litany for Children 90

Living in Society 71

Living with People of Other Faiths 76

Love Is Like Yeast 102

Love Is Made Perfect In Us 49

Love Thy Neighbour? 58

Marginal God 105

Monday Afternoon at the Job Centre 66

Move Us On 51

Mr Vasapa 68

Multi-cultural Living 75

My Name Is Goodness 100

Neighbours 67

On Entering a Manila Slum 60

On the Edge 52

One Family 69

One Village 78

Praise Be to God! 49

Prayer Walk 55

Proclaim Jubilee 57

Racism 78

Seeing Christ 48

Sing Me Your Bethlehem 99

Street Cred. 65

Sunday Night, after 'Phone Calls 54

Taking the Roof Off 95

The Good Samaritan 98

The Promised Community 104

Transform Us 50

Voice-over God, Our Lover and Creator 107

Waves of Change 72

We Are All Alone 53

What Have They Done? 79

You Ask Us to Wait 73

You've Got to Be Joking Me 94

Proclaim Jubilee!

A Growing Opportunity 111

A Loan to Die 117

A Penny for Your Thoughts 126

A Prayer for Economic Justice 130

A Vision of Shalom 113

Baa-baa . . . Barmy World 122

Bringing His Justice 128

Coin Considerations 123

Forgive Us Our Debts 119

God of Rice and Chapatti 114

Grace 114

Grant a Release 120

In the Beginning Was Globalization . . . 130

Jubilee and Celebrations 134

Living with the New Economic Order 129

Paddy Fields 116

Prayer of Confession 127

Shake the Foundations 135

The Golden Idol 125

The Homeworker 118

The Millennium Dream 131

The Ploughman 115

The Time for Jubilee 133

The Use of Money 124

To Blossom Like the Rose 132

Whole Person, Whole Community, Whole World

A Few Hesitant Steps 173

A Litany of Thanks 141

A Prayer for Abundant Life 142

All One in Christ Jesus 150

Beatitudes for a Place of Healing 174

Being There 145

Beyond: A Love Poem 161

Disability: Gift and Struggle 144

Dreaming Denied? 153

Forever Creating 167

Happy Are Those Who Are Merciful to Others 158

Head-injured Survivors and Their Carers 171

Hope Not Frustration . . . 172

Just Being Human 155

Let Nothing Be Lost 178

Light 162

Monday's Angel 143

On Baby Milk 170

Prayer of the Barren Woman 168

Rainbow 148

Sensitive God 143

Sexuality 151

Sharing in the Work of Healing 139

Spiders and Eternity 169

Stewardship of Self 164

The Dream of Wholeness 146

The Evolving Mystery 149

The Gatherer 163

The Kiss of Life 147

Turn to Me and I Will Heal You 175

What Peter Knew . . . 176

Wholeness 159

Words 165

Words With Mother 151

Wrestling the Unnamed to a Blessing 157

Become People for Justice and Joy

A Dalit's Cry 186

A Human Being 202

A New Dawn 199

A Place at the Table 185

A Prayer for Homeless People 205

Aboriginal Land Rights 189

Become the Church for the Stranger 224

Children 201

Don't Call Me a Stranger: The Cry of a Migrant 190

For a Young Man and His Mothers 204

For Oppressed People 191

Gypsies Are Your Creation 212

Home Is Home and Bush Is Bush 210

I Am a Southern Sudanese 198

I Am Dirty 211

Jean's Story 216

Let Justice Flow . . . 183

Let There Be Shalom 227

Our Lady of the Refugees 193

Our Responsibility 207

Pray for People 192

Prayers for Detained Asylum Seekers 215

Prisoners of Conscience 214

Refugee 194

Share Together 219

She Had Come from Afar 196

So Cold 208

Speak to Me in the Body 226

Stranger, Standing at My Door 197

Sunday Morning 206

The Newspapers Say It All . . . 222

The Ogunwobi Family 217

The Slaughter of the Innocents 203

The Squatters' Prayer 209

Thoughts 225

Uprising Is Christianity 220

Voices of the Indigenous People 187

We Are Called to Be the Church 227

Who Are These Strangers? 213

Who's Right? 223

The Whereabouts of Peace

A Calling to Faith 260

A Prayer for Our Pilgrimage 264

A Prayer for the Travellers 265

A Prayer of Peace 243

An Ordinary Man 249

At the Ceasefire 251

At Times of Trouble or Catastrophe 244

Being on the Side of the Angels 231

Blessed Are the People Who . . . 263

Cross Makers 255

Everyone Will Live In Peace 233

Getting My Pages Straight 259

God of Our Contemporaries 253

God of Peace 235

Hope for Rwanda 247

I AM 257

I Want to Soar High 263

In the Face of Violence and Terrorism 245

Kindness 263

Let There Be Peace 242

Living with Self and Others 256

Nothing Else 262

Patience 261

Peace is . . . 236

Peacemakers' Prayer 253

Peniel 259

Pitch-dark World 245

Reconciliation 240

Reconciliation Prayer for Australia 241

Repentance 238

Repentance Speaks Simply 236

Shalom 266

Spirit of Peace 232

Support My Dreams 246

Sweet Peace 251

The Tangled Thicket 257

Wash Hands – Be Clean? 252

Light for the World

A Contribution of Vital Significance 269

A Guided Rocket 289

A Reflection on Parenthood 278

An Errant Engineer 274

Basic Questions 286

Celebrate Wisely 272

Communication 299

Connections 300

Copyrighting Genes . . . 274

Drawing Energy 302

For Benjamin 280

God Help Us to Use Technology Right 283

God of Computer and Test-tube 273

God of Money and Machine 291

Healing in Our Computer Age 295

Heaven and Earth 281

Jubilee Hymn 301

Let Your True Light Shine 271

Newborn 273

Obsession 291

Progress 292

Space 282

Thanksgiving for Our Computer Age 293

The Barrier 287

The Fruit of Knowledge 277

The Web 297

There Is One Voice That Matters 302

Widen Our Vision 286

You Are Like a Light for the Whole World 271

Wisdom is Calling

A Highway Shall Be There 326

A Litany for the Millennium 335

A Morning Psalm 307

A Mother's Prayer 344

A Prayer for Australia 348

A Prayer for Twenty-Four Hours 342

A Psalm of Salvation 341

A Spirituality for Women 313

A Thanksgiving for Australia 347

An Evening Psalm 343

An Increasing Hunger 314

Ash Wednesday Liturgy 349

Be Near Us, Loving God 361

Becoming a Child 340

Benefiting from Diversity 372

Christ Is Living in Our World 309

Circles 328

Deep Silence 370

Divine Wisdom 365

Entrance 307

For All the Saints 377

God 375

God of All Love 332

Good Friday 350

Greenwood of Wisdom 368

Homemakers 344

Hymn for the Millennium 310

Hymn of Grateful Recall and Renewed Commitment 378

I Have Heard Your Cries 362

I Rise to This Day 341

Incarnation 339

In the Meantime 379

Interfaith Dialogue 372

Is This God Really Wise? 318

Jubilee Song 310

Like a Windchime 376

Listen! 305

Litany of the Lord's Prayer 350

Living on the Edge 334

Lord, Teach Us 324

May All Sentient Beings 376

Millennium 377

New Light 325

On the Third Day 331

Orthodoxy 369

Pilgrim God 381

Prayer and Mission 339

Prayer of an Old Chief 316

Ripples of Prophets 371

Spirituality 312

Stillness 327

The Holy Trinity for the Twenty-First Century 380

The Light of the World 376

The Lord's Prayer – *Four Variations* 352

The Poet and the Elder 323

The Sound of God 325

The Trunch Prayer 372

The View from the Mountain 318

The Water of Life 321

The Wayward Spirit 375

These I Want 320

True Riches 330

Unconditional Love 357

Wisdom, Grace and Favour 345

Wisdom Is Calling 359

Wisdom Made Known 360

Wisdom Without Compassion 358

Wild Strawberries 355

With Drums and Trumpets 308

Woman Wisdom 364

Magnificat for a New Millennium

Magnificat for a New Millennium 385

Acknowledgements

* Text can be copied for use in worship on a one-off, non-commercial basis using this acknowledgement.

** Used by permission

A New Heaven and a New Earth . . .

A Restless Star, © Jill Jenkins.

All Creation Is Yours, © Rev Nigel Collinson.

An Urban Version of Isaiah 35, © Heather Pencavel.

Back to Earth, © Norm S. D. Esdon.

Cathedral, © Harry Wiggett.

Climate Change, © Uniting Church in Australia, National Commission for Mission.

Creation Song, © Jan Berry.

Daybreak, © Ann Lewin.

Ecology-Theology, © Audrey Bryant.

Enchantment in the Suburbs, © Alan Nichols.

For the Man and for the Woman, Colin Gibson. © Hope Publishing Company, administered by Copy Care, PO Box 77, Hailsham, BN27 3EF. **

Fulfilment, © Bernard Thorogood. **

God Give Me a Dream, © Bob Warwicker.

I Saw a New Heaven and a New Earth, © Betty Lynn Schwab.

Intricate Wonders, © The United Church Publishing House,
  from *Circles of Grace* by Keri K. Wehlander, 1998,
  pages 30–31. **

Marking the Swallow's Fall, © Norm S. D. Esdon.

Mining and the Environment, © Uniting Church in Australia,
  National Commission for Mission.

Multi-coloured Glory, © Stephen Brown.

Next Year There Will Be No Nest, © Peter Trow. *

Pilgrim Bread, © Joy Mead.

Rays of Hope, © Ed Cox.

Rivers, Mountains and Trees, © Garth Hewitt, Christian Aid,
  Regional Coordinator, London and the South East.

Simplistic? © Margot Arthurton.

Spirit of Creation, © Diane Clutterbuck.

Spirit of God, © Betty Radford Turcott. **

Stargazing, © Jean Mayland.

Striding Out, © Miriam Bennett.

The Land Is Holy, © John Johansen-Berg, Founder and Leader of
  the Community for Reconciliation.

The Myth of Farming, © Les A. Howard.

Theoland, © Shanthi Hettiarachchi, Interfaith Coordinator for the
  Grassroots programme based in Luton, UK.

They Heal Their Bodies . . . They Heal the Earth, © Aruna
  Gnanadason.

Tread Gently, © Jenny Spouge. *

Tree of Life, © The United Church Publishing House, from *Joy is our
  Banquet*, by Keri K. Wehlander, 1996, pages 81–82, 84. **

Trees, © Heather Johnston.

Trinity of Earth, Sky and Sea, © Heather Johnston.

We Are Responsible . . . , © Professor Sir Ghillean T. Prance FRS, Director, Royal Botanic Gardens, Kew, UK, 1998.

We Recycle, © Norm S. D. Esdon.

What Have We Done? © Katrina Maclean.

Your World, © Rev Nigel Collinson.

Love Is Made Perfect In Us . . .

A Creed of Commitment, © Catholic Fund for Overseas Development, London, UK.

A Malagasy Story, © Naliranto Ranaivoson.

A New Village? © John Hunt.

A Work of Love, © Peter Millar, Iona Abbey, 1998.

An Ordinary Day, © Valerie Shedden.

And What Is Love? © The Very Reverend Roger Dawson.

Birthing a New Creation, © Helen Richmond, Minister of the Uniting Church in Australia and Methodist Tutor in Mission Studies, United College of the Ascension, Birmingham UK.

Bread and Wine, © Norm S. D. Esdon.

Children in the New Millennium, © Elizabeth S. Tapia.

Christian People Sing Together, © Marjorie Dobson.

'Community', preface to A Work of Love by Peter Millar (see above), taken from *The Sky is Red* by Kenneth Leech, published and © 1997 by Darton, Longman and Todd Ltd and used in the UK and Commonwealth by permission of the publishers, and by Darley Anderson Books outside the UK and Commonwealth.

Community of Love, © Garth Hewitt, Christian Aid Regional Coordinator, London and the South East.

Confession, © Janet Lees, an ordained minister of the United Reformed Church in the UK.

God of Town and Village, © Jenny Spouge. *

I Saw You, Jesus, © Joseph Pulikal sdb from *I Saw You Jesus* published by Kristu Jyoti Publications, Bangalore, India. **

Illumined By Love, © Marlene Phillips.

Inside Out, © Margot Arthurton.

Into Egypt, © Kate McIlhagga.

Jesus Falls the First Time, © Cedric Rebello SJ from *Up a Million Calvaries*, published by Asia Trading Corporation, Bangalore, India.

Keziah, My Goddaughter, © Stephen Plant.

Lamentation and Dreams of a Streetchild, © Elizabeth S. Tapia.

Litany for Children, © Rosemary Wass.

Living in Society, © Tenzin Gyatso, from *Love, Kindness and Human Responsibility*, Paljor Publications, India; ** followed by one-liners for Personal Meditation, © The Venerable Martin Wallace, Archdeacon of Colchester, UK.

Living with People of Other Faiths, © Uniting Church in Australia, National Commission for Mission.

Love Is Like Yeast, © Peter Trow. *

Love Is Made Perfect In Us, © Betty Lynn Schwab.

Love Thy Neighbour,? © *Crosspoints*, Sri Lanka. **

Marginal God, © Stephen Brown.

Monday Afternoon at the Job Centre, © Heather Pencavel.

Move Us On, © Stewart Henderson, September 1997. Commissioned by BBC 1 TV and reproduced with permission. This poem was first broadcast on *First Light* the day after the funeral of Diana, Princess of Wales.

Mr Vasapa, © Ed Cox.

Multi-cultural Living, © Ian Gillman.

My Name Is Goodness, Patricia Boyle, a Dominican Sister and staff member of the Pastoral Institute, Multan, Pakistan. © *In God's Image*. **

Neighbours, © Derek H. Webster. *

On Entering a Manila Slum, © Vin McMullen.

On the Edge, © Kate McIlhagga.

One Family, © John Johansen-Berg, Founder and Leader of the Community for Reconciliation.

One Village, © Shanthi Hettiarachchi, Interfaith Coordinator for the Grassroots programme based in Luton, UK.

Praise Be to God!, © Dorothy McRae-McMahon, Uniting Church in Australia. **

Prayer Walk, © Rowena Webster.

Proclaim Jubilee, composed by the people of St Michael's Church, West Derby Road, Liverpool, UK. **

Racism, © Peter Comaish.

Seeing Christ, © Rev Susan Hardwick, an Anglican priest and author of a number of books.

Sing Me Your Bethlehem, © Norm S. D. Esdon.

Street Cred., © Edgar Ruddock.

Sunday Night, after 'Phone Calls, © Gillian Hunt, Australia.

Taking the Roof Off, © Janet Lees, an ordained minister of the United Reformed Church in the UK.

The Good Samaritan, © Pat Marsh.

The Promised Community, © Jean Mayland.

Transform Us, © Michael McCoy.

Voice-over God, Our Lover and Creator, © Fred Kaan. Commissioned by and written for the 23rd General Council of the World Alliance of Reformed Churches, Debrecen, Hungary, 1997.

Waves of Change, © Rev Nigel Collinson from *The Land of Unlikeness*, published by Foundery Press.

We Are All Alone, © Brian Louis Pearce from *Battersea Pete*, published by Magwood.

What Have They Done? © Goodwin Zainga.

You Ask Us to Wait, © Ed Cox.

You've Got to Be Joking Me, © Pat Marsh.

Proclaim Jubilee!

A Growing Opportunity, © Michael Taylor, OBE, former Director, Christian Aid. Currently, President and Chief Executive of Selly Oak Colleges, Birmingham, UK.

A Loan to Die, © Richard Becher.

A Penny for Your Thoughts, © The United Church Publishing House, from *Joy is our Banquet*, by Keri K. Wehlander, 1996, pages 98–99. **

A Prayer for Economic Justice, © Rev Philip Freier.

A Vision of Shalom, © Betty Lynn Schwab.

Baa-baa . . . Barmy World, © Ed Cox.

Bringing His Justice, © Lesley K. Steel.

Coin Considerations, © The United Church Publishing House, from *Joy is our Banquet*, by Keri K. Wehlander, 1996, pages 95–96. **

Forgive Us Our Debts, © Stephen Brown.

God of Rice and Chapatti, © Jenny Spouge. *

Grace, © Margot Arthurton.

Grant a Release, © John Johansen-Berg, Founder and Leader of the Community for Reconciliation.

In the Beginning Was Globalization . . ., © Heather Pencavel.

Jubilee and Celebrations, © Uniting Church in Australia, National Commission for Mission.

Living with the New Economic Order, © Uniting Church in Australia, National Commission for Mission.

Paddy Fields, © Alison Stedman.

Prayer of Confession, © Betty Lynn Schwab.

Shake the Foundations, © The United Church Publishing House, from *Circles of Grace*, by Keri K. Wehlander, 1998, pages 44–47. **

The Golden Idol, © Uniting Church in Australia, National Commission for Mission.

The Homeworker, © Anne Morris.

The Millennium Dream, © Rev Susan Hardwick, an Anglican priest and author of a number of books.

The Ploughman, © Alison Stedman.

The Time for Jubilee, © Garth Hewitt, Christian Aid, Regional Coordinator, London and the South East.

The Use of Money, © Marjorie Dobson.

To Blossom Like the Rose, © John Johansen-Berg, Founder and Leader of the Community for Reconciliation.

Whole Person, Whole Community, Whole World

A Few Hesitant Steps, © Samuha, Bangalore, India. Contact at 44 Delfcroft, Ware, Herts, SG12 0BH, UK.

A Litany of Thanks, © The United Church Publishing House, from *Joy is our Banquet*, by Keri K. Wehlander, 1996, pages 93–94. **

A Prayer for Abundant Life, © Marion Best.

All One in Christ Jesus, © Uniting Church in Australia, National Commission for Mission.

Beatitudes for a Place of Healing, © Janet Lees, an ordained minister of the United Reformed Church in the UK.

Being There, © Pat Marsh.

Beyond: A Love Poem, © Ruth Harvey, Director, Ecumenical Spirituality Project, Council of Churches for Britain and Ireland.

Disability: Gift and Struggle, © Vicki Terrell.

Dreaming Denied? © Musa W. Dube Shomanah.

Forever Creating, © Les A. Howard.

What Peter Knew . . ., © Joy Mead.

Wholeness, © John Johansen-Berg, Founder and Leader of the Community for Reconciliation.

Words, © Ruth Gledhill.

Words With Mother, Winnie Ma, © *In God's Image*. **

Wrestling the Unnamed to a Blessing, © Norm S. D. Esdon.

Become People for Justice and Joy

A Dalit's Cry, Jeevan Babu. From *People's Reporter*, Bangalore, India. Permission sought.

A Human Being, © Naliranto Ranaivoson.

A New Dawn, © John Johansen-Berg, Founder and Leader of the Fellowship for Reconciliation.

A Place at the Table, Shirley Erena Murray. © 1998 Hope Publishing Company, administered by Copy Care, PO Box 77, Hailsham, BN27 3EF, UK. **

A Prayer for Homeless People, © Heather Pencavel.

Aboriginal Land Rights, © Bernard Thorogood. **

Become the Church for the Stranger, from *Internally Displaced Communities and the Challenge to the Churches in Asia*, Christian Conference of Asia 1996.

Children, © Bernard Thorogood. **

Don't Call Me a Stranger: The Cry of a Migrant, © *National Council of Churches Review*, India. **

For a Young Man and His Mothers, © Betty Lynn Schwab.

For Oppressed People, © Uniting Church in Australia, National Commission for Mission.

Gypsies Are Your Creation, © Louise Pirouet.

Home Is Home and Bush Is Bush, © Bartholomayo Bol-Mawut, Deng, Kenya.

I Am a Southern Sudanese, © Rev Canon Clement Janda.

I Am Dirty, © Sue Brown.

Jean's Story, © David Haslam.

Let Justice Flow . . ., © Anthea Dove.

Let There Be Shalom, © Christian Conference of Asia, Hong Kong.

Our Lady of the Refugees, Source Unknown.

Our Responsibility, © Rev Susan Hardwick, an Anglican priest and
    author of a number of books.

Pray for People, Thanks to Mrs Beulah Shakir, Editor/Compiler ©
    In God's Image. **

Prayers for Detained Asylum Seekers, 1) Anonymous and 2) ©
    Louise Pirouet.

Prisoners of Conscience, © Salvador de Madariaga, Source
    unknown.

Refugee, © Margot Arthurton.

Share Together, © Christian Conference of Asia, Hong Kong and
    Uniting Church in Australia. From *Becoming the Church of the
    Stranger*, 1997. **

She Had Come from Afar, © Joy Mead.

So Cold, © Stephen Brown.

Speak to Me in the Body, © Jan Berry.

Stranger, Standing at My Door, Shirley Erena Murray. © Hope
    Publishing Company, administered by Copy Care, PO Box 77,
    Hailsham, BN27 3EF, UK. **

Sunday Morning, © Norm S. D. Esdon.

The Newspapers Say It All . . ., © Jean Mayland.

The Ogunwobi Family, © David Haslam.

The Slaughter of the Innocents, © Jan Berry.

The Squatters' Prayer, © Anil Netto, Aliran, Malaysia.

Thoughts, © Jenny Spouge. *

Uprising Is Christianity, © Alan Nichols.

Voices of the Indigenous People, © Anne Pattel-Gray.

We Are Called to Be the Church, © Christian Conference of Asia, Hong Kong. From *Becoming the Church of the Stranger*, 1997. **

Who Are These Strangers? Colin Gibson. © Hope Publishing Company, administered by Copy Care, PO Box 77, Hailsham, BN27 3EF, UK. **

Who's Right?, © Marjorie Dobson.

The Whereabouts of Peace

A Calling to Faith, © Dorothy McRae-McMahon, Uniting Church in Australia. **

A Prayer for Our Pilgrimage, © Peter Trow.

A Prayer for the Travellers, © Raúl Fernández-Calienes.

A Prayer of Peace, © Stephen Brown.

An Ordinary Man, © Margot Arthurton. Written for the Bosnian Arts Project and sold to raise funds for Medical Aid in the former Yugoslavia.

At the Ceasefire, © Margot Arthurton, as above.

At Times of Trouble or Catastrophe, © Kate Compston.

Being on the Side of the Angels, © Fred Kaan, 1998.

Blessed Are the People Who . . ., P. Jacob from *Continent of Hope* published by © Catholic Fund for Overseas Development. **

Cross Makers, © Ed Cox.

Everyone Will Live In Peace, © Betty Lynn Schwab.

Getting My Pages Straight, © Norm S. D. Esdon.

God of Our Contemporaries, © Peter Trow. *

God of Peace, © John P. Brown, 1997. *

Hope for Rwanda, © John Johansen-Berg, Founder and Leader of the Community for Reconciliation.

I AM, © Norm S. D. Esdon.

I Want to Soar High, © Beena Thomas. Permission sought.

In the Face of Violence and Terrorism, © Rev Philip Freier.

Kindness, © Alan Litherland.

Let There Be Peace, © Betty Radford Turcott. **

Living with Self and Others, © Les A. Howard.

Nothing Else, Traditional Jewish story adapted by Derek H. Webster.

Patience, © Ruth Harvey, Director, Ecumenical Spirituality Project of the Council of Churches for Britain and Ireland.

Peace is . . ., Oscar Romero from *Continent of Hope*, published by © Catholic Fund for Overseas Development. **

Peacemakers' Prayer, © Norm S. D. Esdon.

Peniel, © Peter Trow. *

Pitch-dark World, © Naing ye Kaung.

Reconciliation, © Ian Gillman.

Reconciliation Prayer for Australia, composed by Aboriginal People who formed the Indigenous Theology Working Group 1997.

Repentance, © Marjorie Dobson.

Repentance Speaks Simply, © Glenn Jetta Barclay.

Shalom, © Rev Susan Hardwick, an Anglican priest and author of a number of books.

Spirit of Peace, © Rev Susan Hardwick, as above.

Support My Dreams, © Uwamaholo Lekheng. St Peter's Church, Harold Wood, Essex, UK. **

Sweet Peace, © Margot Arthurton. Written for the Bosnian Arts Project and sold to raise funds for Medical Aid in the former Yugoslavia.

The Tangled Thicket, © Pat Marsh.

The Whereabouts of Peace, © Fred Kaan, 1998.

Wash Hands – Be Clean? © Edgar Ruddock.

Light for the World

A Contribution of Vital Significance, © John Polkinghorne FRS, 1998.

A Guided Rocket, © John Johansen-Berg, Founder and Leader of the Community for Reconciliation.

A Reflection on Parenthood, © Rev Sarah Brewerton, a minister of the United Reformed Church in the UK and part-time hospital chaplain to the Central Manchester Healthcare Trust, UK.

An Errant Engineer, © John Johansen-Berg, Founder and Leader of the Community for Reconciliation.

Basic Questions, © Rev Susan Hardwick, an Anglican priest and author of a number of books.

Celebrate Wisely, © Rev Nigel Collinson from *The Land of Unlikeness*, published by Foundery Press.

Communication, © Pat Marsh.

Connections, © Miriam Bennett.

Copyrighting Genes, © Peter Comaish.

Drawing Energy, © Bob Warwicker.

For Benjamin, © Rev Sarah Brewerton, a minister of the United Reformed Church in the UK and part-time hospital chaplain to the Central Manchester Healthcare Trust, UK .

God Help Us to Use Technology Right, © Bob Warwicker.

God of Computer and Test-tube, © Jenny Spouge. *

God of Money and Machine, © Jenny Spouge. *

Healing in Our Computer Age, © Betty Lynn Schwab.

Heaven and Earth, © Stephen Brown.

Jubilee Hymn, © Jan Berry.

Let Your True Light Shine, © Bob Warwicker.

Newborn, © Margot Arthurton.

Obsession, © Bob Warwicker.

Progress, © Marjorie Dobson.

Space, © Peter Comaish.

Thanksgiving for Our Computer Age, © Betty Lynn Schwab.

The Barrier, © Duncan L. Tuck.

The Fruit of Knowledge, © Jan Berry.

The Web, © John Johansen-Berg, Founder and Leader of the Community for Reconciliation.

There Is One Voice That Matters, © Bob Warwicker.

Widen Our Vision, © Rev Susan Hardwick, an Anglican priest and author of a number of books.

You Are Like a Light for the Whole World, © Betty Lynn Schwab.

Wisdom is Calling

A Highway Shall Be There, © Rev Nigel Collinson from *The Land of Unlikeness*, published by Foundery Press.

A Litany for the Millennium, © Rev F. Gerald Downing.

A Morning Psalm, © Derek H. Webster.

A Mother's Prayer, © Bob Commin from *Someone Dreaming Us*, Mercer Books, 5 Roslyn Road, Rondebosch 7700, RSA.

A Prayer for Australia, © Rev Philip Freier.

A Prayer for Twenty-Four Hours, © Heather Johnston.

A Psalm of Salvation, © Derek H. Webster.

A Spirituality for Women, © Libuseng Lebaka-Ketshabile. From *Challenge*, Aug/Sept 1997, an independent ecumenical magazine published by Contextual Publications, Johannesburg, South Africa. **

A Thanksgiving for Australia, Lenore Parker. © 1995, the Anglican Church of Australia Trust Corporation. From the text of *A Prayer Book for Australia*, published under the imprint of Broughton Books by E J Dwyer (Australia) Pty Ltd. **

An Evening Psalm, © Derek H. Webster.

An Increasing Hunger, © Bill Kirkpatrick.

Ash Wednesday Liturgy, © Rev Philip Freier.

Be Near Us, Loving God, © Stephen Brown.

Becoming a Child, © Derek H. Webster.

Benefiting from Diversity, © Linbert Spencer.

Christ Is Living in Our World, © Richard Becher.

Circles, © John Johansen-Berg, Founder and Leader of the
Community for Reconciliation.

Deep Silence, Garth Hewitt, © Chain of Love Music.

Divine Wisdom, © Elizabeth S. Tapia.

Entrance, © Ann Lewin.

For All the Saints, © Janet Morley. First published by Christian Aid.

God, © Valerie Shedden.

God of All Love, © Joy Mead.

Good Friday, © Derek H. Webster.

Greenwood of Wisdom, © The United Church Publishing House,
from *Circles of Grace*, by Keri K. Wehlander, 1998,
pages 69–72. **

Homemakers, © Betty Radford Turcott. **

Hymn for the Millennium, Shirley Erena Murray. © Hope
Publishing Company, administered by Copy Care, PO Box 77,
Hailsham, BN27 3EF, UK . **

Hymn of Grateful Recall and Renewed Commitment, © Fred Kaan.

I Have Heard Your Cries, © Jean Mortimer.

I Rise to This Day, © Bob Commin from *Someone Dreaming Us*,
Mercer Books, 5 Roslyn Road, Rondebosch 7700 RSA.

Incarnation, © Derek H. Webster.

In the Meantime, © Norm S. D. Esdon.

Interfaith Dialogue, © Shanthi Hettiarchchi, Interfaith Coordinator for the Grassroots programme based in Luton, UK.

Is This God Really Wise? © Dorothy McRae-McMahon, Uniting Church in Australia. **

Jubilee Song, © Ed Cox.

Like a Windchime, © Norm S. D. Esdon.

Listen! © David Adam, 1998.

Litany of the Lord's Prayer, © Beaulah Shakir, Young Women's Christian Association, Lahore, Pakistan.

Living on the Edge, © The Venerable Martin Wallace, Archdeacon of Colchester.

Lord, Teach Us, © Rev Nigel Collinson.

May All Sentient Beings, © Tenzin Gyatso from *Love, Kindness and Human Responsibility*, Paljor Publications, India. **

Millennium, © Bernard Thorogood. **

New Light, © The United Church Publishing House, from *Circles of Grace*, by Keri K. Wehlander, 1998, pages 30–31. **

On the Third Day, © John Johansen-Berg, Founder and Leader of the Community for Reconciliation.

Orthodoxy, © Ian Gillman.

Pilgrim God, © Kate McIlhagga.

Prayer and Mission, © Martin Wallace.

Prayer of an Old Chief, Jen-wen Wang and translated by Vivian T. Su from *Taiwan Church News*, Presbyterian Church in Taiwan. **

Ripples of Prophets, © Shanthi Hettiarachchi, Interfaith Coordinator for the Grassroots programme based in Luton, UK.

Spirituality, © John Johansen-Berg, Founder and Leader of the Community for Reconciliation.

Stillness, © Hauptkirche St Michaelis, Hamburg, Germany.

The Holy Trinity for the Twenty-First Century, © Derek H. Webster.

The Light of the World, © Norm S. D. Esdon.

The Lord's Prayer – *Four Variations*, © Derek H. Webster.

The Poet and the Elder, © Derek H. Webster.

The Sound of God, © Miriam Bennett.

The Trunch Prayer, inscribed in Latin on John Goyle's screen placed in Trunch Church, Norfolk, dated 1502. **

The View from the Mountain, © Amado L. Picardal.

The Water of Life, © Kate Compston.

The Wayward Spirit, © Valerie Shedden.

These I Want, © Romeo L. del Rosario.

True Riches, © John Johansen-Berg, Founder and Leader of the Community for Reconciliation.

Unconditional Love, © Kate McIlhagga.

Wisdom, Grace and Favour, © Glenn Jetta Barclay.

Wisdom Is Calling, © Kate Compston.

Wisdom Made Known, © Jan Berry.

Wisdom Without Compassion, © Rev Susan Hardwick, an Anglican priest and author of a number of books.

Wild Strawberries, © Derek H. Webster.

With Drums and Trumpets, © John Johansen-Berg, Founder and Leader of the Community for Reconciliation.

Woman Wisdom, © Dorothy Macneill.

Magnificat

Magnificat for a New Millennium, Fred Kaan © Stainer and Bell Ltd.